Advance praise for

Desperate to Be a Housewife

જ

'A wonderful page-turner of a memoir. Beautifully written, very moving and proof that Meg Bortin must get cracking on the next one.'
—— Tony Barber of the *Financial Times*

'I read this book in one sitting. It's a terrific read – an involving picture of a very interesting period with a very attractive heroine.'
—— Julia Watson, author of *Russian Salad* and *American Pie*

'Meg Bortin's adventures are passionate, full of tenderness and fun. I enjoyed every twist and turn and read the entire saga in one sitting.'
—— Jim Haynes, author of *Everything Is* and *Thanks for Coming*

DESPERATE TO BE

A HOUSEWIFE

৶

MEG BORTIN

MIRABELLE BOOKS

Oakland ৶ Paris

MIRABELLE BOOKS

Oakland ❧ Paris

ISBN-13: 978-0615897592
ISBN-10: 0615897592

Cover illustration by Michelle Schwartzbauer
Cover design by James Eric Jones

The names and minor identifying details of the people portrayed
in this memoir have been changed to protect their privacy.

www.megbortin.com/desperate

To the memory of my mother,
Barbara Louise Harris Bortin

AUTHOR'S NOTE

The names of the people portrayed in this memoir, including
my own, have been changed. Exceptions are historical figures.
The events recounted are as they happened.

Ay, now am I in Arden; the more fool I: when I was at home,
I was in a better place: but travellers must be content.

— William Shakespeare

CONTENTS

FLIGHT

The captain was still speaking when the plane went into a vertical dive. We were several miles above Kabul and had been making a gradual descent through clouds when a gruff Russian voice crackled through the intercom. We would have to corkscrew in, he said, because Afghan guerrillas on the ground armed with Stingers – "supplied by the Americans" – would most likely try to shoot us down. Whoa! Down we pitched. Everyone aboard was whooping, roaring, laughing, gasping. How many whiskies had we tossed back during the flight? It was a planeload of journalists en route from Moscow to cover a war, but no one had prepared us for this. Out the window bright lights shot through the sky beneath the fuselage. Not to worry, the pilot said. Our plane was firing off flares to try to deflect the heat-seeking Stingers. Not to worry? Those Stingers had proved remarkably effective in the Mujahedin's war against the Soviet occupiers of Afghanistan and their puppet government in Kabul. Our Tupolev jet was a perfect hot target.

Heart pounding, mouth dry, eyes fixed on the fireworks below the wing, I clung to the man beside me, a seasoned road warrior from the Times of London, who had gone pale. Down, down we spiraled. It was May 1987, and our Ariana Afghan Airlines plane had been chartered by the Soviet Foreign Ministry to take Moscow's international press corps on a Kremlin-sponsored tour of the war. The ultimate irony, I thought, gripping the armrest with my free hand. Here we were, a planeful of Western hacks – British, French, German, Italian and, like me, American – facing possible instant death thanks to the generosity of the U.S. government in arming the Afghan rebels.

Our descent would last no more than a few minutes but it was time enough for me to wonder what had brought me to this pass. I remembered my father and his best friend, Al, telling me and my brother bedtime stories when we were kids back in Wisconsin. These stories usually starred Tom Sawyer and Huckleberry Finn. My dad would conjure up an impossible situation – the two boys in a barrel about to go over Niagara Falls, say, or caught by a tribeful of Indians ready to scalp them – and just when it seemed there was no way out, he'd say, "Take it, Al." By some miraculous sleight of word, aided by dry martinis, those boys always managed to escape. Was this childhood ritual responsible for my reckless confidence that all would be well in the end? That instead of settling down I could go off to Paris, become a reporter, move to Moscow and ultimately board the plane of an airline no one had heard of, to be fired at by Stingers and live to tell the tale?

Thoughts cartwheeled crazily through my mind as we hurtled downwards. How did I, Mona Venture, come to be on that plane? I, Mona Venture, born in Manhattan, raised near Lake Michigan, where no one could have foreseen such a moment, least of all me? Well, a lot of time had passed since then. Now I was 37, and this was far from my first brush with potential calamity. Yet whatever came my way, from bliss to disaster, I was never really out there for the thrills. No, that was not what I'd been looking for. It was something quite different. Something that would have astounded those closest to me. I may have been seen as a graduate of the ready-for-anything school, but that was only part of the picture. In my heart of hearts – and I have trouble even writing these words, so far are they from my public persona –

during all those years, no matter what anyone else may say, I was actually … desperate to be a housewife.

Yet here I was, plunging to earth, single, childless, and scared out of my mind. I stifled a scream as a flare flashed by. What had gone wrong? I had to face facts. I was heading toward 40 with ever less hope of reaching the promised land – the loving husband, the houseful of kids. My destiny, or so it had seemed back in Wisconsin.

And now any moment we could be blasted out of the sky. Why hadn't I concentrated on the main thing? I'd always expected to have a partner for life, and I'd never stopped longing for children. But I'd swerved somewhere toward the end of the '60s. And now I was paying the price. All the excitement of being a foreign correspondent suddenly seemed as pale as the man beside me. He was trembling as he tried to wrench open another mini of Jack Daniels.

If I hadn't been too terrified to talk, I would have told him that I'd swerved for a reason. I'd wanted to experience the world – and I'd had a good ride. I knew what it was to love a man, indeed I'd loved more than a few. I had my career and plenty of friends, some of them right here on board. We were covering Mikhail Gorbachev's USSR, one of the hottest stories around. It was a time of momentous change, and we were in the heart of it.

Yet all the momentous change in the world couldn't alter the fact that I was, as my mother liked to remind me, still single. No husband, no children, not even a serious lover despite the waves of sexy correspondents coming through Moscow, despite living in a major metropolis of eight million people, half of them men. And now I'd never be a mother. Not if we crashed.

Don't think about that! We were falling, falling, falling. Trying not to panic, I let the memories crowd in.

Men. It wasn't as though I hadn't tried. Ever since my awkward teens I'd been looking for Prince Charming. While my friends went off to the high school dances I stayed home scouring Mademoiselle magazine for tips on how to improve my appearance – and be like everyone else. Much to the scorn of Ben, my artistic younger brother.

One day, after I'd ditched my glasses for contacts, my prince did come. He was tall and blond, captain of the basketball team. I thought I'd faint of happiness when he gave me his ring to wear on a gold chain around my neck. We talked about marriage, but it was just too soon. We were only 17. It was perfect while it lasted – nearly a year. The relationship ended when I declined his invitation to surrender my virginity.

By then I was a student at the University of Wisconsin in Madison, one of the most political campuses in the country. It was 1968 and the women's movement was just taking off. Even someone as conventional as I was couldn't help but be intrigued by the notion that women could abandon their aprons for professions formerly reserved for men – men like my father, a doctor. But would that mean jettisoning happily-ever-after? Did women have to choose to be liberated or married? It was a dilemma. I wanted to be both.

And look how that turned out. Here I was, still wondering where was the prince. Every single love affair had stopped short of the happy ending. Of course, before each break-up had come a beginning of passion so bright as to make the whole adventure appear worth the dare. But with my longing for children as sharp as it had ever been, here I was, far from home and hurtling through space. If home meant anything at all. For the last thing I wanted was to return to Wisconsin. Desperate to be a housewife, sure, but like my mother? No way.

"What's that?" someone shouted as a bolt of light seared the sky. Everyone gasped, and the knot in my stomach grew tighter. Squeezing my eyes shut, I willed myself to concentrate.

My mother. She had disliked every man I ever brought home, and told me so. This was despite her degree in psychology, which she earned at the University of Wisconsin, although she would probably say that her main achievement in college was meeting my father. When I moved overseas, it only made matters worse. She was a sophisticated woman – glamorous, people tell me, strong-willed and ahead of her time. She was clever, energetic and cool under pressure. Yet she worried constantly. I had to take her proclivities into account, managing our relationship by telling her as little as possible that risked upsetting her. I may have put an ocean between us – she still had the knack of destroying my confidence. No way did she know I was on this plane to Afghanistan, for example. Why court the danger of reproach? She'd been distressed enough when I phoned her from London with the news that I'd be moving to Moscow.

"But sweetie, it's a Communist country!" she protested.

At that point I'd been living abroad for more than a decade. Almost without intending to, I'd carved out a kind of independence she could never have dreamed of. I'd known romance, heartache and, occasionally, love. Against all expectation, I'd become a successful newswoman. But my mother was not impressed that Reuters wanted to send me to the USSR to cover one of the world's top stories. All she wanted was for me to come home, meet Mr. Wonderful and provide some grandchildren. She wanted me to hurry up and follow the script. And be like her.

The very idea of sex outside marriage was unthinkable to her. That was the price she paid for getting what she wanted – the loving husband, the houseful of kids. Brought up by prosperous second-generation Jews from Mitteleuropa, she had defied them by falling in love with my father, whose Russian Jewish roots were not quite up to her parents' standards. Even though as a medical student he had a certain cachet. She was 21 and still a virgin when she married him.

A jolt pitched me back to reality. The Tupolev was shaking now. When would this torment end? I gripped the armrests with all my might and plunged back into the past.

My father. Immunologist, fisherman and fabulous teller of tales. I hated the fact that I'd let him down. But try as he might, he didn't understand what had propelled me abroad, and couldn't forgive me for disappointing my mother. Even though I'd just been imitating him, in a way – his curiosity about the world, his drive to make it a better place. Maybe it was because he was dealing with illness all day that he lived so hard and fast. He knew the risks and yet he smoked (Philip Morris), drank (martinis and, later, French wine), and stayed up far too late working on research projects at his massive teak desk. Still he was up early every morning to shower, shave, breakfast and leave for work.

"I'm off to the horse-pistol," he'd say, and for the longest time I pictured his office as some sort of saloon, with swinging half-doors and a bar manned by a cowboy. How could a doctor take care of people in such a setting, I wondered, until someone finally pointed out that he meant "the hospital."

He adored my mother, wined and dined her, and brought her jewels on her birthday. They had met on a blind date in Madison and it had been magic from the word go. After the war they thought about settling in San Francisco, but chose New York for the quality of the training hospitals there. Which explains why that city is where I was born.

Another jolt! Out the window I saw mountains in the distance, with deadly bursts of light. Oh my god – could that be the Stingers? As we neared the earth, the past was flitting faster and faster before my eyes, back to the very beginning.

My entry into the world began at a Buster Keaton movie on the Upper West Side of Manhattan. No, actually it began the night I was conceived, in a tenement in Hell's Kitchen, where my parents, unable to afford anything better on an intern's salary, got cozy, perhaps in an effort to stay warm, for it was February 1949, a time of hope with the war four years past and progress looming for America. The neighbors threw the garbage out the window, my mom told me later. She was eager to move on and my forthcoming arrival provided the stimulus for them to find a better place uptown.

One evening in early November, with the due date a couple weeks away, my parents left their small apartment on Central Park West to go to the movies. My mother hesitated when she felt the first contractions but after a while she poked my father and said, "Sweetie, I think it's time." Everyone around them was laughing at Keaton's shenanigans. She just wanted to get to the hospital.

"Shut up and watch the movie," my father said pleasantly. He had delivered plenty of babies and knew how long it took. They watched the film right to the end, walked home, got my mom's bag and at last took a cab to the hospital, where 10 hours later I was born.

Musing on this story, told to me lovingly many times, it's hard not to imagine that my beginnings explain why my search for love and happiness has so often involved laughter in the dark...

Screams shattered my reverie. Everyone on board was shouting again. Whoa! Here came land. I braced for the crash, hoping I'd live – until, as the earth rose to meet us, our pilot leveled out and set the plane down sweet as can be. A few bumps, and that was it. We were safe.

Then everyone was talking and laughing again, playing it cooler than cool, even if we actually felt like kissing the Afghan tarmac.

Once we landed I thought my memories would dissipate, but to my surprise they lingered on. My mom, my dad, my brother Ben. My loves, glorious and less so. The heartbreak, the longing. The wild nights and sober awakenings. My quest for understanding. The distance I'd traveled in search of a way to feel at home in the world.

Now, midway through life's journey, I felt strong but vulnerable, confident but uncertain, surrounded by friends but alone. Had I lost my bearings as I navigated the minefield of changing roles for women? Was it me or my entire generation? One thing seemed clear. I was indelibly marked by my era, a woman ready for anything – anything, that is, except the prospect of growing old without love.

As I contemplated this prospect, questions engulfed me. What had I done wrong, or right, when I veered off the path of marriage and family? How would I ever emerge from this thicket of contradictions? And the most tantalizing question of all — could there still be a happy ending?

SEX

1970

When I got up, my mother was ironing. It was early, the light still pale. Spruces soared dark and blue beyond the snow-covered field.

"Good morning, Mom," I said. She didn't look up. Her ironing hand pressed down harder, gliding angrily over the linens. Shit, I thought, heading past the round white table into the kitchen for coffee. If only I'd kept my mouth shut. Still, it was her own damn fault. She'd been asking me for months whether I'd slept with Jake, and I'd always lied – until last night.

She had caught me at a weak moment. I was home for the weekend from Madison, they'd had some friends over for dinner, I'd indulged in a couple of cocktails, and when the guests departed, she struck.

"So, sweetie," she said as we were clearing away the ashtrays and lipstick-smudged glasses, "I know it's none of my business, but I just keep thinking about you and Jake."

"Yes?" I said, sitting down on the edge of the couch. Embers lingered in the black marble fireplace. We were alone in the family room. My dad and Ben had gone to bed.

"Well," she said, lighting a cigarette, "you know, Mona, you hear so much about college students and sex these days, and I worry about

9

you. I don't want you to get hurt. You're not sleeping with him, are you?"

It was March 1970, my third year at the University of Wisconsin, and I'd left my mother's plans for me behind. Yes, I'd joined a sorority when I'd arrived. And I'd stuck it out for a second year, too, even after Dow Chemical came to recruit on campus and all hell broke loose and I realized there was a war on in Vietnam. Even after Johnny, the golden ski bum of a boy I met on a trip to Aspen, took me home to his place and rolled me my first joint. Even after my roommate, the arrestingly beautiful Suzy Esterhazy, got pregnant and told me everything she knew about sex.

But not anymore. Now I had quit the sorority, packed away my little black dress and taken up with Jake Spielman, an East Coast radical with long tawny hair and green eyes to die for. Jake was perfect in every way – he was political, he played baseball and he played the violin. We protested the war together. We read Marx together. We smoked marijuana and tried mescaline together. We were 20 years old. And yes, we were lovers.

My mom was waiting.

"Do you really want to know?" I asked, suddenly swept by the desire to shed my hypocrisy and come clean. Was I a liberated woman, or what?

My mother sat still as a stone as I told her.

"Things aren't the same as when you were a student," I began, rushing with brash abandon into what could only turn into a train wreck. "Women are sexually liberated now. I love him, he loves me. We're happy together. It's not the end of the world."

Her pale blue eyes clouded over with the vision of her baby girl nestling in the chest hair of this heathen man.

"Is he going to marry you?" she asked, her voice quavering.

"That's not on the agenda right now," I replied, keeping to myself Jake's views on the subject. He had said that he would never marry me because a) marriage was too bourgeois, and b) so was I.

"Liberated women don't need to be married," he admonished me. Besides, Jake said one day when we were lolling in bed, "A good revolutionary needs to be prepared to pick up a gun and shoot her parents. You would never do that, right?"

Right.

That evening, as my mother's face took on a crumpled look, I kind of wanted to shoot Jake. But life with a campus radical was far too exciting.

I was a liberated woman, I reminded myself. I squeezed my mother's hand and went to bed.

Now, armed with coffee, I came back and sat down at the white table. The iron flew faster and faster. Overnight, my mom's shock, disappointment, or whatever it was had turned to fury.

"Promise me you won't tell your father," she demanded. "It would kill him."

I had never been able to face down my mother. So I made the promise, and for two years I kept my word. This was foolish, I realized later. Wasn't my father the one who, as I was leaving for college, had reminded me there was such a thing as the pill? He was a doctor and knew the ways of the world. He might have understood.

But not my mom. For her, like her parents before her, sex before marriage was the ultimate sin. She had disliked Jake from the moment she saw him, and now she had a reason to hate him. As for me, I'd wrecked everything. She never forgave me.

I was studying with Jake at his house when the phone rang. It was my roommate.

"Your mom called," Suzy said. "She sounded kind of upset."

Now what? My mother had this knack of phoning at inconvenient moments. There we'd been, Jake and I, reading comfortably on his bed, his hand brushing over my jeans in a friendly way, moving up inside the thigh over the seam, then down, and up again, closing in until my entire leg was an erogenous zone.

We were just setting our books aside and reaching for each other when the call came.

"What did you tell her?" I asked.

"I said you were at the library," Suzy replied. "You'd better wait a while before calling back."

Jake lived in a two-story wooden house with a porch facing Lake Mendota. His three housemates had rooms upstairs, but Jake had drawn the short straw when they moved in that fall. His bedroom was on the ground floor, separated from the living room only by a light green cotton bedspread with raised squiggly patterns – enough of a screen to hide us from view but totally ineffective as a sound barrier. When we were alone in the house, as we were that afternoon, we could make love without inhibition. Our study session had been heading in that direction, but now the spell was broken.

"Hi, Mom," I said when the call went through. "Suzy said you phoned."

She didn't waste time.

"What were you doing yesterday afternoon?" she demanded.

"Yesterday? I was at class. Why?"

"Grandma called from Sedona. She and Grandpa saw you on the news last night. There was a report from Madison on a big anti-war demonstration. They saw you! You were wearing a khaki army jacket and shouting slogans."

"It couldn't have been me," I lied, although the jacket – Jake's – still smelled of tear gas. I'd washed it out three times but couldn't get rid of the acrid odor.

In fact I had gone to class, but when the march went by some of us just picked up our books and went out into the spring afternoon. Who could resist? There were hundreds, maybe thousands, of student demonstrators on Bascom Hill, all chanting "War machine off campus!" and "Remember Kent!" With passions already high against the war in Vietnam, the United States had just invaded Cambodia, electrifying the student protest movement. Then National Guard troops had opened fire on students at Kent State University, killing four. It was too outrageous to be believed – American troops shooting American students!

Jake and I melted into the crowd as it headed slowly down the hill toward Langdon Street. The authorities were braced for trouble – police troopers in riot gear lined the hill. As more and more students poured out of their classrooms, things got tense.

"Pigs off campus!" someone yelled, and the chant rolled through the crowd.

Jake threw me his jacket as the police began moving forward.

"Put it on," he shouted. "This could get hairy."

A noise like firecrackers ripped through the crowd. I didn't realize what was happening until the burning started. Tear gas! I fumbled to get my contact lenses out of my eyes without falling over in the terrifying crush of people running away. Everyone was screaming. Where was Jake? My heart pumped madly as I dashed down Langdon Street. I'd lost Jake! There was no more shouting, just the sound of feet pounding as frightened students made for cover. I was desperate to get away from the terrible stinging stench, the burning on my face and in my eyes.

Later someone said the police had used mustard gas. As I'd never been gassed before, I didn't know.

"Are you sure you weren't there?" my mother asked. "Grandma said they could swear it was you."

"Well what if it was?" I said. "There were jillions of people on the hill yesterday, Mom. Our government is waging war in Vietnam, and now we've invaded Cambodia! That's wrong! This is supposed to be a free country, but at Kent State they shot students at a demonstration! And maybe I did walk through the protest after class. But there's no way Grandma and Grandpa could have picked me out of that crowd, even if I'd been there."

"Well, let me tell you something, Mona Venture," my mother snapped, getting out the big artillery. She only used my full name when truly furious. "Grandma saw a close-up of your face. So what does this mean, young lady? Are you lying to us about everything these days?"

No, I wanted to answer, not everything. Just everything I care about. Things like taking a stand against a government capable of dropping napalm on women and children in a faraway land in the name of democracy. Of mutilating and massacring hundreds of unarmed civilians, like what happened when Charlie Company went crazy at My Lai. And now, invading another sovereign country. And killing students for exercising their right to freedom of speech! The world had gone topsy-turvy since I got to Madison. Democracy was a value I grew up with and believed in, but now it seemed devoid of sense. What were we doing killing civilians in Southeast Asia? If students didn't protest this immoral war, who would?

"Forget it, Mom," I said. "We'll talk next time I'm home."

Sure we would. I had tried talking with my parents about Vietnam, but it was no use. They were from the World War II generation. Hadn't the United States saved Europe and stopped Hitler's massacre of the Jews? Hadn't we sent our boys to die on the beaches of Normandy and Guadalcanal? Weren't we the most upright, honorable, selfless country in the world? My parents could no more question the government, especially in matters of "defense," than they could view the earth as flat. If President Nixon had decided that we needed to send our troops to Southeast Asia to fight Communism, he had to be right. That was how they saw it.

Meanwhile I was studying Third World national liberation movements and reading Lenin.

"But Grandma said the police used tear gas," my mother went on. A note of concern crept into her voice. "Are you okay?"

"Yes, I'm fine, don't worry. But this war is wrong."

I hung up.

"Your parents are so reactionary," Jake said. "They're really giving you a hard time."

How could he understand? His parents were liberal East Coast intellectuals while mine were conservative Midwestern professionals. Never mind that everyone was Jewish. Our families were from separate planets, and he and I had grown up in different worlds. Being a lefty was easy for him. For me, it was a giant leap into an unknown place where you had to carve out morality for yourself since all the standards you'd known through life were being proven false daily by the hypocrisy of the U.S. government and the American public at large.

I pitied my parents. My father the doctor, dedicating himself to helping people, my mother the perfect homemaker, devoting herself to her children before beginning a midlife career. Only two generations away from "the old country," they represented everything that was best in America. In their architect-designed, glass-walled house down a country lane in a leafy corner of Wisconsin, with their formerly well-behaved daughter, their son and their spaniel named Sparky, they had been living the American dream. But now they were caught in a time-warp. They couldn't let go of their belief in "America right or wrong."

Neither could my friends from high school days.

"Mona's gone off the deep end," they were saying – meaning she's into sex and drugs and in the streets protesting the war. It was so hypocritical. These same kids were off fucking like bunnies and avoiding the draft while pretending to buy into the values of the previous generation. Not me. Make war, not love? If that's what Americans like my parents thought, their world wasn't the one I wanted to be in.

June came to Madison, and activism faded as the sky over Lake Mendota took on a sparkling blue. Little boats dotted the rippling water. Students lolled on the hill. It should have been a perfect day, but it wasn't.

I had been to a see a doctor. As I was taking the elevator down, everything went black. They say you get spots before your eyes, but it was more like a checkerboard. I struggled against it but the squares of dark grew bigger until they merged. When I woke up on the floor of the elevator, a nurse was standing over me. I was still woozy as she helped me to my feet. We went back to the doctor's office, where she had me lie down on a bed. He came to take a look at me.

"This is a normal reaction," the doctor said. "Just lie here for a while until you feel better. It's probably best if you call someone to come get you."

I had gone to the appointment alone. I'd asked Jake to come, but he had an important class. That sort of pissed me off. After all, I was doing this for him as much as for me. But feminism was just getting started, and birth control was seen as the woman's problem. I had started taking the pill when we first became lovers, but discovered I was part of the alleged minority whose equilibrium was affected by the daily dose of hormones. I would find myself crying for no reason – not my usual style. When I finally went to the doctor about it, he prescribed a daily dose of vitamin B6 to counteract the side-effects of the hormones. A few months later, fed up with taking so many pills, I decided to switch to an IUD.

Already in 1970, there was no shortage of doctors in Madison willing to insert intra-uterine devices into the wombs of college students under the age of 21. Friends of mine had IUDs, and they assured me it was no problem. So I went gamely off to my appointment and agreed when the doctor suggested that he give me a Dalkon Shield, a new kind of IUD that was said to be super-effective. The shield was the size of a thumbnail, made of white plastic with little barbs along the sides and a string like a kite's tail. The doctor gave me a pill to relax me, then had me spread my legs into the stirrups.

I wasn't prepared for the pain. They used clamps to force my cervix open wide enough for the shield to pass through. It didn't take long, but the cramping was excruciating. Afterwards the doctor had me lie there for a few minutes, then told me to get dressed. I wrote a check, left the office and fainted.

Now, lying on the doctor's bed, I wondered if I'd made a mistake. Maybe IUDs weren't so inoffensive after all. Or was I just being a baby? There was no way to tell. The feminist bible "Our Bodies, Ourselves" hadn't been published yet. The only politically aware literature on the effects of birth control was in the form of leaflets – not easy to obtain.

Well, I thought, welcome to adulthood.

This was the last thing I would have imagined all those months ago when Jake invited me home after a concert. It was our second date, and I'd been nervous all day. I could feel where things were heading.

Before going out I checked my appearance in the mirror – shaggy hair, bright eyes. God, why did I look so young?

"This is it," I told Suzy as I left our room. "I'm going to sleep with him tonight."

We heard Bach's Double Violin Concerto. Afterwards, transported by the exuberance of the music, I floated down the street on Jake's arm.

His housemates were conveniently out when we got to his place. We sat on the couch and he rolled a joint. I lay in his arms as we smoked it, snuggling into him, letting him slip his hands inside my shirt, unhook my bra. I was shivering. Our tongues found each other.

"Want to see my blue light?" he asked after a while. I was so turned on it was hard to speak.

"Sure," I mumbled, wondering what was so special. It was a naked blue bulb hanging over his bed. We quickly stripped to our underwear and climbed in. As we kissed some more, Jake wriggled out of his shorts and let his hands drift down my body. They were reaching for my panties – he wanted them off.

"Wait," I whispered. He ignored me, pressing impatiently against my thigh as he struggled to remove the offending garment.

"No, wait!" I yelped, wrenching myself free.

17

"Wait for what?" he snorted in surprise. He was annoyed, but I had to tell him.

"It's just that I'm a virgin."

Jake looked at me oddly and started to laugh.

"That's a good one," he scoffed.

"What's so funny?" I said. "It's true."

"Oh yeah?" said Jake. "That's not what I hear. Didn't you go out with Larry Levy from A E Pi? He told me how much fun you were in bed."

Jake had a job washing dishes at the Villa Maria, a girls' residence, and clearly he had fraternized with some of the fraternity boys who worked there. He was right – I had gone out with Larry, even spent the night with him a couple of times, but we didn't "go all the way."

In the aquarium glow of his blue light, Jake eyed me incredulously as I told him what he obviously wanted to believe was a yarn.

"Okay," he finally said. He rolled over and buried his head in his pillow.

"Wait!" I said. "Come here." I curled up behind him, caressing his chest, his taut belly, then – oops. He'd gone limp.

"Turn over," I said. "Let's make love."

"But you're a virgin!" he bleated.

"Yes," I said, "but tomorrow I won't be."

I caressed him until he was ready, then let him try to guide himself inside me. I was so tense he couldn't get in and when he did he came immediately. That's it? I thought. He kissed me tenderly.

"It's always fast the first time," he said. "I'll be ready again in a few minutes."

And so he was.

The next afternoon we went for a walk along Lake Mendota and ended up on a pier that we had all to ourselves.

"Well," I asked, "am I still a virgin?"

Jake laughed. But then he turned serious.

"I want to ask you something," he said. "Are you on the pill?"

I wasn't. Why should I be? I had never had sex with anyone before that night. Jake wrinkled his brow and lowered his voice.

"I hope you're not pregnant," he said.

"Oh my god," I gasped. "Do you think it could happen so fast?"

Pregnant! The word was terrifying and exciting. Creating a life inside my body? This is what I longed for. To have a man and a family. A career, maybe, once I graduated, but that would be secondary. The main thing was to have children – lots of rambunctious children.

But not now. Not now.

For the next week until I could get a doctor's appointment we made love every night, coitus interruptus style. Then I got the pill, and now the IUD. Welcome to adulthood.

By the time I met Jake I'd been in Madison for two years and the learning curve had been brutal. As a freshman I'd enthusiastically joined Kappa Alpha Theta, where my sorority sisters were fetching and gregarious with a sophistication I hoped was contagious. At the initiation ceremony they dressed me in a white robe and gave me a Greek name. At the formal dinner, nobody mentioned sex, religion or – especially – politics.

But it was impossible to ignore politics my freshman year. During the Dow protests in October '67, the route up Bascom Hill to my Russian midterm took me past National Guardsmen with unsheathed bayonets. Dow was providing the U.S. Army with napalm, which, I learned, burns people alive. When spring came, Martin Luther King was gunned down in April and then Bobby Kennedy in June, sending virtually the entire campus into mourning. Between the two assassinations came the Paris student-worker protests of May '68. French students were tearing up the streets and brandishing posters proclaiming, "Be realistic! Demand the impossible!"

By my sophomore year, when black students went on strike to demand the creation of a Black Studies department, I was starting to pay attention. The momentum built up for months. One February day, when I was studying at the Theta house, voices rang through the air. Through the bare boughs outside my window I saw a big march heading down Langdon Street. It was the black students and hundreds of supporters. I hesitated a split-second, threw on a coat and ran outdoors.

"On strike, shut it down! Power to the people!" the marchers chanted.

A light snow was falling, softening their voices. My first demonstration, but it wasn't frightening – it felt right to be there.

"Mona!" Loud and clear, a voice I knew. I looked around and there in the crowd was Johnny, the golden boy I'd skied with in Aspen.

"Right on! Power to the people!" he chanted. Was that really me joining in? Swept up in the jubilant din, my arm linked in Johnny's, I stumbled on the secret truth about demonstrating – it was fun. And powerful too, for the movement gave birth to a Department of Afro-American Studies, one of the first in the country.

A few months later, in the summer of 1969, I went abroad to Avignon, in the opulent south of France, where the culture shock was profound and delicious. My post-'68 political awakening was so intense that when I returned to Wisconsin at summer's end, I'd changed. I let my hair flow loose, gave up dresses for jeans, dropped out of the sorority, signed up for a class on Marx and another called Physics for Poets, and promptly encountered Jake in both. His shock of honey-brown hair, his smattering of freckles, his intelligent brow, his vulnerable grin, his jaunty lope, his brown leather jacket, the bandana he sometimes knotted around his neck – it all added up to a neon sign flashing, "You have got to meet this man."

Jake must have noticed me noticing him, for in short order he invited me out for coffee. We went to the Student Union, a comfortably scruffy building beside the lake. I trembled when his hand brushed mine as we took our cafeteria trays. Within days – or was it minutes? – I was hopelessly and irremediably in love.

&

And so I became part of Jake's household. His housemates were New York Jews — Alan, the whimsical one, Phil, the studious one, and Jerry, the funny one from the Bronx with a sheepdog called Mopsy. I admired their easy self-esteem. Their accents, their humor, their irony, their upfront insolence — all this was new and seductive. Or maybe seductive because not really new. For though I'd been raised in Wisconsin, where I spent my high school years trying to pass as anything but Jewish, I must have retained from earliest childhood a trace of that New York kind of attitude. At Jake's place, I felt a kind of a resonance of how Manhattan could have been.

During the day we went our separate ways, but we regrouped at night to party. The wine was lousy ("What's the word? Thunderbird. What's the price? A quarter twice!") but the grass was cheap and abundant. We listened to music nonstop — The Band, Jefferson Airplane, Crosby Stills Nash and Young, the Doors, the Stones, Bob Dylan, Jimi Hendrix, the Dead, the Who, Janis Joplin, Santana, Joni Mitchell, Otis Redding, Frank Zappa, the Temptations, the Beatles, Aretha Franklin, Laura Nyro, Marvin Gaye, Martha and the Vandellas, the Four Tops, the Paul Butterfield Blues Band, the Incredible String Band, Canned Heat, the Fugs, Country Joe and the Fish, Pink Floyd, Joan Baez, Sha-Na-Na, Diana Ross and the Supremes, the Byrds, Buffalo Springfield, Judy Collins, and the list goes on. We ate to music, drank to music, studied to music, made love to music, slept to music half the time because we faded out even as the music played on. It spoke directly to us. "I, I feel free," sang the Cream, and the music was liberation, a door into a world where anything was possible. I'd missed Woodstock in the summer of '69, but even in France I'd realized it was a defining moment — as much so as the other huge event of that summer, man's first step on the moon.

With music as its liquid fuel, Woodstock lifted an entire generation off the earth as we had known it at a time when we were collectively searching for clues. The search was a mystery tour, not always magical. Alan and his girlfriend, Lisa, turned to Hari Krishna, walking barefoot, chanting and asking for money in a line of newly recruited Buddhists. The Scientologists got Harvey, a friend of Jerry's who until then had sought salvation by getting high and screeching along to Coltrane on a battered sax. A woman I knew, Sally Katz, joined the Labor Committee, a political cult run by a man calling himself Lyn Marcus – the closest American equivalent to Lenin-Marx. Others linked up with New Left groups like SDS – Students for a Democratic Society, a major player in the anti-war campaign.

As for me, I protested the war without joining any political group. I marched in every demonstration, taught at consciousness-raising sessions and put my knowledge of French to use translating articles about Vietnam from Parisian newspapers like Le Monde, considered more reliable by the movement than the American mainstream press. We ran those articles off on mimeograph machines, handing them to students as they went to class and, when the National Guard was called out to keep order, delivering them to the guardsmen with a smile and, sometimes, a flower.

Yet I, too, was searching for clues, in fact desperate for answers at a time when the countercultural earthquake rolling through America was toppling certitudes left and right. I felt I had to relearn everything I'd been taught. Phrases like "land of the free and home of the brave" took on a somber cast. What did it mean to be free? Free to get sent to Vietnam? To face discrimination if you weren't born white? When I thought about the inequalities in American society, it just infuriated me. I'd grown up in a world of privilege and wanted to give something back. But how? Meantime everyone around me was talking about liberation. Yes, I wanted to be "liberated," but how was that supposed to take place? Was liberation to be found in the women's movement, which was just getting started? Maybe, but at 20 I was far too enamored of men to be angry at them. In sex? I was a neophyte, too inexperienced to judge. In politics? We were trying to help the Vietnamese but they were pretty far away. Closer to home there were workshops on ecology, but I was a French major, not a scientist. I sought answers everywhere – in music, at the movies, in conversation with Jake. He was my lover, but also my mentor, my guide. He knew Mao's "Little Red Book" nearly by heart. He had studied the U.S. labor movement. He understood about class struggle and the military-industrial complex. I learned from him. I worshipped him.

The Kent State killings in May 1970 effectively finished off the school year in Madison and campuses across the nation. En masse, students went on strike. Our junior year behind us, Jake invited me home to New Jersey to meet his parents in June. The very thought made my heart skip a beat – wasn't this usually a prelude to marriage?

We left in a beat-up rental van with Alan, Lisa and Jerry and headed east through the afternoon and the night, taking turns driving as we passed through Chicago, Gary, Cleveland, Pittsburgh, Philly, and finally headed into New Jersey, the tape deck running full blast. It was the closest I'd come to a hippie road trip. We may not have had flowers in our hair, but we wore beads and bell-bottoms and Jake and I made out in the back of the van when it wasn't our turn to drive. By the time we rolled into his parents' driveway in a leafy suburb, I was wrecked – exhausted, exhilarated, scared.

Would they like me? It was already summer vacation for Jake's parents, who worked as professors in New York City. His younger brothers were still living at home. They all came out to greet us.

"So you must be Mona," his mom said with a warm smile. "Welcome!"

They took us inside and ushered us to the basement game room where there was a spare double bed. Not like my parents, who made Jake sleep in Ben's room when he visited. Here we were acknowledged as adults – if not man-and-wife, man-and-woman.

Our three days in New Jersey went by in a blur. We spent plenty of time in bed, recuperating from the drive and the tense spring, and discovered afterwards that the ceiling of our basement hideaway was as effective in blocking sound as Jake's squiggly curtain. His family heard us making love day and night – and laughed about it at the table.

"Sounds like you two haven't been bored down there," his bespectacled father rumbled. In my family, this would have been a scandal. But Jake's parents seemed accepting, even envious of our pleasure.

There was no pressure about marriage. We were on a visit home between our junior and senior years, that's all. And yet. So what if I'd gone from Mademoiselle to tear gas? I knew what it meant if your boyfriend took you home to his parents. I couldn't imagine not marrying Jake. He was my lover, my only lover – I didn't want any other man. This was for life.

Wasn't it? He and I didn't discuss it, but I felt things were heading in the right direction. We would be seniors and, after that, we could get married. I wanted to wear my mother's wedding dress. If Jake and I got married, maybe she would forgive me for taking the leap into premarital sex. She was under the illusion that my father still didn't know about Jake and me sleeping together, but I was sure he suspected. He just didn't ask.

Jake had some business to attend to in New Jersey, so I flew back to Madison a few days ahead of him. I had a summer job at the UW Library and was sharing a little house with a couple of friends. When Jake got back he came straight over to visit and we resumed our amorous activities where we'd left off.

It was hot in my room that July despite a big screened window that let in the occasional breeze. I was lying on my single bed reading one afternoon a few days after Jake's return when I noticed the itch. At first I thought I was imagining things, but it was undeniable – an itch right in my crotch. And not only that. When I went to the bathroom, it smelled like cheese. God! Why did this happen? It must be an infection. I went to the clinic and they took a look at me.

"So, young lady, you have a boyfriend."

The doctor didn't ask, he stated the obvious.

"Yes," I murmured. I was embarrassed to be there.

"It's summertime," the doctor continued. "Maybe your boyfriend's not here. Have you been sleeping around?"

Certainly not! I blushed to the roots of my hair.

"Why do you ask?" was all I could say.

"Because you have a walloping vaginal infection here. It's not VD but it's the same principle. Doesn't just get there out of nowhere. Someone must have passed it on to you."

"But that's impossible!" I squawked. "The only man I've ever slept with is my boyfriend."

"And what about him?" the doctor asked sternly. "Has he been seeing anyone?"

"No, I'm sure he hasn't," I said, but my pulse began racing. Had he? I had to know.

I left the clinic, got my prescription filled and headed over to Jake's house. He wasn't there, but I was prepared to wait.

"What's wrong?" Jake said when he saw me on the front porch. He could tell I was upset.

"I had to see the doctor today," I said quietly. "Somebody's given me an infection. And I haven't slept with anyone but you."

Jake said nothing. But his eyes took on the kind of hang-dog look Mopsy had the day he ate the blueberry pie Jerry had left out to cool.

"So what's the deal?" I asked. "Have you been sleeping around?"

Jake reluctantly met my gaze.

"Do you remember Marie?" he asked.

Of course I remembered her. An old high-school friend of his from New Jersey. He had introduced us when she strolled past his parents' front yard one day. She had curly black hair and big firm tits that bounced merrily when she walked.

"You didn't," I said.

"It doesn't mean anything," he mumbled.

"Do you mean to tell me that as soon as I left New Jersey you hopped into bed with another woman?"

He didn't deny it, but went into the house.

When I rose to leave, the tears came. I stumbled across town to my small bed and stayed there until morning. Jake brought me bagels and flowers – he was trying to be nice. But as far as I was concerned it was no use. I had trusted him completely, absolutely. He had wrecked everything.

I didn't break up with Jake, but our relations went into a cool spell. Even in confusing times like the summer of '70, there were certain bedrock principles, weren't there? Like, you were faithful to the one you love. Stung by Jake's betrayal but doubting my own feelings, I tried using a Maoist technique then fashionable in our circle: criticism and self-criticism. Was he just plain wrong – a cheating rat, as my parents would say? Or was I wrong to be reacting this way? Was I hopelessly old-fashioned? Did the sexual revolution give partners permission to sleep around? Even if they hadn't agreed on that ahead of time?

Words like commitment and trust swirled through my head in the many hours I spent alone. I'd left Madison for the month of August. My parents were traveling in Europe, Ben was away at camp and I had been appointed cat-and-dog sitter. There were no friends around except Laura, a former sorority sister. When she phoned to propose we go out on a Friday night, I jumped at the chance.

She took me to to the kind of bar I normally avoided – neon lights, loud music, men on the make. In virtually no time we were picked up by two young doctors. Around midnight one of them invited me to his place. He had a little red sports car and a lot of attitude, which would have bothered me more if I hadn't had so much to drink. As he led me to bed, I found myself musing in some dark corner of my brain about payback time. If I had doubts, I suppressed them. After all, Jake had done it. Wasn't this what sexual liberation was all about?

Whatever transformative erotic experience I may have been expecting, it did not transpire. The doctor had his way with me, turned over and started to snore. It made me feel like the cheap one-night-stand he clearly took me to be. When he drove me home in the morning, down the leafy lane leading to my parents' stunning glass house, his interest in me brightened. He wanted to stay in touch, he said. I smiled sweetly and handed him a wrong number. He and his little red sports car could take a hike.

Once inside the house I headed straight for the shower and stayed there a long time, trying to wash the stain of what I'd done from my body. Still, the feeling lingered in my soul. I dried off, dressed and got on the phone to Jake in Madison.

"When are you coming back?" he said. "Let's make everything good again."

We were cautious in what we said, but the subtext was clear – he couldn't wait to see me, and I felt the same way. How could that be? He had slept around. I should be furious. And now I'd also been untrue. But in my heart I'd been wedded to Jake since the first time we slept together. Wasn't the phrase "for better or for worse?" I couldn't wait to get back to campus – to be with the one I loved.

On August 24, 1970, four young men enraged by the Kent State killings stuffed a van with ammonium nitrate and fuel oil and detonated it outside Sterling Hall in Madison. The bomb exploded outside the university's Army Math Research Center in the pre-dawn hours, killing a physicist with no connection to army research. The blast destroyed the center, damaged buildings in a wide radius and was heard by Jake and everyone else in town. He phoned me that morning at my parents' place.

"Have you heard about the bombing?" he asked.

I had. My parents were back from Europe and my mother, who listened to National Public Radio, was already asking me to transfer to another university.

"Please, sweetie," she said. "Think it over. Madison's too dangerous. Dad and I will pay for it. You can go anywhere you like."

Nice try, Mom. She wanted so badly to get me back into the role she had scripted – a good girl in a good school with a good man, anyone but Jake Spielman. But it was too late. This was 1970, not 1940. The way she saw life may have been right for her in her time, but it wasn't right for me in my time. No way was I going to let that bombing separate me from the man I loved. The next day I kissed my parents goodbye and boarded the Badger Bus back to Madison.

Jake and I resumed our relationship but we had less time together now. We overlapped in only one course – European Social History by Professor Harvey Goldberg, a leftist whose lectures on Rosa Luxemburg and her revolutionary comrades in Berlin were so spectacular that he was acclaimed like a rock star when he entered the hall. I found a job copy editing at The Daily Cardinal, the university paper, so it was usually past suppertime when I got home. I was sharing an apartment near campus with three like-minded women, about a 10-minute walk from Jake's place. He and I slept together a few times a week, not every night like before. This worked for him, but there were nights when I couldn't handle the absence. Sex was a powerful drug, and I wanted it all the time.

"Jake," I said on the phone one wintry evening, "I've finished my work for tomorrow. Let's meet up."

It was early December, the time of year when darkness fell early, nights stretched into infinity and the longing became unbearable.

"Sorry," he said. "I can't tonight. I have a big test in the morning."

"No problem. I'll help you study," I said. "I'm getting my coat on. I'll be right over."

Before he could object I hung up. The wind whipped my face on the walk over. Icy sleet was falling – it stung the skin. By the time I reached Jake's, I was frozen. I couldn't wait to get inside and make something warm to drink. But when I rang the bell, he came to the door with a stern look.

"You can't stay here tonight," he said. "I told you, I need to study. You'll just distract me."

"No, I won't," I lied.

I needed him. It was a physical thing, overwhelming any modicum of respect I should have felt for him or for myself. I couldn't help it. I was desperate to feel his warmth – around me, inside of me.

"Let me in, Jake, I'm freezing," I said.

"Okay," he said. "Just for a minute. But then you're going to have to leave."

He brought me coffee.

"Come here," I said when I'd warmed up, hoping to change his mind with a long passionate kiss. But he gently pushed me away.

"Don't try that," he said. "I know what you're up to." And with that, he sent me out into the night.

A wave of desolation came over me – a sense of emptiness so intense that I walked across the street from his house and sank onto a frozen bench facing the lake. I stayed there a long time, sitting motionless as the sleet turned to snow, drifting down and covering me in flecks of white. A couple of times someone stopped to ask if I needed help.

"No, no," I stammered, "I'll be fine."

But would I? Or was I destined to end up like my father's mother, interned for much of her life in a psychiatric hospital disguised as a home for the emotionally fragile?

Thinking about that helped me pull myself together. I got up, brushed off the snow and walked home, saying nothing about the incident to my housemates, merely making a hot cup of tea before going to bed. But as I lay there I was haunted by the image of myself in the snow, of my aching need for Jake. I was supposed to be a liberated woman, but it was blazingly obvious I hadn't become one. Wasn't the idea that we would take control of our bodies? What a joke. I'd become a prisoner of sex – my liberated body had taken control of myself.

And what about Jake? Did I really love him, or was I merely dependent – hooked, addicted to sex and the idea of love? He was always saying that I was overdependent. Maybe he was right. Maybe that's why he held back. We had been together over a year and he had never once said the words "I love you." That only deepened my need.

By the the end of our senior year, with the conflicts in our relationship still unresolved, Jake and I decided to go our separate ways. He would head east in the autumn to study history at Rutgers, while I would stay in Madison, taking a break from studies to try to figure out what to do next. My choice of French as a major suddenly seemed very wrong. Why hadn't I chosen a more meaningful subject, medicine for example? I could have followed in my father's footsteps, becoming a doctor and helping people. But how could I have thought of that? There were no women doctors where I grew up. No role models. It hadn't entered my mind as a possible choice.

Over the summer, as an odd prelude to separation, Jake and I rented a tiny house and lived together for the first time. To cover my share of the rent I took a job as a waitress at Gargano's pizzeria. On a whim I signed up for an intensive chemistry class, just to see whether I could handle pre-med. Intensive meant a year's course in eight weeks.

In our rare moments together, Jake and I read to each other — in bed, as we had no living room. At night we were discovering the Marquis de Sade, but morning was when the reading got hot. The New York Times had begun publishing the Pentagon Papers, the hidden backstory of the Vietnam War. Even for anti-war activists like us, the disclosures were startling. The Times rolled out article after article detailing how deeply deception had figured in the conduct of the war. With the revelations broadcast nightly into homes across America, it soon became clear that publication of the Pentagon Papers was jump-starting opposition to the war among the public. It was a lesson in the power of the press, and a turning point in the Vietnam-era battle for hearts and minds. To those of us who had courted social dismay by joining up with the "radical fringe," it felt like a victory.

When Jake left for Rutgers at summer's end, I dropped the idea of pre-med. The intensive chemistry course had convinced me that the far more rigorous path to a medical practice would be incompatible with having children. By the time I completed my residency and could think about starting a family, I'd be 30. At the time that seemed incredibly old. With no clear alternatives in mind, I supported myself waiting tables at Gargano's, took a dance class, looked into grad schools and tried not to think too hard about the future.

Jake and I talked on the phone most days. He was lonely at Rutgers and wanted me to visit. I resisted at first. What was the point? He wouldn't commit to anything. But he persisted, and in October I agreed to go see him for a week.

"But where will you stay?" my mother asked when I phoned to tell her I was flying out to New Jersey.

"With Sally Katz – remember her?" Sally had met my parents once when they visited Madison. Now she was at Rutgers, in New Brunswick. That satisfied my mother. At least I was keeping up appearances.

During my week with Jake, he asked me to come live with him. We found an apartment and picked up some second-hand furniture. By the time I got back with my things, a kitten had taken up residence. We named her Clara Zetkin, after one of Harvey Goldberg's revolutionary heroines.

So there we were. Even if we weren't married, I was living with Jake. A door had opened onto the future – the kind of future I most desired, with a man and, later, I was sure, a family. I'd left Wisconsin behind. My days as a single woman were over. I felt that my life was finally about to begin.

MEN
1972

Jake was lying on his side in our double bed, his back to me. I nestled up to him.

"Not now," he moaned, pulling the pillow over his head. "I need to sleep."

Okay, I thought, notching up another sexless night.

Maybe moving to New Jersey hadn't been such a great idea. My father had stopped speaking to me as soon as he realized I wasn't living with Sally Katz. That had been in November, right after I moved into our yellow stucco house across the street from Dunkin' Donuts and an Esso station. Now it was February, and I was on my second job. Sure, going into New York every day had been fun at first. But I wasn't cut out to be a secretary, never mind the two-hour commute each way. I'd since found work as a substitute teacher at a tough high school closer to home. But the cops who patrolled the halls kept hauling me to the principal's office because, at 22, I looked so young they took me for a delinquent student.

At home, Jake and I had settled into a modus vivendi that came perilously close to the bourgeois model he abhorred. He went to class. I did the shopping and cooking. Sometimes he did the dishes or took out the garbage. Once a week we hosted a Marxist-Leninist study group attended by his some of his grad school friends. As I was the only one who could read Louis Althusser in French, the group had to take me seriously. Otherwise, I realized, I would have been perceived as "the wife." For at these gatherings, Jake served the wine, I served the cheese and crackers. We were like a married couple, only we weren't married. And now no sex.

I tried talking with him about it. "What's wrong?" I asked. "Why is this happening to us? I want you back."

But he just said his course work was tiring him out.

"Maybe we should split up," I said. But as I'd moved all the way to New Jersey this didn't seem realistic. Besides, he kept insisting he wanted us to stay together.

One night in March, Jake having refused my advances yet again, sending my frustration level into the stratosphere, I dressed hurriedly, ran outdoors and jogged to the Raritan River. It felt like my mind was exploding. On the bridge I could hear sounds, loud piercing sounds, almost as if I was screaming. But I wouldn't go into the streets and scream – would I? The sounds poured forth into the inky darkness. It was 2 a.m. and luckily no cars drove past. Only as the sounds subsided, my energy spent, did I look over the railing at the pitch-black water below. No, I wasn't about to jump.

On the cold walk home, visions of my grandmother and the shock therapy she had endured filled my mind. Was this where I was heading? I let myself quietly into the house, curled up on the couch and slept. The next day I accepted Cornell University's offer of a full scholarship to enter grad school in French. I could have chosen Columbia, in Manhattan, but that would have allowed us to prolong our nonmarital version of conjugal hell. Cornell, on the other hand, was in Ithaca, in the picturesque Finger Lakes district, a five-hour drive away.

The knowledge that Jake and I would separate in the fall gave a spark of new life to our relationship. Or maybe it was the arrival of spring, the daffodils that came up in our yard. Whatever it was, Jake began seeking me out again. Wondering idly whether sex was all it took to make me happy, I mentally restored him to his place as my partner for life. One day he surprised me by proposing a trip to Europe in May, when his semester ended. We could visit friends in Paris and Bologna and stop in Florence as well. I'd never been to Italy, and as for Paris – City of Light, city of love – nothing could be more romantic. So what if we'd be living apart in the autumn? I was definitely in the mood for romance.

We flew into Paris on a rainy May morning and checked into the Hotel Henri IV on the Place Dauphine. It was one of those cold gray springs that catch you by surprise. Forget chestnuts in blossom, bring on the sweaters and gloves.

"Let's go for a walk," I said when we'd dropped our bags in our room, a fifth-floor garret that smelled of beeswax on dark wood. Jake looked great – he was wearing his leather jacket, the one I loved. As we strolled along the Seine under a fine drizzle, I took his hand. Mistake. He shook himself free. End of romance.

The rest of Paris was a miserable blur. The cafés, the unicorn tapestries at the Cluny Museum, our arty friend with a collection of old-fashioned bicycles – it all felt meaningless. Without love, what did anything mean? I thought about flying back to the States, but that, too, seemed absurd. We'd be going on to Italy to visit one of our Madison friends, Dan Greenbaum. He'd spent the last year in veterinary school in Bologna. I was counting on the change of scene to change my mood.

Dan was waiting at the station, all smiles, when we arrived by train on a sparkling May day. He had come with his housemate, Adam, a vet school friend. We piled onto their Vespa motor scooters, bags and all, and headed through Bologna's sunny historic center to their apartment at the edge of town.

When did it start? Over lunch, as Dan and Jake caught up on the last year? Over coffee, when Dan and Adam regaled us with a hilarious description of vet school, Italian style? Adam spoke with a soft East European accent. He was, it turned out, Transylvanian – a Hungarian Jew by culture, born in a disputed area that was now part of Romania. As he spoke I drank in his golden skin, his gentle smile, his wide blue eyes. It was my first encounter with someone from that part of the world – land of my ancestors, for I was part Hungarian myself, on my mother's side. Was that why, when Adam picked up his guitar, the Hungarian folk songs he played sounded so dizzyingly familiar, their melancholy strains so haunting? After a while Dan went out on an errand, taking Jake with him. The shutters were down against the heat, letting tiny slats of sun into the room. The filtered light, the plaintive lilt, the heat, the quiet, just Adam and me, his blue blue eyes...

They talk about love at first sight being a thunderbolt. I sat there light-headed, unable to speak. Adam was singing now, his voice calm and rich. It drew me in. I wanted more. The notes he coaxed from his guitar flew into my heart, leaving me stunned.

We were still sitting there when Jake returned. He must have sensed something, for he was tense the rest of the day and unmoved by the story Adam told over dinner – how his family had escaped from Communist Romania under cover of night, crawling through barbed wire at the border. They had been persecuted in Romania as both Hungarians and Jews and were hoping for a better life in Israel. When they got there Adam was drafted into the army just in time to fight in the Six-Day War. He had been shot in the foot, hence his slight limp.

Night faded to morning and we were going on a picnic, taking the Vespas up into the hills south of Bologna. Jake rode off with Adam. I clung to Dan as we set out behind. He waited until they were a good distance ahead before starting to talk.

"You know, Jake and I have been friends a long time," Dan said, shouting over the roar of the wind and the scooter.

"Yes?" I said, holding my breath.

"Well, I'm fond of Jake," he said. "But I love Adam."

Uh-oh, I thought. Was he about to tell me that they were gay?

"So," Dan continued, "I'd do anything to help Adam, even if it might mean hurting a friend. He asked me to talk to you. He wants to know how you feel about him."

My heart was racing.

"Something happened," I said. "I don't know. It's really strong."

"Good," said Dan, "because Adam wants to be with you. I'm sure you can work it out."

We arrived at our picnic spot, a sun-splashed knoll dotted with tiny flowers. We were high in the hills, above a majestic panorama of golden fields and green-black cypress trees. We unfolded a linen tablecloth and unpacked our lunch – bread, cheese, olives and wine.

Adam found a way to take me aside, behind an old stone shelter once used by shepherds.

"Did Dan talk to you?" he asked.

"Yes," I said, and melted into his arms. His skin was hot when we kissed.

Later that afternoon, Adam was in the kitchen making Hungarian fish soup. We had bought the ingredients on the way home. In the living room, Jake had a word with me.

"Let's get out of here," he said quietly. "I don't know what's going on, but we have to leave."

Adam was chopping onions when I went to the kitchen to tell him we were taking the morning train to Florence. Was it the onions? His eyes clouded.

"Don't go," he said, his breath warm on my face.

"I have to," I told him. "But I'll come back."

I sat at the kitchen table and watched as Adam made his soup: onions, garlic, sweet red pepper, paprika, tomatoes, white wine, and finally the fish. We said little. From time to time Dan or Jake came in for a glass of wine, but mainly they left us alone. When the soup was ready, the four of us got through dinner somehow. During the night Jake reached for me in bed but I turned away.

Morning. We had an early train. We were at the door, ready to go. My watch. My Omega watch, a gift from my parents. Suddenly it wasn't on my wrist. No. It was buried under a pile of mail on the hall table. Jake hadn't noticed. We said our goodbyes. The train was a local, not very full. Only when it had pulled out of the station did I turn to Jake: "What time is it?"

From our stifling hotel room in Florence, we phoned Dan. Yes, they had found the watch. Jake objected when I said I'd go back alone the next day, but I insisted. It was not negotiable.

Adam met me at the station and took me straight to bed. We made love hungrily, tenderly, laughing together, telling stories, luxuriating in the long afternoon. When it was time for me to return to Florence, I again promised I'd come back.

"Stay now," said Adam.

"No," I said. "I can't leave Jake before we get back to Paris. It's only 10 days."

Would it have been less cruel to abandon Jake on the spot? We got lost going to San Gimignano in Tuscany, sat under a striped umbrella beside the Adriatic south of Rimini, then traveled on to Nice and the French Riviera. Only when we boarded our train to Paris did I tell him he'd be flying back to America alone.

We had reserved a room at a small hotel on the Rue Gît-le-Coeur, literally "lies the heart," as in, "Here lies the heart...," a phrase once used on tombstones. When night fell, Jake said he was going out.

"If you won't change your mind," he said, "I'm throwing myself in the Seine."

How did I get through that night? Sleep never came. When the sun was up, when I'd had my café au lait and was fretting, wondering what to do – call the police? go out? – Jake's key turned in the door.

"Finally!" I said. "Where were you?"

He'd gone to Shakespeare & Company, just down the street. The bookstore people had let him sleep on a mattress upstairs. He was unshaven and looked a wreck. Clearly he had forgotten we had a meeting that morning. It was ironic, it was surreal, but my parents were flying in from the States, and so were his. They had never met. In an arrangement meticulously choreographed by my mother, we were all to gather for coffee at Jake's parents' hotel.

"Forget it," Jake said when I reminded him. "I'm not going. Tell my parents whatever you want."

I met my mom and dad at their hotel and watched their faces light up when I told them Jake and I were through. We could have canceled the meeting with Jake's parents, but my mother wouldn't hear of that. She'd been waiting to meet them for more than two years and wasn't about to miss this opportunity.

The hotel café where we met was dim, with orange leatherette banquettes and brown formica tables. Jake's mom and dad looked crushed when I told them the news.

"But we wanted to meet you anyway," my mother said brightly. "We just found out, too."

And so I left them, having coffee, chatting about what might have been. Next stop: Alitalia, for my ticket.

Adam and I were ordering dinner at a casual family restaurant – our last night in Bologna before heading home in opposite directions to summer jobs in Tel Aviv and Wisconsin. My Italian had improved during our time together, but I couldn't read everything on the menu.

"What's this?" I asked, pointing to something called *coglioni*.

"That's balls," Adam announced. "Bull's testicles."

Suddenly I felt queasy. Three years before, in Provence, I'd been served chicken-head soup – which now seemed delightful compared to bull's balls.

"Do people really eat that?"

"Sure," Adam said. "In fact, I'll order it."

"Oh, don't," I said. "You don't need to. I believe you."

But he did, casting a shadow over 10 days of bliss. We'd had the apartment to ourselves after Dan left for the summer. Sometimes, when Adam played his guitar, I had let my mind wander to subjects like the chances against two people from such dissimilar origins intersecting on the giant grid of life. It seemed so improbable. Despite differences of nationality, language and culture, we had found each other and we were in love. Adam declared it, over and over, in English, Italian, even Hungarian, insisting that I repeat it: "*Szeretlek.*"

Occasionally, when I least expected it, a troubling thought pierced my lovestruck haze. What if I'd fallen for Adam because he was so different from Jake? The two of them were opposites – Adam sunny, Jake serious, Adam whimsical, Jake pragmatic, Adam gentle, Jake rigorous. Adam was a dreamer, hopeless at practical matters like managing money. Which was no problem in our instant romance. But what if Adam turned out to be too much the opposite? Certain things I liked in Jake seemed to be lacking in Adam. Jake's tough-mindedness, for example. As exasperating as it was to be countered by him, it was thrilling the way he could stand up to people, especially me. I could be tough myself and felt I needed a man capable of challenging me. Otherwise I'd be the dominant one – and that wouldn't work. But as quickly as these subversive thoughts surged up, I'd banish them.

Now, on our last evening together, as Adam tucked into his plate of cooked testicles, new doubts invaded at me. Would we make it through the next few months? Our plan was simple. I'd do a semester of grad school at Cornell and then take a leave, come back to Bologna and live with Adam. He wanted children. We could start a family while he finished vet school and – who knows? – maybe even get married. I would see about my education later.

In the morning I caught a train to Rome and a plane back to America. The next day, sitting with my mother at the white table, looking out on the soft beauty of a Wisconsin June, I told her about my future with Adam. She listened raptly and studied the photos I'd brought back – his open smile, his relaxed demeanor, his goodness and simplicity shining through. And he was Jewish. She couldn't have been happier about this turn of events. At last I was back on track.

≥≥

The worst part of that endless summer may have been the job I found temping as a secretary – staggeringly boring – or it may have been the disappearance of sex. There was some consolation to be found in the news, for The Washington Post was beginning its investigation into a bungled attempt by five men to bug the offices of the Democratic National Committee at the Watergate building. As details emerged and The Post established links between the Watergate burglars and White House Republicans, the anti-war movement went on alert, for it looked like this hilarious yarn might one day implicate the president himself. But for the moment soldiers and civilians were still dying in Vietnam, Richard Nixon was still in the Oval Office, and not even the joy of Watergate could make up for the absence of sex.

To compensate for the lack of a physical connection, Adam and I wrote to each other every day. Real letters, sent via the international post. There was no email, no Internet. Personal computers didn't exist yet.

Back in my childhood home, the prodigal daughter returned, I clung to Adam's letters like a shipwreck survivor to a plank. Only the knowledge that I'd find one waiting for me in the evening allowed me to get through my office chores.

We developed an odd synchronicity. It took five days or so for a letter to travel between Wisconsin and Israel. Yet if I mailed a question to Adam in the morning, I'd often get his reply the same evening. I started thinking about extrasensory perception. Was our love so strong that he could anticipate my questions? The phenomenon was uncanny, and it worked both ways. We joked that we were cosmically linked.

At last it was time to leave for grad school at Cornell. During a scouting trip in the spring I'd found an apartment in a brown-and-white clapboard house perched on a leafy gorge. My new bedroom overlooked a rushing waterfall. But there was no light my first night in Ithaca. The previous tenants had cut off the power. The next morning

I went to the electric company to open a new account, then bought a can of paint. I wanted my bedroom blue.

With no electricity in the house I couldn't put the stereo on, but the roaring of the waterfall outside my window filled the room with sound. It was a hot September day. I was up on a ladder painting a wall when a song I detested popped into my head: "Happiness Is a Warm Gun" by the Beatles. I tried to get rid of it but it persisted, irritatingly, until finally I dug out my old battery-run transistor radio and put on some other music.

A week later, I received a small packet from Adam with a cassette inside. He was still in Tel Aviv – vet school didn't resume until October – and phoning was expensive, so sometimes we talked to each other on tapes. I waited until evening to curl up on my bed with my tape player. Adam talked to me for a while, then said he'd play a couple of songs on his guitar. I listened dreamily. He spoke up again: "Now I'll play you something by the Beatles." In the split-second before the song came on, I knew. "Happiness Is a Warm Gun."

I didn't sleep that night. It was just too weird. I told myself it couldn't be ESP – could it? I tried to remember exactly the time when the song had popped into my head. The next morning I phoned Tel Aviv, never mind the expense.

"I got your tape," I told Adam. "Do you remember when you recorded it?"

He worked it out. The date was right. We added in the time difference and confirmed that he'd been recording the song I loathed at the exact moment it entered my head.

I tried not to think about it, but something shifted inside me. Could I really marry Adam? The mixed feelings that I'd repressed during the summer were suddenly and uncomfortably back.

The trees lining the gorge outside my bedroom window were turning scarlet and gold. It was several weeks into my first term at Cornell's amusingly named Department of Romance Studies and I was finding the pace hard going. We were expected to read a century of French literature every six weeks. After slogging through medieval poetry and Old French we had lurched into the 16th century, tackling the essays of Michel de Montaigne and the bawdy tales of Rabelais.

One evening when I was home reading, there was a rap at the back door. It was late, nearly midnight, but I wasn't surprised.

"Come in," I called, rising.

It was Radomir.

"Hey, you," he said in his soft Croatian accent, taking hold of my waist as the screen door banged shut. He was wearing a purple T-shirt and tight jeans, his uniform for tackling the hills of Ithaca on his bicycle. It was mid-October and the nights were brisk, but he had worked up a sweat pedaling uphill to my place. I called him my midnight rider.

I poured us a couple glasses of wine.

"What are you reading?" Rad asked, picking up Volume I of the complete works of Rabelais, its jaunty yellow cover emblazoned with an image of Gargantua eating a pilgrim he had mistakenly mixed in with his salad.

"'How Rondibilis declared Cuckolddom to be a natural privilege of marriage,'" he read, only slightly garbling the French. "Sounds promising."

Leaving his wine aside, he took my hand and said, "Let's go to bed."

I had been seeing Rad for about a month. He was a grad student, appropriately, in high-energy physics. When I met him at a party shortly after arriving in Ithaca, it felt as though Adam had reincarnated in the form of this supersexy Croatian, whose golden skin and East European accent so intensely conjured up my Transylvanian lover. But where Adam was easygoing, uncomplicated, Rad was kinetic, electric – hyperintelligent, cocky, wired.

In my longing for Adam, with the roar of the waterfall stoking the sexual craving that had invaded me after months of abstinence, it was easy to let myself confuse the two East Europeans – so magnetic, so delicious in their foreignness.

Rad was long and lean, his muscles hardened by bicycle riding. I liked to watch him undress. We had fallen into the habit of reading sexy novels to each other in bed – wordplay as a prelude to foreplay. We had already tried Henry Miller. That night, armed with the Rabelais, we repaired to my blue bedroom. When we were naked, we kissed, letting the tips of our tongues caress, our bodies brushing against each other, my soft curves and his springy tension forming a perfect synergy. He was already hard when we slipped beneath the sheets of my single bed. We settled in comfortably alongside each other. It was my turn to read. As I began, I stroked him, the foreskin silky against my hand.

"'Haven of grace (cried Rondibilis) what are you asking me? If you will be a cuckold? My friend, I am married; you will be shortly; but inscribe this word in your brain, with a stylus made of iron, that every married man is in danger of becoming a cuckold.'"

Rad laughed. He was caressing me, too, making me wet with wanting him. I tried to concentrate on the text.

"'Cuckolddom is one of the natural privileges of marriage,'" I continued. "'A shadow follows a body no more naturally than cuckolddom follows married people, and...' – oh, forget it," I said, handing him the book. "Your turn."

"Later," he said, and pulled me to him.

In the quiet moments after sex, nestled in Rad's arms, I often found myself thinking about Adam. I still loved him, I assured myself. I felt faithful to him in spirit if not in body. But how could that be? I was spending night after night with another man. Was my passion for Rad undermining my feelings for Adam? When does the merging of two bodies become the merging of two souls?

I certainly wasn't in love with Rad, I told myself. Our relationship was an erotic adventure, nothing more. But his libertine spirit was infectious. After my misadventures in monogamy with Jake, Rad was a revelation. While we in the West were talking about sexual liberation in the '60s, the East Europeans had been living it. With Rad, I felt I was making up for lost time. I still intended to join Adam in Bologna — though maybe not as early as planned. Graduate school was intellectually challenging, exciting. I now thought it best to finish two semesters before taking a leave.

My friends didn't understand.

"What are you doing with that guy Ruddigore?" one asked when he came up from New Jersey, intentionally mangling Radomir's name. He knew about the problems I'd had with Jake and thought I'd solved them with Adam. But life was not that easy.

Rad came by a couple times a week. He had a place across town that he shared with a muscular black psychology student and a pretty Latina sophomore named Anita with whom he was suspiciously friendly. I avoided going over there.

Not that I was jealous, god forbid — that wasn't part of the deal. But I couldn't help feeling a pang one November night when Rad, hopping into my bed, told me about the party he'd been to the evening before.

"I met this incredibly beautiful Indian woman named Vanhi," he said. "She has hair down her back to the floor."

"Well?" I said. "Did you sleep with her?"

"Of course."

I took it badly. Even if we weren't in love, I didn't feel like sharing him with every beautiful woman on campus. I started paying more attention to the timing of his visits. It rapidly became clear that he was spending every third night with me. I could all too easily imagine how he was spending the other two. Wanting to check it out, I appeared unannounced at his physics lab.

"Careful," he said sharply as I entered.

"What is it?" I asked.

Rad strutted to the doorway. There, taped to the top of the doorjamb, was hanging a single strand of very long black hair.

"Vanhi stopped by and we made love on the table," he said. "I found this after she left."

The next afternoon Rad came over to my place. He needed a haircut and I'd offered to do it. He took a seat, we discussed the look and I set to work. We got to talking.

"So you're sleeping with Vanhi," I said. "Are you sleeping with Anita too?"

"She's fantastic," he said. "Even if she's really young."

"So you make the rounds among the three of us," I said, snipping away. "We're kind of interchangeable."

"No!" he exclaimed. "You're all different."

As he enumerated the many ways he enjoyed Vanhi and Anita and me, his hair got shorter and shorter.

"Oops," I said, laying the scissors aside. He looked like a plucked chicken. I handed him a mirror.

Rad jumped up from the chair, frowning. "What have you done?" he exploded.

"Sorry," I said. "It just happened."

We didn't sleep together again.

When did I fall out of love with Adam? When he ate the bull's balls? When our paranormal communication connected us via the wrong song? When my sexual bond with Rad became so strong that it propelled memories of Adam into a far corner of my consciousness? Rad may have been a three-timing Lothario, but he was fabulous in bed and had a worldliness, an intellectual sophistication, that Adam couldn't equal. Matching wits with someone of Rad's brainpower had been thrilling. I realized I'd acquired a taste for the excitement of that sport.

Just before Christmas, appalled at my own heartlessness, I wrote to Adam to tell him I wanted to put things on hold.

"Everything's changed," I said in my letter. "I don't feel the same as when we met. I need time to think."

It was so easy to put that letter in the box, then go on about my life as a grad student with a heavy reading schedule. With Rad gone, distractions were fewer.

At times, I even found myself wondering about Jake. One day I called him.

"What's new?" I asked when he answered the phone.

"I've joined the Labor Committee," Jake said.

"You're kidding." When we were together, we had scoffed at the pseudo-Marxist antics of the Labor Committee, a group once described in The New York Times as so far left it was actually on the far right. Recent news items about the Labor Committee had been disturbing. The group's leader had apparently developed conspiracy theories, sometimes with an anti-Semitic tinge, and lately I'd been reading about "Operation Mop-Up," in which Labor Committee gangs were physically beating up members of other leftist groups. I couldn't believe that someone like Jake, an ultrarational man with socialist ideals, would set aside logic to join what increasingly looked like a group of extremists.

"No, I'm not kidding," he said. "Remember Sally Katz?"

Of course I did. She was the "friend in New Jersey" I'd allegedly stayed with on my first visit out to see Jake.

"What about her?" I asked.

"You know, I was kind of depressed after we split up," Jake said. "I ran into Sally at a demonstration in September and we went out a couple of times. Then she took me to a Labor Committee meeting. She started organizing for them last year. The meeting was great. When I saw what kind of work they were doing, I wanted to join."

"The kind of work they were doing? Including beating up Puerto Ricans? Well, good luck," I said. "Lyn Marcus is certifiable."

"It's not Lyn Marcus anymore," Jake said. "It's Lyndon LaRouche. He went back to his real name. And he's not crazy. It's American society that's gone off the rails. He's trying to change things."

No, I thought when we hung up, Jake's the one who's gone off the rails. He must have been so shocked by our break-up that he needed to enter a cult.

We didn't speak again until late spring. This time he phoned me.

"There's something I need to tell you," Jake said.

"Yes?" I asked warily.

"I didn't want you to hear about it from somebody else," he continued.

"What is it?" I said. "Are you okay?"

"Yes," he said. "I've never been better. Sally and I are getting married."

Now it was my turn to be shocked.

"I thought marriage was too bourgeois," I said.

"That was an infantile attitude," Jake replied. "Sally made me see how wrong I was. Besides, the Labor Committee approves of marriage between two members."

Oh my god, I thought as I hung up. Jake's getting married! But not to me – to Sally Fucking Katz.

My head was spinning. Even though Jake was now part of my past, I still intensely regretted that our relationship had failed. What's wrong with me? I thought. Why had she been able to make him see how wrong he was? Why hadn't I?

Or – or –maybe I was lucky to have escaped marriage to the kind of man who could join a sect. Anyone working with Lyndon LaRouche had obvious character flaws. I hated to admit it, but maybe my mother had been right about Jake.

Or – or – the most subversive thought of all – maybe I'd been lucky to escape marriage, period. Maybe Jake's initial take on the matter had been wise. Maybe feminists were right to disparage wedlock as institutionalized monogamy. One thing I'd learned since leaving Jake: in our earthly paradise, life is for tasting. With Adam and Rad I had feasted from a tree of knowledge of the senses laden with plump ripe fruit. The boughs were lush and heavy, with so much still to be tasted. At 23, I was curious, voluptuous and hungry.

છ

Summer came, and with it the chance to go back to Paris. I'd been accepted into a Columbia University program called "Psychanalyse et Littérature." Participants were housed at Reid Hall, a vine-covered building in Montparnasse. My room, on the top floor, had long, thin atelier windows looking down onto a leafy courtyard brightened by red geraniums. Our ground-floor classrooms surrounded the courtyard.

The program came with an impressive list of professors. Jacques Lacan, the god of French psychoanalysis, came as guest lecturer one day and told us about the death of his dog. But the real action was not in class. Structuralism may sound dry but in fact it was teeming with sexual innuendo. Eros held sway throughout the six weeks of our program. The hip anti-psychiatrist Félix Guattari had a little-concealed affair with a student, a chic brunette. I hooked up with the idiosyncratic David Kaiser, a tall New Yorker who dressed all in black, except for the days when he dressed all in white. He had the keys to a friend's apartment down the street. We repaired there to listen to Hendrix, smoke hash and make love on the living room floor.

Everyone knew David and I were seeing each other, but that didn't stop another student from courting me. Jeremy wouldn't take no for an answer.

"Come to dinner with me tonight," he pleaded after class one day.

"I'm sorry, I just can't," I said. "I have to write a paper."

That night, when I was sleeping, there was a tap on my atelier window. Startled, I rose to see what was happening.

There stood Jeremy on the narrow ledge, four stories up, looking half-crazed.

"What are you doing?" I whispered, terrified he would fall.

"Let me in, Mona," Jeremy demanded, a mad glint in his eye. What choice did I have? I opened the window. In he came, grinning like a conqueror. He wrapped me in his arms and drew me to bed, where the inevitable came to pass. One time only.

When the program ended, I went down to Bologna to see Adam.

"It's not a good idea," I told him when he phoned me in Paris to ask me to come.

"Please," he said. "I still love you. I need to understand what happened."

Adam met my train and as soon as he saw me, he knew. It was over. A year had gone by since we first met, and much had transpired. Even if I was unable at the time to express it, by then I knew I needed more from life than a wedding ring and a houseful of kids. Yes, I still wanted to be married – someday – but I'd entered a rich and complex universe since leaving Italy the previous summer and was far from through exploring its possibilities. I was just starting to liberate myself from the expectations I'd grown up with. I didn't yet know how, but I wanted to do something that mattered. I couldn't just run off to Bologna and tether my life to Adam's. I needed to find my way in the world, and that would take time. Adam and I cried together, but he understood, at least I thought he did. It was just unbearably sad to see how sad he was.

When I returned to Paris, I had a week left in France. David was gone, but he had kindly arranged for me to use his friend's apartment. The owner, Antoinette, was away in Provence. Her former husband, Wim, would come by for the keys when it was time for me to leave. That was the plan.

But in fact Wim stopped by the day I moved in. I opened the door to find a slight man with sandy hair, piercing blue eyes and a wiry body. When he arrived I had been making an apple tart, struggling to get the pastry right. Wim took off his blue-jean jacket, rolled up his sleeves, and said, "Let me help. I'll show you how Antoinette used to do it."

I stepped aside and watched, fascinated, as he plunged his hands into the bowl of butter, egg yolk, sugar and flour. In three minutes flat, the tart pan was lined with a perfect pâte sablée. We talked as we worked. By the time we'd cut up the apples and sprinkled them with sugar, I knew the mattress on Antoinette's living room floor would soon be back in use.

Wim was German, but you wouldn't know it. He'd moved to Paris as a student, married young and cast off all he could of his heavy national heritage. Now, at 35, he could have passed as French – his accent, his look, everything was perfect. He worked as a professor of linguistics at a branch of the University of Paris in Vincennes, on the city's eastern edge. More experimental than the Sorbonne, Vincennes had been set up after May '68 in response to the demands of radical students for reform of the French university system.

Wim turned out to be an engaging intellectual companion as well as an imaginative lover. He was fascinated by an American novel then in vogue in French psychoanalytic circles, "The Other" by Thomas Tryon. Wim clearly found my otherness alluring – he had never before been with an American, or a Jew. I, too, had wondered what it would be like to sleep with a German. But Wim, who had lived through the Nazi era, had lost all trace of Germanness. During our week together he cooked for me, read Le Monde with me, talked politics with me at his favorite café, the Academy of Beer on the Boulevard du Port Royal. One day he took me out past Vincennes by train to have lunch at a riverside restaurant called Chez Gégène where they specialized in tiny fried fish and accordion music. When it was time for me to fly home, Wim asked if he could visit me. He had never been to the States. We agreed he would come over in winter.

Back at graduate school in Ithaca, I fell out of love with Romance Studies. The work felt divorced from reality: structuralism, metalanguage, psycholinguistics and all the trendy theoretical baggage that went with French literature as it was being taught at Cornell. More and more I felt I'd been wrong to choose a subject that could lead only to a job as an academic. Yet I had accepted the department's offer of a fellowship for study in Paris beginning the next fall.

I thought back to my first semester at Cornell. When we reached the 17th century in our marathon literature program, I'd been too busy with Rad to complete the assigned reading: the major plays of Racine, Corneille and Molière, the philosophical works of Descartes and Pascal. And others. All in six weeks. The night before the exam I'd gone to the library, where I read the relevant chapters of the Larousse Encyclopedia of French Literature. The exam wasn't bad – I figured I'd pass. But in fact I received an A and glowing comments from the professor.

Confused, I went to my student adviser and admitted that I hadn't read the works covered by the exam.

"Don't ever tell anyone else about this," he cautioned. "It could wreck your career."

Now I was really confused. I had cheated, confessed and been told to keep quiet. Was this what academia was all about?

Wim came to Ithaca just after Christmas but that did nothing to improve my mood. The connection we'd forged in the lightness of Paris disintegrated in the long, dark, snowbound evenings of upstate New York. We were like strangers to each other by the time he left. At 24, I felt my life was frozen.

When spring came, the glory of nature renewing itself only made me feel worse. The lilacs bursting into bloom, the rush of crystal streamlets through the gorges, the fresh leaves popping out on campus – all these reminders of the real world we inhabit made my intellectual endeavors at Cornell seem utterly surreal.

One sunny day, instead of writing the paper I'd been assigned on Julia Kristeva, a semiotician and darling of the French chattering classes, I found myself ripping sheet after unfinished sheet of nonsense from my typewriter and wondering when French literary criticism had segued into mental masturbation. It was the spring of '74, America was still in Vietnam, Watergate had failed to topple President Richard Nixon, and here we were, Cornell's geniuses of Romance Studies, getting off on wordplay.

Overcome by a wave of nausea, I put down my pen and went back to my student adviser.

"You can have your Paris fellowship back," I said. "I'm leaving Cornell. I wasn't cut out to be an academic."

"You're wrong!" he said. But I was out of there.

Somehow I made it through the Ithaca summer. I found a job posing nude for art classes, daring myself to cast off the self-consciousness about my body that neither multiple lovers nor feminism had managed to dispel. I did volunteer work at Planned Parenthood, where I got rid of my Dalkon Shield – the device, found to cause problems from infection to infertility, had been withdrawn from the market and would soon be the object of a huge class-action lawsuit. Hoping for enlightenment, I consulted an astrologer, fasted, made love with a philosopher. To pass the time I went skinny dipping with hippies in the tingling waters of a deep stone quarry.

I was on hold, waiting for September. I had booked my air ticket to Paris months earlier, long before dropping out of grad school, and I still intended to go there. In August, when Nixon at last announced his resignation to avoid impeachment over Watergate, it felt like the end of an era. I wanted to leave, to make a clean start, to try to resolve some of the contradictions that had left me feeling so alienated in America. To try to resolve my own contradictions about men. Yes, sex was a powerful drug, but – bottom line – it wasn't enough. Despite all my entanglements, I still felt an emptiness inside me. I needed to get away, to clear my head, to try something new.

At summer's end I gave away my possessions, keeping only what fit in my knapsack – some clothes, two frying pans, four books. Scared but excited, ready for anything, I hopped on a bus to New York, took the E train out to JFK and boarded an Icelandic Airways jet to Europe.

PARIS

1974

"So that's what I'm doing on this plane." I was trying to keep my voice down, but the roar of the jet engines made that difficult. Besides, after two of those little bottles of wine and who knows how many mini Jack Daniels, who cared? The passenger beside me had taken my hand and was rubbing his thumb over my fingers, his face close, his sandy hair flopping over attentive gray eyes. We'd been talking since the plane lifted off from Kennedy, through the half-light of a Reykjavik dawn, and now most of the way to Luxembourg.

"Tell me, Mona," he teased. "Are you running away from America, or is it from men?"

"Don't be so negative," I smiled. "I'm escaping to Paris – not from, but to."

His name was Ted and he looked like a cowboy, with stitched boots, a rugged sweater and worn jeans. He was a couple years older than me, en route to Italy with his guitar. I had noticed the rough-hewn angles and planes of his face when I first sat down. Now, 10 hours later, a light-colored stubble had poked through. We'd spent the night laughing, drinking, telling tales.

Ted drank in my stories – Jake, Adam, Radomir, Wim. The sexiness filled him with wanting, and me too, but there we were, strapped in, our seatbelts buckled for landing. We were sharing our first kiss when the plane bumped down on the Luxembourg runway.

"I don't want to leave you at the airport," Ted said huskily as sleepy travelers gathered up their hand luggage. "Let's get a room."

Behind us a rangy dark-haired twentysomething raised an eyebrow, making me blush.

Soon Ted and I were in a taxi, breezing through the tiny kingdom's capital to the foot of its palace where, the driver assured us, we'd have the choice of many hotels.

We collapsed into bed, too exhausted for anything but sleep. When I awoke Ted was kissing the nape of my neck. We dissolved into each other, all the pent-up desire of the night before cascading through the late afternoon into evening. We made love again after a candlelit dinner beneath the palace.

But the next morning we decided to move on.

"Goodbye, and good luck," Ted said at the station as I boarded my train for Paris. He stood and waved. I watched until he could be seen no more.

It was so odd. I could still feel the memory of him deep inside me, yet I knew I'd never see him again. I had no address in Paris. I had no idea where I'd be staying, nor for how long. It was September 1974, I was 24 years old, and this rackety old train was carrying me away from all the bearings of my past, even this last fleeting encounter.

Of course, it had been my choice to come to this new place – actually this old place, Europe – where, I was hoping, I could find some understanding of what matters in the short span we are allotted here on earth. Was it love, or freedom, or equality, or righting the wrongs of the world? Like so many hippies, "revolutionaries," feminists, ecologists and other idealists who had survived the upheaval of the '60s, I was still struggling in the '70s to reconstruct a life.

My brief tryst with Ted had reminded me how wonderful it was to be with a lover – to be held, caressed, enwrapped in the gravelly tones of a man's pleasure. Why couldn't it ever last? I had to face facts – I wanted a stable relationship with a man but my efforts to stay in one had, frankly, failed.

The train rumbled through the gentle hills of eastern France and into Champagne country, where leafy vines glistened in the September sun. So now I was moving to France. Would anything change? I remembered a French expression that suddenly seemed all too appropriate – *la fuite en avant*. Literally "fleeing forward," though it connoted so much more: leaving the past behind to run headlong into the next adventure, consequences be damned.

It wasn't a long train ride from Luxembourg to Paris, only three hours. As I neared my destination, I remembered something else – something I'd experienced during previous travels. When I spoke French I wasn't the same person. Seeing life through the lens of a foreign language imposed a different perception of reality. This altered everything, even one's sense of self.

My mood lifted as the train pulled into the Gare de l'Est and familiar Paris smells enveloped me – espresso, Gauloise cigarettes and French petrol fumes in a heady mix. When I descended into the Métro, I caught the electric whiff of rubber wheels and realized I'd know where I was even blindfolded. In a way, I was coming home.

It was a straight shot on the Métro to the Place Saint-Michel. In my guide book I had earmarked an inexpensive hotel on the Rue des Ecoles – with any luck they'd have a room available. On my back I had my knapsack. Over my shoulder, a handbag and small carryall. Nothing, really. And so, divested of all but my memories, weary but hopeful, I checked in to an uncertain future.

For two days I barely left the hotel, sleeping off jetlag and the effects of my mini-liaison with Ted. I had been careful to ask for a room with a balcony, and there I had my meals – cheese, bread and fruit that I picked up downstairs at a small grocery store, with wine in the evening. It wasn't a luxury – in Paris, wine was cheaper than water.

I finally emerged on a sunlit morning and was crossing the Rue des

Ecoles when a bicyclist, ringing his bell madly, nearly knocked me off my feet.

"*Attention!*" I cried, jumping back in alarm. "Careful!"

How do you say asshole in French, I was wondering, when the rider cried out, "Hi Mona!"

"You!" I exclaimed. It was the rangy dark-haired guy from the plane. "How did you know my name?"

"Are you kidding?" he grinned. "I was sitting behind you on the flight over. I know your whole life story!"

His name was Louis, he was a grad student and he'd be living in France for the year, studying with a paleontologist. He seemed like a nice enough guy despite having eavesdropped. Never mind. It was my fault for spilling everything to Ted, convinced no one in earshot would cross my path again.

"Where's your friend?" Louis asked over café au lait. He brightened when I said Ted had gone on to Italy.

Louis had straight black hair, dark eyes and a protruding chin that gave him a caveman air. Maybe that explained his choice of profession, I thought, as I agreed to meet him that evening for dinner. When he biked away, I virtually danced down the street. A friend in Paris! Of course there was also Wim – he lived a couple of blocks from my hotel. But I wasn't about to call him. We had hardly corresponded since his visit to Ithaca, and when I wrote to tell him I was coming to Paris his reply had felt decidedly cool.

For a week I spent my days house-hunting – tricky without a phone. My room didn't have one, and at the front desk I had to shout into an antiquated mouthpiece, my imperfect French resounding through the lobby. The places I saw were shabby, dark, hole-in-the-wall rooms without even a toilet. You had to share a toilet in the hall, the kind with foot pads where you had to squat. The few nice places I saw were beyond my means. I met Louis for dinner a couple of times, but he was leaving for the south of France and would be gone most of the autumn.

My solitary routine was getting oppressive. The day after Louis left, I felt as though the walls of my hotel room were closing in on me. So what if I was living under the eaves in a picturesque garret in Paris? I'm not spending another evening alone, I thought at the front desk as I dialed Wim's number.

"How long have you been here?" he demanded in surprise. "Why didn't you call?"

Wim already had dinner plans but suggested we meet for a drink afterwards at a café, Le Métro on the Place Maubert.

After a long day and another balcony meal alone – my last, I hoped – I pulled on a striped top and jeans and slipped into the Parisian night. It was a short walk to the café. Through the window, I saw Wim at a table – with a man. Disappointed, I paused. After all these months I wanted Wim to myself.

But there was nothing to be done. So I put on a bright smile and went in to join them.

"You're looking good," Wim said, kissing me on both cheeks. "This is Dieter, a friend from Berlin. Dieter, Mona."

Dieter. Of course. Wim had told me about his gay German friend. They were close, he confided, so close that they had briefly been lovers. The summer before, during my fling with Wim, I'd found it sexy to be sleeping with a bisexual man. Now, confronted with the reality, I felt strange.

Dieter clearly knew about me too. His grave eyes studied me from behind steel-rimmed glasses. He had straight chestnut hair and a flat, sensual mouth with a tiny separation between the lips. I could see why Wim found him attractive.

We ordered beer and the conversation quickly turned to apartment-hunting. Dieter, too, had just arrived. He was doing doctoral research, by coincidence on Julia Kristeva. He needed a place for at least nine months, and so did I. Neither of us had a phone.

"Why don't you two help each other look?" Wim suggested. "Antoinette's out of town this week. You can use her phone."

When we met early the next morning, Dieter had Le Figaro under his arm. Over espresso at a bar's zinc counter we read the ads aloud to each other. We each wanted a one-room flat, preferably in the Latin Quarter. But the one-rooms on offer were expensive and few. My eyes drifted down the page.

"Listen to this," I said. "'Spacious two-room apartment, one bedroom, living room with dining cove that could serve as second bedroom, kitchen, bath, charm. Rue des Boulangers.'"

Dieter checked his Paris street guide. It was near Wim's place, just up the street from the Rue des Ecoles. Our eyes met. This was crazy. Should we?

"Let's go," said Dieter as we quickly paid the barman. It was 7:30 a.m., prime time for apartment hunters. We dashed across the street and up five floors to Antoinette's familiar apartment, its walls still thick with my memories of David and Wim. Dieter dialed the number.

"The apartment's available," said the landlord. "But another couple" – couple! – "is coming at 9, so I'd suggest you get over here right away if you want to be first."

Down the stairs we chased again. Okay, we'd have to pretend to be a couple. Why not, if the place was right? It wasn't expensive, the neighborhood was perfect, and there were advantages to having a housemate. Like Wim and all the student rebels of '68, Dieter was a leftist – reliable enough credentials in my eyes. We concocted a story on the way over, walking so fast we were breathless when we arrived.

Rue des Boulangers is a winding cobblestone street that rises from the Rue Monge and descends sharply toward the university of sciences at Jussieu. The buildings have massive wooden doors, some broad enough to accommodate the horsedrawn carriages of years past. It's a secret of Paris that behind its forbidding facades lie hidden gardens. At the address the landlord had given us, the heavy blue door swung open onto a leafy courtyard that drifted back to Building D, where the apartment was located. Too good to be true, I thought. Up a waxed oak staircase to the third floor we ran. Trying not to laugh, we rang the bell.

"You're first," the landlord announced as he checked us out. The place was bright, with a view onto the courtyard greenery and roofs of the Latin Quarter. The furnishings were basic but adequate. The landlord didn't question our tale that we were a couple.

"It needs a fresh coat of paint and new carpeting," he said. "If you take care of that, you can move right in and I'll knock 10 percent off the rent."

By the time the next would-be tenants trooped up the stairs, Dieter and I were signing the lease. We'd known each other less than 12 hours. The next day we moved in.

Now that I had a place to live, I needed a job. I'd heard that the American Center in Montparnasse had a good bulletin board. So I traipsed over to Boulevard Raspail and found an ad posted by a Frenchman who was looking for an American cleaning lady, someone who could find peanut butter to make sandwiches for his half-American son. No problem, I thought, copying down the address. The next day I met Monsieur Vidal, a 40ish businessman whose American wife had divorced him. He hired me on the spot.

But 30 francs a day – $6 at the time – wasn't enough to live on. At 12 francs an hour that's what I made cleaning up after Monsieur Vidal and his 10-year-old, scouring their bathtub, washing their clothes, ironing, shopping and cooking their evening meal. Sometimes I made enough food for four and took the two extra portions home for Dieter and me. But stealing was against my nature. I found another job.

The Académie de la Grande Chaumière was an art school just a block away from Reid Hall. Nude modeling had proved an easy way to make money in Ithaca, and in France models didn't need working papers – notoriously difficult to obtain. But I mainly loved the idea of joining the circle of women who'd posed in Paris, where so many of the world's great artists had worked.

I was nervous when I entered La Grande Chaumière. A long hall led to a desk where the director's assistant, black hair piled high on her head, cheeks rouged, presided imperiously over the school's comings and goings.

"So you'd like to model," said the woman. "Take off your clothes — here." She pointed to a screen beside the desk.

I complied, doing my best to appear at ease when she peered behind the screen. She frowned but nodded approval.

"Come next Tuesday for the 3 p.m. drawing class."

When I returned, I was ushered into a spacious studio with a small stage layered with worn Persian rugs and a couple of furs. A gas heater was positioned beside the stage, its blue flames creating a warm aura. Artists were setting up their easels. The place looked like it hadn't changed in a hundred years. I slipped out of my clothes behind a screen and emerged to pose facing floor-to-ceiling atelier windows that looked onto a quiet garden. As the artists began sketching I felt like I'd stepped into a painting by Renoir — comfortable, relaxed, appreciated.

A third job came via one of Dieter's grad school friends, Rachelle, a sultry French woman swathed in antique silver jewelry. She was studying psychoanalysis with Jacques Lacan. In Rachelle's intimidating presence, I felt overwhelmed by my ignorance — of French culture, politics, psychoanalysis, literature and pretty much everything else. I was trying to read the newspaper Libération every day, but it had so much impenetrable lefty newspeak that I often gave up. After more than a month in France, I was still hopelessly out of it.

At dinner one evening, Rachelle announced that she knew of a feminist editor who needed an errand girl. So that's how Rachelle sees me, I thought with a wince. My doctoral studies had paralleled hers and Dieter's, but in the eyes of the world I was a cleaning lady now. Why not be an errand girl, too? I could use the money.

Rachelle was waiting. I flashed a smile.

"Great," I said. "When do I start?"

Even with three jobs there was time to go to class. In October, I signed up for a course at the Sorbonne with Sarah Kofman, a French philosopher whose work on Nietzsche I had discovered at Cornell. Although American feminists largely detested Freud, Kofman was a *nouvelle Freudienne*. She had studied with Jacques Derrida, one of the deconstructionists whose work I had embraced and then rejected in Ithaca. In addition, Kofman was Jewish. I was fascinated by the mind of this woman who had sought, so soon after the war, to deconstruct Nietzsche, the German philosopher who perhaps most influenced Hitler.

Living in France in the autumn of 1974, the Holocaust felt very present. Thirty years earlier, Jews were still being gassed in Hitler's death camps and the Nazis had only just been driven from Paris. Now that I was next door to Germany, I intended to go there. It was visceral: I *needed* to understand. Why did Hitler's Reich come to power? How did the unspeakable happen? This is why I'd studied German before leaving Ithaca. I wanted to be able to ask first-hand.

Kofman was a slight blonde woman with a forceful voice. Her philosophy class met in a darkened amphitheater in the Sorbonne's main building. It was so dim it was hard to take notes, so I merely listened. My attempts to get to know the other students were fruitless. They were Parisians and already had plenty of friends.

Thank goodness I had Dieter. We shared our Parisian life easily. The apartment on Rue des Boulangers was painted now – it had taken far longer than either of us expected but the place looked great, except for the tatty carpet. I slept on a sofa bed in the dining cove. No problem, given my sexless existence. Dieter had the bedroom, where he brought handsome conquests he picked up at gay bars along Boulevard Saint-Germain.

Sometimes Dieter also brought home women he'd met as a student radical in Berlin and Paris. He introduced me to Liese Faber, a fair-haired German studying for a Masters in French. Through them I met Chantal Rosenblum, a French high school teacher of Polish Jewish descent. As for Wim, he sometimes came to dinner, nothing more. The love triangle was broken.

I spent most of my time alone, and felt better about it some days than others. I had thought when I flew over to Europe in September that I would shed my alienation like an old cloak upon reaching France. No more immoral war! No more McDonalds! But it hadn't worked out that way. There was so much anti-American feeling in Paris that I sometimes told people I was Canadian. It was easy to pass – easier than explaining that not every American appreciated the policies of the U.S. government. I played with the idea. Could I pass as French? I wanted to be like the self-assured young French women I observed all around me. But even if my accent had not made that impossible, I quickly realized, it would only be role-playing. I couldn't absorb their self-confidence by osmosis. Yes, I was alienated by my country's involvement in Vietnam, by its fast food, big cars and spendthrift ways. I was alienated by America's lack of irony, its self-important vision as the greatest country in the world, even if I loved it for its idealism. But I'd be kidding myself to blame everything on the country I'd left behind.

My alienation was inside of me. I knew it, even if I tried most days to repress that uncomfortable truth. No matter how far I'd gone toward becoming a sophisticated, independent woman, I still felt just as awkward in certain situations as I had as a young teen. I still needed to find my place in the world – to accept myself for the person I was or, better, to allow myself to become the person I wanted to be.

Hadn't that been the attraction of France? It was a land of wit and grace, of taste and savoir-faire – qualities I wanted to acquire. Still, I recognized with relief, I was wearing my alienation better in Paris than I had in the States. Which made sense, in a way. Far easier to feel foreign in a foreign land than to feel out of place in your own country.

As fall edged toward winter, I found myself longing for companionship, preferably male companionship. Paris was supposed to be the capital of romance, but I hardly knew any men. There was Monsieur Vidal, my paunchy employer, whose unwanted advances I'd had to deflect more than once. There was Jules, who picked me up at a bus stop outside Monsieur Vidal's place one gray November day. Jules had the aristocratic good looks of a Renaissance nobleman, with a velvet jacket and flowing black hair. He hopped on the bus, chatted me up on the ride to my literary errand-girl job and waited for me at a bar. The next day I took him to bed at Monsieur Vidal's place. Serves the old coot right, I thought while intertwined with Jules on the living room couch. But Jules had since evaporated into the Paris air. Then came Alejandro, a sexy Argentinian student I met at a demonstration against the Pinochet regime in Chile. He tried to rape me in his dorm room on our first date.

Now it was December, and night fell early – Paris, it turned out, was as far north as Montréal. I mainly stayed in. Looking for solace, or maybe wisdom, I read and reread one of the four books I'd brought over from the States – "What is Called Thinking?" by Martin Heidegger – with no discernable impact on my worsening frame of mind. Christmas was looming. I dreaded the prospect, I confided to Liese.

"Don't stay here alone, Mona," Liese exclaimed. "Come with me to Germany." She had an old car and was dropping Dieter in Essen, then driving on to her parents' place near Bremen, in the north. After Christmas we could go on to Hamburg where Liese's sister, Beate, a New Left activist, would let us sleep on the living room floor of her tiny apartment.

I phoned my parents to let them know I was going to Germany for the holidays. Predictably they disapproved.

"Be careful, sweetie," my mother said. "They still don't like Jews over there."

Maybe. That was why I needed to go.

Liese, Dieter and I rattled into Germany the day before Christmas.

Feeling like a spy who had penetrated the enemy heartland, I took in everything around me, and said little. The buildings, the dress, the food, the demeanor – everything was so different in Germany that I felt I was on another planet. Everything here was heavy, and yet the young people I met were more welcoming than in France, where everything was light. I had tried out my German shortly after we crossed the border, and found I could make myself understood. That was at a gas station. I had gained confidence in the ensuing week, but still preferred to listen. There was so much I needed to know.

Now it was January 1, 1975, and I was, well, in bed with the enemy.

"Tell me more," I murmured, snuggling into Ralf's embrace.

"My father? Yes, he was an officer, but in the army, you know. He wasn't in the SS or the Gestapo."

"Well, he was a Nazi," I persisted.

"Yes, of course," said Ralf. "He had to be. Everyone in the army was in the party. Besides, people believed Hitler was going to save the country."

"But surely he must have known what was happening to the Jews," I said.

It was okay. Ralf was not an anti-Semite – his politics didn't allow that. I had met him at Beate's radical-chic New Year's Eve party, where the cream of Hamburg's New Left turned out. I felt safe exploring this territory with him.

"After Crystal Night," I said, "when they smashed up Jewish shops all over Germany and burned down the synagogues, surely every German knew the fate that awaited the Jews. How could your father have served a regime that allowed such things to happen? And then sent Jews to be gassed in camps?"

"He didn't know about the camps," Ralf said. "At least that's what he told us. He never wanted to talk about the war, though. He won't talk about his experiences, even to me."

"Do you think I could meet him?"

"Come here, Mona," Ralf said, silencing me with a drowsy kiss. "Let's talk later. I need to sleep."

Fair enough. It was four in the morning and we had been intermittently talking and making love since the party. I had to admit that seducing Ralf had been cynical – one of the most cynical things I'd done in my 25 years. But the temptation had been too strong. A handsome blond German with merry blue eyes just waiting to be picked up. In my sex-starved state, how to resist? And sex hadn't even been the main attraction. While we flirted, he'd confided that he was the son of a Nazi officer. Wasn't this why I'd come to Germany? To hear about the war?

With the Rhine wine flowing, the music throbbing as body-to-body guests gyrated in Beate's apartment, Ralf had been such an easy catch. First we talked. He wanted to know where the American left was headed. And would the Vietnam War ever end? I wanted to know what Ralf and his lefty friends thought of the violent Red Army Faction. Then we danced. As the clock neared midnight I wrapped myself around him, letting my pelvis brush his in rhythm to the beat. We kissed when the clock struck twelve.

"Come to my place?" Ralf whispered. I had a quick word with Liese and went to find my coat.

Now, in Ralf's bed, as he snored softly beside me, I felt like I had committed original sin. I hadn't let him enter me at first – not before I gave him a long lazy blow job, enjoying my power over his body. When he came, I held him close and told him I was Jewish.

"Have you ever made love with a Jewish woman before?" I asked.

"Actually, no. But I want to," Ralf said with fervor. "Just give me a few minutes."

As we lay together I told him about my family, how my father's grandparents had fled Russia in the 1890s to escape the pogroms, how my mother's Austro-Hungarian grandparents had left even earlier in hopes of improving their fortunes in the States. My entire family had left Europe a generation before the outbreak of World War I.

"So they didn't lose anyone in the Holocaust," Ralf remarked.

"But that makes it no less real," I said sharply.

"I know," said Ralf. "I didn't mean it wasn't. But you're right, I shouldn't have said it like that. I have so much to learn from you."

I took the cue and drew him to me. I let him kiss me as I reached down to verify what I felt pressing against my belly. Yes, he was ready. I helped him slip inside me, feeling the familiar shock of penetration as he made his way to my very center. After a while we switched places and I was on top. I pulled away, teasing him by refusing him entry until he could wait no longer. He gripped my waist and pulled me to him until our bodies fused. Now we were in rhythm.

"I can feel your heartbeat," Ralf said in the afterglow. That was when I asked him about his father.

Now, as I drifted toward sleep, I let memories of my trip to this strange Teutonic land flit through my mind.

There had been the journey from France, with Liese at the wheel of her old crate, Dieter in front beside her, driving northeast through Aix-la-Chapelle – the Germans called it Aachen – to the depressing industrial heartland, frozen white in the December cold. Beate came down from Hamburg for Christmas with Liese's family, and the occasion should have been festive. But although Liese's mother prepared a lovely holiday dinner, with goose and red cabbage, her father sat through the meal without speaking. As he ate he shot what I took to be suspicious glances my way. He had been wounded as a youth in the war, and walked with a limp. Did he resent me because I was American, or because I was Jewish? I didn't possess enough German to ask, and besides I was a guest in his house.

"Don't worry about my father," Liese reassured me. "He never says much."

But if I didn't worry I wondered about it. What was it like to be shot at the age of 18? I imagined his terror as he lay amid the rubble of Berlin, bleeding from the leg, teeth chattering, not knowing whether he'd be rescued. At least it was a Russian soldier, not an American, who had fired at him 30 years ago. But what must he think about this guest, his daughter's friend, whose country had defeated the Reich? After all, it wasn't his fault the war broke out. To my surprise, I felt a secret sympathy for this taciturn man.

Then there was the one-legged, white-haired veteran I had passed on the street in Hamburg. He was on crutches, his pant leg turned up at the knee. His keen blue eyes, his aristocratic demeanor, his bitter elegance caught my glance. Intrigued, I turned on my heel and followed him to a bar near the port. He didn't notice as I found a table in the back. Over tea, I observed him. He sipped slowly from a large stein of beer, looking out to sea. Who had he been in the war? A Nazi officer, surely. Perhaps in the navy. Maybe he'd been a member of the SS, Hitler's elite troops, or even, god forbid, the Gestapo. But I didn't dare approach him to ask.

And then, tonight, Ralf, my Aryan lover. He had received the postwar political education that all young Germans got in school. Even through the lens of his leftist politics, he seemed to have no hang-ups about being with an American.

But he had no first-hand knowledge of Jews. There simply were none left to know in his environment. Still, it was hard for him to open up about his father — mainly because his father had said so little.

"I think he was an honorable man," said Ralf. "I know he hates Hitler now, for bringing such shame on our country."

We were getting our clothes on in the gray-yellow dawn. It was already 9, and Liese was planning to start the drive back to Paris at 10.

"Mona — let me come visit you in France," Ralf said, hugging me one last time before we left the warmth of his flat for the icy streets. "We can talk about the war some more."

"Okay," I lied. "We'll see."

The man sitting on the window ledge in Chantal's kitchen was wearing a navy blue sailor's sweater with buttons on one shoulder. He was thin, with curly black hair, twinkling brown eyes behind wire-rim glasses and a significant nose over a black mustache. No one introduced him when I arrived with Liese and Dieter — clearly they already knew each other. They bantered easily together as Chantal made lunch, cauliflower with a creamy cheese sauce. It was steamy in the kitchen, cheery and warm, and it felt good to be in from the cold.

As the others chatted, I glanced at the man in the window. When our eyes met, for only a second, a jolt hit my belly. Something electric filled the air.

Lunch was about to be served. When the curly-haired man went to wash his hands, I turned to Dieter.

"Who is he?" I asked quietly.

"Jacques? He's Chantal's brother. I thought you knew."

No, I mused, and I would never have guessed. Chantal Rosenblum had pale blue eyes, frizzy auburn hair and a lilting voice. She bore absolutely no resemblance to her brother, who spoke in gruff tones and looked startlingly like the ink drawing of a Polish rabbi my parents had back in Wisconsin. As Jacques and Chantal conversed over lunch, I wondered how two people who had grown up together could be so different. By the time we finished the meal I was feeling high, and we hadn't had wine.

"Tell me about Jacques," I asked Dieter when we left, trying to sound nonchalant. "Is he with someone?"

"Why," Dieter teased, "are you interested?"

I blushed. "Come on," I said. "Just tell me."

"He was living with someone for a long time, but they split up about a year ago."

"Who was it? What was she like?"

"Jeanne. Very good-looking. Blonde. Kind of intense. They were at university together, at Nanterre. I think they got together during May '68."

"I wonder how old he is."

"He's about my age," said Dieter, who was already 28. Three years older than me.

"Hurry up, you two," called Liese. In her car she had a big roll of carpeting that we'd bought at a discount store in the suburbs. She wanted to get us home with it. And we needed to get it down on the floor of our apartment. It was already mid-January, and the landlord was pressing us to finish the job.

The next morning, when I arose, Dieter was having tea in the kitchen, alone for once. He winked at me.

"Chantal phoned last night after you went to bed."

Electricity again. I was wide awake.

"And?"

"Jacques started asking Chantal about you as soon as we left. He asked her to find out whether I thought you'd go out with him."

"So? What did you say?"

"I said I thought you would. He'll probably call you."

All day I waited, but the phone didn't ring. By evening, unable to stand it, I went out for some air. My steps took me down to the river, to the quays along the Seine.

Staring pensively at the inky ribbon of water, I didn't notice the man come up beside me until he spoke.

"Are you sad?" he asked in accented French.

"Not at all," I replied tartly, annoyed by this invasion of my privacy. But he looked unthreatening, even interesting, blond with a long thin ponytail and a small gold hoop in one ear. I didn't move away.

"That's my home," he said, pointing to a houseboat just below. "Would you like to take a look?"

"No thanks."

"Well, would you join me for a beer?"

Why not, I thought. It's much better than sitting at home waiting for that blasted Frenchman to call.

We repaired to a nearby café and the man with the ponytail told me about his life adrift. He was a Dutchman, a sailor, and swore he had a parrot on the boat. Going from port to port, he lived from day to day, taking odd jobs as they came along. He didn't believe in accumulating material things. Or even immaterial things, he took pains to point out, like a relationship. His name was Nico. After several beers he asked to walk me home.

"Can I come in, Mona?" he asked when we reached my door. He slipped his hand casually around my waist. To my annoyance I felt a tingle of pleasure move up my spine.

"No," I said firmly. "Not tonight."

Dieter was reading when I entered the flat alone.

"Well?" I asked.

"Nothing," he said. "No phone calls."

I crept away to bed. Dieter and I had switched places so I now had the bedroom, its mattress on the floor taking up most of the space. I liked the deep blue carpeting we'd chosen. At least something in the room felt peaceful.

The next morning sunlight was streaming into the room when I awoke. I didn't feel like getting up, but I had to. Chantal and some other friends were coming to dinner and I had volunteered to cook.

"Why don't *you* call *him?*" Dieter said when I emerged looking downcast. "You could invite him to join us tonight." But then he remembered that Jacques didn't have a phone.

I was in the tub when the call came.

"It's him," Dieter shouted. "What should I tell him?"

But I was already bounding to the phone, wrapped in a towel.

"*Oui*," I said into the receiver, utterly failing to conceal my happiness. "*Oui, ce soir, c'est possible.* I'm free tonight. But you come here. We're having friends over. Come at 7 and stay for dinner."

I floated down the street, did the shopping, then got busy in the kitchen. In mid-afternoon the doorbell rang. Who could that be, I thought, vaguely irritated at the interruption. I brushed off my apron and pulled the door open.

It was Nico. With a bouquet! And this time he wasn't taking no for an answer.

"Come here, Mona," he said, throwing his arms around me. "I'm not leaving Paris till I've had you."

I pushed him away, trying to get him out the door.

"Nico, I can't see you now. I'm cooking. We're having company tonight. And besides, I think I'm in love!"

"In love?" sneered Nico. "You didn't mention that last night." He sank into an armchair, impervious to my request that he leave immediately. I was cajoling him, promising I'd see him another day, when the bell rang again.

"Now what?" I moaned.

I opened the door and gasped. It was Jacques! With a pretty box from a pastry shop. Trying not to panic, I blocked his way.

"You're early," I smiled. "By several hours." The last thing I wanted was to let him in with another man in the house.

"I know," said Jacques. "It's just that I couldn't wait! I needed to see you, Mona."

He swept past me into the living room – and stopped dead at the sight of Nico.

"But perhaps I am intruding," Jacques said stiffly. "Here." He thrust the box at me. "I'll come back later."

"No, no," I cried. "Please stay! He was just leaving."

But Nico showed no inclination to leave. He sat there in his armchair, clearly amused, as Jacques headed for the door.

"I know what," I said, blocking his way again. "Let's all have a nice cup of tea, and then we'll go for a walk." Cooking could wait.

But Jacques would have none of it. When he left, I turned on Nico.

"Now look what's happened," I snapped. "You should have left. You don't even believe in love, and now I may never see him again!"

"Don't worry," said Nico. "He'll be back. I could tell by the way he looked at you. Now let's go to bed."

"No!" I cried. "I can't. Now you'll just have to leave. Here's my number. Call up the next time you're in Paris."

Even with Nico finally out of the house, I was a wreck. I somehow managed to finish cooking and put on the long skirt I saved for special occasions.

Dieter returned from the library at 7, and our guests arrived. All except Jacques. By 8, with dinner ready to go on the table, I thought I'd die of nerves. Then the bell rang.

We made light conversation through dinner. When I rose to clear the table, Jacques followed.

We were alone in the kitchen. "Who was he?" Jacques asked.

"Just some guy I met last night when I was taking a walk."

"But how did he get your address?" Jacques insisted.

"I let him walk me home. Mistake!" I replied. "But don't worry. He's a Dutch sailor. He doesn't even live here."

We took some plates back to the dining cove along with the pale green pastry box. I untied its pink ribbon. Inside was a magnificent pear tart.

"From Bourdaloue," Jacques announced proudly.

I knew nothing of Bourdaloue – one of Paris' best patisseries, I later learned – but I knew enough to realize that a tart could be more than a tart. Taking my time, I cut six slices and passed them around the table. My face was warm with the realization that Jacques was watching me. Our eyes locked as we lifted our spoons and let the delicious flaky pastry and the sweet wet pears melt into a foretaste of desire.

After dessert, the guests proposed we all go out for coffee. I preferred to stay in, but I was overruled. At the café, I couldn't concentrate. I couldn't wait to get home and take Jacques to bed, to feel his body against mine. This day had been so long! But in the street, Jacques surprised me.

"Au revoir," he said, kissing me on both cheeks. He was leaving!

"Don't you want to come home with me?" I asked. So much had happened in the last 24 hours, I felt lost.

"No," he said. "Not tonight. I'll call you."

❧

I tossed for hours before succumbing. Men! It was impossible to tell what they wanted.

It felt like I'd just drifted off when the phone started jangling beside the bed. I fumbled for it in the dark.

"Mona? Did I wake you?"

It was Jacques, the sound of his voice as sweet to me as nectar to a starving bee.

"What time is it?" I was wide awake.

"Six. I couldn't sleep. I kept thinking about you."

"Mmmm. Me too."

"I need to see you. I can be there in half an hour."

In the winter darkness I quickly slipped on my striped top and jeans. I made coffee but felt too nervous to drink it. Would he ever get here?

When the bell rang, Jacques hesitated in the doorway.

"Any other guys here today?" he asked, peeking inside.

I smiled.

"No. Just Dieter. Let's go."

Bundled against the January cold, we headed into the brisk morning, first to a bar for café au lait and croissants, then down to the river. The sun was just coming up. We tarried as we strolled down the Quai de Montebello where I had met Nico two nights ago – his houseboat was gone now. We stopped to browse at Left Bank book sellers just opening their stands as we followed the Seine to the venerable Pont Neuf.

"The New Bridge," said Jacques as we crossed, "but in fact it's the oldest bridge in Paris." He was wearing a cap, the tweedy kind with a brim that French taxi drivers wear.

Before reaching the Right Bank we stopped to take in the morning, leaning against the cold white stone of the bridge. We had passed the tip of Ile de la Cité and could see the slated turrets of the Conciergerie to the east, brilliant in the morning light. To the west was the Eiffel

Tower, soaring against a blue sky dotted with feathery clouds. Below rushed the sun-flecked river. It was turning into a perfect day.

I turned to Jacques. "Where are we going?" I asked.

"It doesn't matter," he replied, taking my hand in his thick glove. "I just want to get to know you."

Holding hands, we continued across the bridge and headed toward Les Halles – unfamiliar territory for me as I rarely left the Left Bank. I remembered Les Halles from my first visit to Paris, with my parents and Ben when I was 17. We had dined at a restaurant beside charming glass pavilions housing the city's huge food market. Now the pavilions had been torn down, leaving a vast muddy hole.

"An Italian director shot a Western down there last summer," Jacques told me as I gazed into the abyss. It was true, the hole was big enough to accommodate plenty of horses. At the center, the winter rains had created a muddy lake.

We turned into the Rue du Louvre and headed north. It was lunch time, but Jacques didn't mention food and I didn't ask. I had butterflies in my stomach.

We reached a broad, crowded avenue lined with cheap-looking stores. "Les Grands Boulevards," Jacques announced, turning right into a mass of people out for a Sunday stroll.

What's so grand about this, I wondered, as we wove a path through the boisterous crowd. But Jacques seemed perfectly at ease.

He steered me into a side street where the atmosphere instantly changed to something warmer, more familiar. I had an odd sense I was nearing home. We entered a delicatessen called Goldenberg's. The smells of Jewish food were deliciously maddening. People bustled and jostled their way to the counter.

"We'll have a picnic," Jacques said as we waited our turn.

I laughed nervously.

"Are you sure you think we should eat outdoors in this weather?"

"Of course not," he said. "We'll go to my place."

My heart began to pound.

He bought caraway rye and big kosher pickles and corned beef and kosher salami and cake and a bottle of wine. As the shop woman wrapped up our package, I realized I was starving.

A few blocks more and we turned into the small street where Jacques lived. His flat was on the third floor. I held my breath as he turned the key in his door, pushed it open and ushered me in.

Sunlight spilled through tall windows into the living room, painting its oak floor with splashes of gold. I sank into a sofa, all my senses aroused. First we had tea with the little pastries Jacques had bought at the deli. We talked and talked, about my family and his, and our past loves. Our studies, our work, our hopes. Politics. Even religion. But not sex.

As evening fell, Jacques unfolded a pink linen tablecloth and – since the room lacked a table – laid it on the living room floor, beside the door to his bedroom. On the cloth he set silver candelabra with white candles, stemmed glasses, white china plates and silver cutlery. I stood in his kitchen and watched as he arranged the food on platters and uncorked the wine. He wouldn't let me help.

We settled ourselves on the floor beside the improvised table. The candles' soft glow filled the room – it couldn't have been more romantic. I let Jacques serve me. We were just lifting a glass when the doorbell rang.

"Oh no," said Jacques.

"You don't have to answer," I murmured. But he did. He didn't have a phone. It could be something important.

He rose and opened the door.

"*Ooh-là*," said the youth who entered. "It looks like I'm interrupting something." He turned to leave.

"Not at all," lied Jacques. "Let me take your coat. Mona, this is Yann. Yann, Mona."

So Yann joined the feast, inserting himself into Jacques' carefully choreographed seduction scene. He was the brother of Jeanne, Jacques' former girlfriend, and he clearly felt at home.

As the two friends chatted, I could hardly eat. The food felt odd in my mouth – I wanted to taste only Jacques. But fate had made that impossible. Watching the candles burn down, I scandalized myself by wondering whether Yann was available. He was a very attractive guy. I was so turned on I would have been prepared to leave with him had Jacques not finally suggested it was time for our guest to go.

I wanted to put the dinner things away, but Jacques caught hold of me and led me to his bed. We undressed by candlelight. I was shivering. On his bed Jacques had an enormous blue satin quilt encased in a crisp cotton cover. We snuggled in under the quilt to finish undressing.

How strange, I thought as Jacques' hands explored my body. We hadn't yet kissed.

I lifted my face to his, and our lips met. His mustache tickling me was the last thing I noticed as our tongues intertwined and we slipped into lovers' oblivion.

LOVE
1975

Jacques-and-Mona, Mona-and-Jacques. Two months, and we were already an item, consecrated not by a ring or any external token but by the way friends had double-barreled our names – other couples like Roger-and-Françoise, Ariel-and-Jacqueline, Yann-and-Christine. Was this what I'd been looking for? Who could tell? It had all happened so fast I hadn't had time to think it over.

Now, two months into our relationship, the thump-in-the-gut way I had felt when I first saw Jacques still hit me with surprising force each time we met. It wasn't just the thrill of being in love with a Frenchman in France. I *liked* Jacques – his politics, his attitude, his quirks. He had a quick intelligence that I appreciated and a sharp sense of irony. He was attentive, warm, generous, energetic. The fact that he was a Jewish intellectual was icing on the cake.

Jacques had a Masters in sociology but was working as a welder – actually an apprentice welder in a government-financed training program. A choice, I presumed, stemming from his time at Nanterre, the most radical of French universities. Something about getting closer to the working class. He left home before dawn Monday to Friday, taking a thermos of coffee with him. He was exhausted when he came back in the evening. I wanted to cook for him, but he wouldn't hear of it. He had a routine – *une semaine de soupe, une semaine de riz*. A week of soup, a week of rice. He did the shopping and cooking on Sundays. On soup weeks he piled carrots, leeks and a slab of bacon into a large pot of water with some thyme. This he ate for the next five nights, accompanied by wine, bread and cheese. The recipe was the same on rice weeks, except he chopped the bacon into cubes and sautéed it with the vegetables before adding brown rice and water. For breakfast he had bread, butter and a whole clove of garlic. Every day!

Jacques didn't like displays of emotion, but he demonstrated his affection in other ways. I found it touching how quickly he brought me into his circle. We'd been together for only a couple of weeks when he took me to meet his cousin's newborn son.

"Too cute!" I exclaimed when I saw the tiny baby in the basket. "May I pick him up?"

I settled myself in an easy chair as the young mother lifted the precious bundle and handed him over. Maxim was just a few weeks old. The father, Jacques' cousin Roger, was a dark gorilla of a man. Françoise, the mother, was petite, blonde and luminously beautiful in that understated way some Frenchwomen achieve. Both were medical students.

I felt fluttery in the home of this charming couple, a tiny flat under the eaves replete with baby. As I held the child I wondered how long it would be before I, too, could produce such a miracle. After all, I was already 25. The fluttery feeling persisted through lunch at a small bistro where the four of us talked and laughed as Maxim slept in his basket beside the table. A wave of longing invaded me. I could feel it in my belly – I wanted a baby. Why was this feeling so strong? It must be hormones, I thought, trying to shake myself back to reality. Jacques and I had only just started seeing each other. It wasn't time yet.

I spent most nights at Jacques' place, returning home to the Rue des Boulangers in the morning to change, clean Monsieur Vidal's apartment – and look for a new place to live. Shortly after Deiter and

I finished redecorating, the landlord had announced we'd have to leave. So we were house-hunting again.

Dieter wanted to move in with the man he'd been seeing. I couldn't move in with Jacques – it was just too new. Through Yann we heard about a top-floor maid's room I could rent. I went to check it out on a sunny February afternoon. It was on the Rue Buffon, across the street from the Jardin des Plantes, Paris's botanical gardens, and would have been perfect had it not been a seventh-floor walk-up, with no phone. But it was cheap and clean. I took it.

Jacques borrowed his father's car to take my things to the maid's room – two rooms, actually, with hexagonal terracotta tiles on the floor. There was a tiny sleeping cove just big enough for a double bed and a main room with table and chairs, a ministove, a tiny fridge and a small space heater. There was no toilet – I had to use the communal squatter in the hall. But the place did have a sink, and beside it a plywood board that served as a counter. Beneath the board was a small bathtub. You could sit in it and read a book – which is what I did most days, to keep warm. The tiny heater didn't really warm the place but there was an endless supply of hot water.

Reading in the tub beside a window that looked out on the snow-covered gardens below felt romantic – I was actually living in a garret in Paris! – but it was lonely. Nobody wanted to climb seven narrow flights of stairs only to find I wasn't there. I could go out and use a pay phone to reach most people, but not Jacques. He had been waiting for the French telephone company to install a phone at his place for more than a year but didn't look likely to get one anytime soon. There was a long waiting list, and the state-run phone company was just not in a hurry. This was the kind of inefficiency that drove Americans in Paris crazy in the '70s.

The phone problem nearly torpedoed our relationship one February day when we planned to go visit Yann and his girlfriend at their cottage in the Loire valley. I went to the train station at the appointed hour, but Jacques wasn't there. Not daring to board without him, I went home depressed, only to find a terse note in my mailbox. Jacques had come to my place to meet me and wanted to know where on earth I'd been.

"Too bad, we could have had a nice time," he wrote.

I waited for hours but he didn't come back. Late that afternoon I went to the post office and sent him a *pneumatique*. They could shoot a letter across Paris through pressurized tubes and deliver it in an hour – the fastest way to communicate in those days. Hearing nothing back from Jacques, I had a bad night. But the next morning he turned up with a bouquet of roses. We left together for the station after coffee.

I had seen Yann a couple of times but had never before met his partner, Christine, a dancer who had dropped out of the Paris ballet scene to adopt a post-'60s back-to-the-land lifestyle. She had chestnut hair tied back in a ponytail and worked hard at being "zen." She and Yann lived in a small stone house with no running water. They had to go out to the well to fetch water for bathing and cooking. The dishes they washed outdoors. They heated the house with a cheery wood fire and made simple food from vegetables they grew in their garden. They needed little money. Even in winter the area was quite beautiful. It was an appealing kind of life.

Like Roger and Françoise, Yann and Christine had been together for years but hadn't wed. This was another legacy of May '68 – young French leftists absolutely did not believe in marriage.

"Why do we need a piece of paper to certify how we feel about each other?" Christine replied testily when I asked if they planned to marry. "As long as we love each other, we'll be together. It's our business, not the business of City Hall."

Thinking it over, I realized I didn't have any French friends who were married. Even if they had children. It was different in the States, where various leftist friends had already made their couples official.

One day I asked Jacques what he thought about that.

"I'll never get married," he said. "It's too bourgeois."

Oh god, I thought, here we go again. But I kept my thoughts to myself. What was the point of arguing? I was in love with Jacques. I wasn't about to leave him over a detail like marriage. Besides, he might change his mind.

Jacques wasn't doctrinaire the way some of his friends were – the ones who became card-carrying members of one or another group when the French new left split into factions: Maoists, Trotskyists, Maoist-Trotskyists... It was confusing, but it mattered because you were judged by the company you kept. Almost as though the literary salons of the 18th century had resurrected in the form of New Left political factions. Jacques had stayed clear of these groups, although a couple of his friends belonged to the Ligue Communiste Révolutionnaire – which despite the name was not Communist, but neo-Trotskyist.

His parents, however, were Communists. Or had been. They left the French Communist Party in 1956 when the Soviet Union crushed liberalism in Hungary – not, I noted, three years earlier, when Nikita Khrushchev denounced Stalin's crimes.

I had heard about the Rosenblum parents from Chantal even before meeting Jacques. They were East European Jews who had fled Poland in the late '30s, just before Germany invaded. Jacques' mother went first to Palestine, was expelled back to Poland by the British, then made her way to Paris as a clandestine immigrant. His father had also come clandestinely to Paris, which is where the two met. They joined the Communist Party and lived frugally but happily among other Polish Jews until the war reached France in 1940. Jacques' father joined the French Foreign Legion, went to war and was quickly captured by the Germans. He survived despite being Jewish thanks to the Red Cross, which supervised the German prisoner-of-war camps where he was held. His mother hid, first in attics in Paris, then in the countryside. Despite being separated they were able to marry via the Red Cross. This allowed Jacques' mother to get a card as "the wife of a prisoner of war," which gave her a measure of protection – not from the Nazis, but from the French police – and probably saved her life. The two were reunited in 1945 when Jacques' father came straggling back to Paris, emaciated but alive.

This heroic past weighed on Chantal.

"It's too heavy being the child of Jews who lived through the war," she told me. "I could never match their courage."

Jacques, too, felt the weight of his family heritage, although he expressed it differently.

"I'm just waiting for them to die," he said one day while putting on his socks.

"You can't mean it!" I exclaimed.

"I do," said Jacques. "As long as they're alive, I'll have the feeling I can never live up to their expectations."

Maybe this is why Jacques imposed a kind of moral rigor on himself and expected the same of others. It was unnerving – I wasn't sure even I lived up to his expectations. Like so many other French people I met, he was both fascinated and repelled by America. He could be stingingly ironic about Americans and it was hard not to take personally. Yes, we were having a sexy affair, but did he like me? I wondered about it.

So I was pleased when Jacques said his parents had invited us to dinner. I dressed carefully and, on the walk over, was surprised to find they lived just around the corner from Jacques' place – in an apartment they were granted by the French government after the war.

His mother emerged from the kitchen to greet us. Elise, as she was known in France, looked me over and smiled approvingly. She was a slight, rather austere woman with gray hair pulled back in a bun. I tried but failed to spot any resemblance with Jacques – except perhaps for her twinkling brown eyes. But his father, Marek, looked so much like Chantal it was uncanny, never mind that he was bald. Same light blue eyes, same dimples, same toothy grin. He worked as a tailor making leather goods – gloves, jackets, coats – and Elise helped out at his workshop.

Their apartment felt familiar at once. It was filled with tchatchkas, and the comfortable smells of Jewish cooking reminded me of my grandparents' place back in Wisconsin. But when I took my seat at the table, the food was most definitely not the same. The main course was roast horse. I couldn't insult Jacques' mother by refusing to eat it. So I forced myself. It was much like beef, if you didn't think about it too hard. This, I surmised, made me part of the family.

In March, Jacques went south to attend the delivery of Jeanne's first baby. I took it badly. We'd been together for two months, and I couldn't get my head around the idea that Jacques would be at the bedside when his ex gave birth. After all, he wasn't the father. That was Thomas, the dashing Pole who had swept Jeanne off her feet a year earlier. But Jacques had given his word and wasn't about to break it. He left me at his place in Paris on my own.

Jeanne and Thomas lived on a farm in the Cévennes, west of Provence. In a back-to-the-land mood, she wanted natural childbirth at home. No hospital, no clinic, just the local doctor and some friends. I didn't hear a word from Jacques for a week – he had no phone, so there were no phone calls, and he forgot to write. Let's face it: I was jealous, and in no mood to be conciliatory when he finally returned.

Jacques looked worse than haggard when he entered the flat.

"I feel like I'm returning from a war zone," he mumbled, and sank down on the couch. His appearance startled me. Instead of giving vent to my grievances, I just asked what happened.

The baby, he said, was fine – a girl, Camille – but the birth had been traumatic.

"Jeanne went past her due date so the doctor decided to induce," he told me. "The contractions went on for hours. It turned out she needed a Caesarian, but it was too late to move her and there was no way the doctor could operate out at the farm. He had to go in with suction cups to force the baby out."

"No, really?"

"Jeanne was screaming – just terrible, unreal – but then Camille was born." He paused for a moment. "But there was a complication. She couldn't expel the placenta – her contractions were too weak. There was a risk of hemorrhage. So the doctor just stuck his fist up inside her and pulled the placenta out. He didn't give a damn how much she screamed."

I winced. "Oh my god! How barbaric."

"I thought I was going to pass out," said Jacques, "but someone had to be there to help Jeanne."

"What about Thomas?"

Jacques snorted.

"Thomas left the room as soon as Jeanne went into labor. He couldn't take it. He just sat there in another room while she was struggling to have their baby. He played his guitar as though nothing was going on."

"How could he desert her like that?" I asked indignantly.

"That's why Jeanne wanted me there, I think," Jacques said. "She was afraid she wouldn't be able to count on him."

I was miserable but said nothing. How could I verbalize what I felt? After everything Jeanne had gone through, my feelings seemed trivial now. It was too confusing. I wanted to be the one having Jacques' baby, not Jeanne! But it wasn't Jacques' baby, I reminded myself.

We never discussed it again, but perhaps Jacques sensed how much this incident had upset me. As I drew into myself, he became more caring, more attentive. When April came, he asked me to move in with him. With only a moment's hestitation, I agreed.

Jacques borrowed his father's station wagon, parked at the Rue Buffon and climbed the seven stories to help me with my meager belongings. When everything was stashed in the car, we set out for the small street in the 10th arrondissement that would be my new home.

"I'm moving in with my French lover," I thought contentedly as we rolled through the lamplight of Paris by night, across the Seine, through the Place de la Bastille and along broad boulevards toward the Gare de l'Est.

Then Jacques picked a fight. The subject was trivial, but by the time we reached his place he had decided I shouldn't move in after all. When he parked outside his building and went in, leaving me in the car with my belongings, I felt hot tears roll down my cheeks.

Hadn't I learned anything? I thought back to when I moved to New Jersey to be with Jake, only to have him turn his back on me. I had wanted to flee but had nowhere to go. Now this psychodrama was repeating itself. The maid's room I'd just left had been rented to a new tenant. My things were in Jacques' car. I couldn't see any choice but to go inside.

I carried my backpack up three flights to Jacques' door and rang the bell. No answer. I rang a few more times, then sat down on the stairs, head bowed like an old woman. After a while I got up and pounded on the door.

"Jacques, let me in!" I shouted. Across the hall a neighbor poked his head out and glared at me.

"What's going on?" he demanded.

"I forgot my keys," I mumbled as, at last, the door swung open. There was Jacques, lips pressed firmly together in a scowl. But he let me in.

I crept to bed. This was so far from the crossing-the-threshold scenario I had dreamed of since childhood that all I desired was oblivion. My prince had come, and look what happened. I longed for a drug, whisky, anything, to help me forget about this fiasco and go to sleep.

The next day, Jacques brought me coffee and croissants in bed. When I told him I'd be moving to a hotel, he begged me to stay.

"I don't know what came over me," he said, once again the charming Frenchman. "I want you to be here."

"No you don't," I retorted. "If you did you would never have abandoned me in the car like that."

"I'm so sorry," said Jacques, kissing me on the forehead, the nose, the cheeks. As he moved his lips toward mine I recoiled, but the thump-in-the-gut got the better of me. It was a Sunday morning. Church bells were pealing, the sun flooded in, birds twittered outside our window. Despite the sadness that had invaded me the night before, all seemed (nearly) right with the world. After a while we made love. Later he helped me unpack my things. All too easily I let the pain fly out of my soul. Had he been a bastard? Definitely. Was I going to leave? No way.

Thinking back, I have to wonder why a woman would stay with a man after such a disturbing scene. And then I remember the blues – the delta blues, the Chicago blues, all those old songs of love gone wrong and women hanging on. Hanging on in hope that he will see the light and mend his ways.

In hope of never losing the magic of his touch.

It was the scent that woke me. We had been driving all night, four of us piled into an old car, windows open to the balmy spring air. Toward dawn a perfume more intoxicating than any I remembered wafted in, teasing me from sleep. Jacques was at the wheel, Ariel and Jacqueline dozing in back.

"What do I smell?" I asked. "It's beautiful."

"Look," said Jacques. "We're in the south. The *genêt* grows wild down here."

Out the window, bushes of broom lush with yellow flowers filled every available space, even the median strip. I drank in the heady odor.

It was the last leg of our journey. In the early evening we had left Paris in Ariel's battered Renault 4L, a tin can of a car that made you aware of every bump in the road. Now, Jacques said, we were just an hour from our destination.

I was too excited to feel fatigued. The dawn turned rosy as we headed into the Gard, an ancient Languedoc area that reached all the way to the Mediterranean and looked as if it hadn't changed in centuries. Rolling fields and vineyards alternated with small villages, their august stone houses and undulating tile roofs reminding me of my summer in Provence six years earlier. We drove through a sizable town, Alès, a smaller one, Anduze, then turned into the woods, down a packed earth lane lined with scrub oak. Cicadas chirped quietly in the early morning heat. White light slanted through the leaves. The beauty took my breath away.

We were in the Cévennes. This was the lane to Floréal, Jeanne's farm.

At first I'd balked when Jacques suggested we go to Floréal over a long weekend in May. But the prospect of a trip with my lover had outweighed any qualms. Being with Jacqueline and Ariel also softened the prospect of spending three days with Jacques' ex. Jacqueline was salt of the earth, a medical student specializing in gynecology. Ariel was an architect. He reminded me of Woody Allen – his looks, his sense of humor. They would keep things in perspective.

When we pulled up to the old stone farmhouse, Thomas was standing there waiting for us. He was a carpenter, tall and muscular with deep-set blue eyes and a shock of blond hair.

"Jacques," he said with a bear hug, "wait till you see how Camille has grown! Jacqueline, Ariel, good to see you. And," he said, looking me up and down, "you must be Mona. Welcome to Floréal!"

We trooped inside and there was Jeanne in the kitchen, nursing the baby.

"Ooh, let me see her!" cooed Jacqueline, as she rushed to admire the child.

"Jeanne," said Jacques with that gruff voice he used when he felt emotional about something. "Look at Camille. How beautiful she is!" He embraced his ex and kissed the baby on the head. I reached for his hand.

"Oh yes," he said, "Jeanne, this is Mona."

Thomas brought coffee, fresh bread and fig jam to a big wooden table where we sat chatting as Jeanne fed the baby. It was a rambling farm kitchen with beams and high windows that let the light flood in.

Jeanne was wearing an old-fashioned linen slip dyed raspberry pink. She had her sandy-blonde hair in a crewcut, much like Jean Seberg in Godard's film "Breathless." The effect only heightened her beauty. She had huge blue-grey eyes, freckles and a mouth that frowned ever so slightly when relaxed, à la Jeanne Moreau. But this Jeanne evoked not just the two actresses, but Joan of Arc – Jeanne d'Arc in French. She had that look of illumination shared by saints and crusaders and madmen.

"Let's get you settled," said Jeanne when we'd finished our breakfast. "Jacques and Mona, you can stay in the *magnanerie*. Thomas will take you. Ariel and Jacqueline, you're upstairs here in the house."

"What's a *magnanerie*?" I asked as Thomas escorted us to an ancient stone barn.

"It's the barn where they used to raise the silkworms," said Thomas. "This is a silk-growing region. Look at all the mulberry trees."

I hadn't noticed the mulberry trees, but once they'd been pointed out I could see they were all around the property. It was mid-morning and already hot.

"Come on," said Jacques. "I'll take you on a tour."

We walked back down the packed earth lane to a house we had passed on the way in.

"This is where Jeanne's mother lives," said Jacques. "When her husband died, she gathered her five children and asked whether they wanted to keep the farm or sell it and split the money. There was no argument. So now Jeanne's mother is here full-time. So is the oldest son, Joseph. He takes care of the vineyard. Yann and the others stop by from time to time."

We walked back to the main house. Grapevines stretched into the distance against a backdrop of forest. The cicadas were making a racket now. Jacques took Ariel, Jacqueline and me to see the vegetable patch, down a grassy path past an outbuilding where Joseph made the wine. The path wended around an old cistern to the garden, where neat rows of onion greens, lettuce, carrot fronds, miniature bean plants and green peas tied to criss-cross stakes formed a pretty pattern against the red-brown earth. Tiny tomato plants were already in flower.

I reached down to pick a tomato leaf and crushed it in my hand, releasing its earthy odor. It made me dream of having a farmhouse and growing my own food.

When we returned to the house Jeanne was outside on the porch washing Camille in a plastic tub. The baby, just two months old, gurgled and cooed in the warm water. She had her father's bright blue eyes and a fuzz of white-blonde hair.

"Could I hold her?" I asked when the baby was dry.

"Here," said Jeanne, handing her over. I settled myself in a wicker chair beneath a wisteria bower heavy with purple blooms and cuddled the child. Longing surged up again. When would I, too, be a mother?

After a leisurely lunch with plenty of wine, Jacques and I retired for a siesta to the *magnanerie*. It was a vast space lit by slats under the roof. Soft white light filtered in. Despite the May heat, thick stone walls kept the barn cool. It was sparsely furnished, with a double bed as centerpiece. Around the walls were chimneys used in the old days to keep the silkworms warm in their cocoons. The sound of insects drowsily buzzing outdoors was like a lullaby.

I led Jacques to the bed. I was wearing a white Mexican peasant blouse with bright embroidered flowers and a pair of old jeans. I slipped out of my sandals and stretched out. Jacques was in an undershirt and blue overalls.

"How do you like it here?" he asked.

"It's gorgeous," I said. "I feel like I'm in paradise."

"I knew it," said Jacques. "That's why I wanted to bring you here."

"It makes me dream of living on a farm like this some day," I ventured, wondering if I'd dare to pop the question.

"Really?" asked Jacques. "I can't imagine you living outside a city. Aren't you afraid of bugs?"

I laughed nervously.

"Only some bugs. But seriously, would you ever consider moving to the country?"

"I don't know," said Jacques. "It depends what kind of work I could get."

I took a deep breath.

"Jacques," I said, "have you thought about having children?"

"Not really," he said, warily. "Why?"

Looking into his eyes, I whispered, "If we had a baby, I could live at a place like this so easily. It would be so beautiful, Jacques."

His body stiffened at the sound of the word "baby."

"Mona, stop! How could we have a kid? We don't have an income. Neither of us has a regular job. How would we support the child?"

"Look at Jeanne and Thomas," I said. "They don't have an income, and that didn't stop them from having a baby."

"They do," said Jacques. "Jeanne gets a share of the money the family makes selling their wine to the local cooperative. It's not much, but it's enough. And Thomas gets carpentry work from time to time."

"Well, we'll both have work soon enough," I said. "It could happen – if you want it to."

"Listen," said Jacques soothingly. "We've only been together a few months. Why are you in such a hurry? Let's see what happens. We have plenty of time."

When we returned to Paris there was a letter from Wisconsin waiting for me. Not surprising – my mom wrote twice a week. But folded up inside was another letter that had been mailed to my parents from Bologna. The return address was Dan Greenbaum, Adam's housemate.

Foreboding flashed through as I tore the envelope open. Jacques had gone out for groceries. I was alone in the flat.

"Mona, I have bad news," Dan wrote. I sank into the sofa. "Adam had a motorcycle accident last Wednesday. They couldn't save him. He died on impact."

Adam dead? I reread the words. It couldn't be. My hands were shaking so hard I had trouble reading on.

"Adam wasn't very happy in vet school here these last couple of years," Dan wrote. "He took to riding around on his scooter at all hours of the day and night. Last week he went out very late. He'd been drinking. The police called me at 3 in the morning. Adam's scooter hit a wall, head on. I wish I could tell you it was an accident but that's not clear. We'll never know whether he did it on purpose or not."

A rush of nausea came over me. Clutching the letter, I made my way to the bedroom. I was too shocked to cry.

Adam, gone.

I remembered his transcendent smile, his warm skin, the touch of his fingers, tips hardened from playing the guitar. How we'd made love over and over that first afternoon when I escaped from Florence. How we'd laughed, how our bodies fit together, how we'd trusted each other.

I had betrayed him. And now he was dead. Great waves of guilt washed through me. It was my fault. I had left him, and now he was gone. I couldn't wrap my mind around it. Adam dead? No!

"No! No! No!" The words were pouring out from the bedroom in long howls when Jacques came back from the store.

Alarmed, he dropped the groceries and came to me.

"What is it?" said Jacques. "Mona! What's wrong?" He shook me. "Pull yourself together and tell me."

I could barely get the words out.

"Adam… died…"

Jacques pulled me toward him, holding me tight. He knew about my relationship with Adam.

"Calm down," he said, "and tell me what happened."

"He ran his motorcycle into a wall, and now he's dead. And it's my fault!" I dissolved into a heap of sobs.

"Hey there," said Jacques. "What do you mean?"

"I let him down," I said. "I broke his heart, and now he's killed himself."

"No, Mona," said Jacques. "You don't know that. Don't torture yourself. You don't know what's gone on in Adam's life since you split up. For god's sake, don't blame yourself!"

"But he loved me, and I left him. It's so sad."

"You know," said Jacques, "people fall in love, and they fall out again. It's an old story. Usually they get over it. Sometimes they don't. That's life."

"C'est la vie" – the way the French have of shrugging off disaster in three words.

"So stop blaming yourself," Jacques said firmly. "If you don't, it will poison the rest of your life."

Eight months into my stay in Paris, my parents paid me a visit. They were en route to Austria, where Ben was studying glass-blowing.

"I cannot believe you have another boyfriend whose parents are communists!" my mother said in the cab into town from the airport.

"Were communists," I corrected her. "They left the party decades ago."

"Doesn't matter," said my mom. "They're still leftists, aren't they? Will we get to meet them?"

From the front seat, my dad laughed at the non sequitur.

"Let's meet Jacques first," he said.

We dropped off the bags at their hotel and went on to La Coupole, the legendary Montparnasse brasserie where artists like Picasso, Léger, Chagall, Man Ray and Sonia Delaunay once dined. Jacques was meeting us there for lunch.

After the mandatory round of kisses and pleasantries, events unfolded as I'd feared they might. My mother was politely invasive.

The more Jacques tried to deflect her, the more relentlessly she probed. When Jacques had to return to work, my parents lingered with me over coffee.

"He seems nice enough," my mother said icily. "Do you think he'll marry you?"

I took a deep breath and tried to smile.

"Mom," I said, "we've only been together a few months. Let's wait and see."

"Well, you're not getting any younger," my mother said. "What are you now, 25? And we want grandchildren! Don't we, sweetie?" she added, turning to my dad. He shrugged – he loved both women in his life and didn't want to take sides.

"It'll be okay, doll," my dad said, using his most affectionate term for my mom. "Let's let Mona take her time. You know what they say. Marry in haste, repent at leisure."

I smiled gratefully at my father. I loved my mom too – she was just harder to manage. Although it certainly helped that she lived in Wisconsin and I was in France. I pointed this out to Jacques that evening when he started giving me a hard time.

"My mother?" I said. "Don't worry about it. She's here now, but most of the time she's there, I'm here, and there's a large body of water called the Atlantic in between."

July came, and with it an invitation to return to Floréal. I had reservations – did I really want to spend a month at the farm of Jacques' ex? But the old criticism and self-criticism reflex kicked in. Wasn't I being boringly old-fashioned? We'd had a good time in the spring, hadn't we? What could be better than a vacation on a commune in the lazy, sensual south of France?

We took the train down this time and were met in Nîmes by Jeanne's brother Joseph, dust-covered from working in the vines. With him was Brenda, an American friend of Jeanne's who was spending the summer at Floréal.

A large, jovial honey-blonde woman, she greeted Jacques heartily, then turned to me.

"So you're the new Jeanne," Brenda said with a laugh somewhere between a sneer and a chortle.

"No," I said, "I'm the old Mona."

What's her problem? I wondered. I'd been pleased to hear there'd be another American woman at Floréal, but now I wasn't so sure.

"Tell me," I asked Brenda as we bumped along, "how did you and Jeanne get to know each other?"

"We met in Paris through *co-conseil*."

"Which is?"

"You don't know about co-counseling?" Brenda asked incredulously. "It's a major movement in the States with branches all over Europe. We help each other by listening in pairs. It allows people to liberate themselves from oppression."

"Like, ah, political oppression?" I asked.

"No, no, no," said Brenda. "Our own internal oppression! People have patterns of distress. We help each other find those patterns and then block them."

As Joseph turned into Floréal's earthen lane, his mother emerged, cutting short the discussion. But I hadn't heard the last of co-counseling.

Our visit started well enough. I learned the ways of the farm – making yogurt every couple of days from fresh milk, making red currant jam from newly picked berries, feeding the baby, washing the baby, rocking the baby. Everyone helped – Brenda, Thomas, Jacques, and a stream of visitors who passed through during the summer.

I mainly helped in the kitchen, fascinated by the earthy life we led. There was the day we picked buds off a bush called a *caprier*, packing them into sterilized jars and dousing them with vinegar. This, I realized in astonishment, was where capers came from. I had thought they were from the sea, like anchovies. Then there was the day we slaughtered the pig. I got out of the way, going for a long walk rather than sticking around to witness the butchery. But I could still hear the animal's terrified squeals, and the silence that followed. When I returned the pig was hanging head down, its blood dripping into a bucket. Jeanne boiled the blood with spices to make *boudin*, the French version of blood sausage. This involved repeated washings of the pig's intestines so they could be used for casings. Some of the meat was chopped up with fat, salted, peppered, sprinkled with saltpeter and packed into more washed pig gut to be hung in the rafters and dried for hard sausage. Some was prepared as bacon. The rest was cut up into chops and roasts and frozen, to be eaten throughout the winter. Another day we picked masses of ripe green beans that needed to be trimmed, boiled and packed into sterilized jars. As the weeks passed, the shelves of the pantry grew heavy with homegrown vegetables – carrots, peas, onions, beets, chard, spinach.

I loved the sense of accomplishment that followed our bouts of picking, trimming and canning. I loved seeing the wild artichokes along the roadside open up their purple thistle crowns to the sky. I loved the sensuousness of the heat, of bathing outdoors beneath an old shower head, of sunbathing nude in the fields, visible only to the heavens.

It could have been perfect, a summer of peace and love. But there were tensions. Brenda couldn't be trusted. She was friendly one moment and snide the next. Jeanne and Thomas were bickering. He wanted to take a job in Montpellier, more than an hour away. Jeanne wanted him to stay to help with Camille.

Worse, Jacques and I were not getting along. He was exasperated, maybe even embarrassed by me. I had thought capers were a kind of fish! I ate meat, but I'd run off when they slaughtered the pig! And every time a bee or wasp flew by, I ran in the other direction. Jacques mocked me as a city slicker.

The others feigned indifference, but they were smirking too. They may have been a band of transplanted French intellectuals – the key word was not "intellectuals," but "French." For modern France was a nation with deep rural roots, and proud of it. Wasn't this the land that produced 365 kinds of cheese, one for each day of the year? Every French schoolchild could rattle off the names of a dozen of them. Until World War II, nearly half the French population had lived in the countryside. Now, 30 years later, even the urban French were close to the land in a way few urban Americans could imagine. Their rural collective memory lived on in the language and the cities.

The tension made its way into our bed. After Jacques turned his back on me several nights in a row, I moved out of the *magnanerie*. There was a small room free off the terrace. It wasn't ideal, but it was better than feeling rejected.

No one seemed to find it surprising that Jacques and I were sleeping apart. Still, the next day Brenda took me aside and suggested a co-counseling session.

"It might make you feel better," she said.

Why not? I thought. Things could hardly get worse.

Off we went to an empty bedroom and Brenda showed me the drill. I ("the client") was to sit crosslegged opposite her ("the counselor"), put my open hands on hers, look directly into her eyes and talk about what was bothering me.

I poured out my frustrations to Brenda.

"I thought I understood the French, but clearly I don't," I moaned. The summer had proved me wrong. Everyone was ganging up on me, starting with my lover. In fact, I regretted coming to Floréal.

It felt good to open up to another American. Too bad I hadn't thought it through ahead of time. I was unprepared for the programmed stage of co-counseling known as "discharge," when "the client" breaks down and cries. Everything came out: my failed relationship with Jake, the death of Adam, my uncertainties about Jacques, my longing for a child. Breaking the rules, Brenda asked Jeanne to join us. The two women egged me on, assuring me that the session would liberate me from my "internalized contradictions." But it merely made me relive some of the worst moments of my life. It was supposed to be confidential, but nothing stayed confidential at the farm.

After the session, I retired to my small room with a headache. It was a balmy afternoon. The wisteria hung low and sweet above a bamboo screen over the terrace. The murmuring of insects and chatter of the cicadas made it hard to hear the conversation beyond my window. I slept.

By evening, feeling better, I emerged in time for supper. In the kitchen, a new guest was at the stove stirring a pot and chatting familiarly with Jeanne. She had long dark hair framing a heart-shaped face, with dreamy eyes that could have belonged to Marlene Dietrich if they had been blue, not brown.

"Hi," I said tentatively.

"Hello," she said, glancing my way. "I'm Colette."

Colette. I remembered hearing Jacques mention her. They'd been at Nanterre together.

"I'm Mona," I said, extending a hand. "Mona Venture."

"Of course," said Colette, flashing a friendly smile. "I've heard about you."

Dinner that evening was a pleasant affair, the tensions melting in the warmth of Colette's presence. Later, I turned to Jacques. We were still on speaking terms, after all.

"Tell me about Colette," I said quietly.

Jeanne and I used to hang out with her and her husband," he said. "They were both students at Nanterre and got married at the age of 19. But it didn't work out. Now Colette has switched to women, from what I hear."

"She seems very nice," I said.

"She is," said Jacques. "She's very special – a lesbian feminist intellectual with a sense of humor."

Like the chemical reaction that occurs when a new element is added to an unstable mixture, Colette's arrival transformed the dynamics at Floréal. She refused to take seriously the psychodramas orchestrated by Brenda and Jeanne. She befriended me and, with the lightest touch of irony, was able to deflect Jacques' arrows.

I moved back in with him. A few days later, Ariel and Jacqueline arrived. Picking up on Floréal's weird ambiance, they invited Jacques and me to come along on a driving tour of the Cévennes.

"Let's go," I urged Jacques. "I can't wait to get out of here."

We packed a few things, piled into Ariel's crate, and off we drove into the mountains. The narrow road up through Saint-Jean-du-Gard and into the chestnut forests of the Cévennes National Park twisted and turned in a dizzying way, with steep hills plunging down to deep valleys below. This would have been fine if Ariel had stayed on his side of the road. But at each turn he drifted into the opposite lane, cutting corners – to save time? – and veering frighteningly back if an oncoming vehicle surged up.

I flinched each time this happened, finally asking Ariel to cool it – and incurring the wrath of Jacques.

"Don't tell him how to drive!" Jacques snapped. "You Americans" – he actually said *Amérloques*, a slur equating Americans with old rags – "pay too much attention to the rules. You even stick to the speed limit! We know how to handle mountains. So give it a rest!"

I shrank into a corner of the back seat. I should have stayed at the farm, with Colette. Peace and love – what a joke!

We spent one night in a mountain retreat where the tensions from the ride turned the atmosphere frigid. Even Ariel's humor couldn't dispel the chill.

When we returned to Floréal the next day, I packed my bags. I was heading back to Paris, alone. From the station in Nîmes, I phoned Wim before boarding my train. He had a big apartment with a spare room. He agreed to let me stay there.

Classical music was booming from Wim's study when I arrived, filling the place with joyous sound. My room was spacious and sunny. But I couldn't get my mind off Jacques. It was so confusing – I knew he cared for me, but the way he had acted in the Cévennes felt like a betrayal. If he couldn't admit that he was in love with me, maybe it was time to move on. For the first time in a year, I started thinking about going back to Cornell to finish my degree.

Wim's place was a stone's throw from the Sorbonne and dozens of book stores. There was a new book I'd read about, "Les Parleuses," a conversation between two feminist writers – Marguerite Duras and Xavière Gauthier. Duras, an edgy author in the prime of life, had agreed to a series of interviews with Gauthier, a young journalist. Through the script of their discussions emerged the notion of a woman-specific form of literary creation.

I bought the book and dived in.

"It's fascinating," I told Wim that evening. "Marguerite Duras believes that women writers create in a way different than men do and should refuse to be judged by the same standards."

"Yeah, it sounds like bullshit, doesn't it," he replied. "But she's supertrendy now. Especially with the feminist crowd."

By the time Jacques returned to Paris, I had read half a dozen novels by Duras. I found her to be thoughtful and provocative without engaging in the psycho/structuro/metalinguistic wordplay that had precipitated my flight from graduate school.

"I could see writing a thesis about her," I told Jacques over dinner. He had taken me to a bistro we both liked – a peace offering of sorts. Removed from the cultlike atmosphere of Floréal, he was acting human again, and I appreciated it. But I wasn't about to sleep with him. It was exactly a year since I'd arrived in Paris, and I needed to take stock.

One day in late September Colette phoned and invited me to a supper meeting of her women's group.

"I'll bring some wine," I said, trying to hide my elation.

Colette was in the avant garde of the Parisian women's movement. She had been an early member of a group called Les Polymorphes

Perverses, founded on the premise that Freud's theories of sexuality proved he understood nothing about women. That was a fairly revolutionary stance in a country whose chattering classes worshipped Freud. It was also funny. Could feminism have a sense of humor? Not in the States, maybe, but here in France the rules were different.

French feminists weren't burning bras, they were wearing them. They also wore dresses, jewelry and – perish the thought – lipstick. I remembered how I'd dressed back at Madison, in the early days of the movement: in jeans and a green army jacket, every day, with no makeup. In the States, women who wore makeup were seen as unliberated. Women dressed like men. But was that feminist? In France, feminists, or at least some of them, believed that women could embellish their natural beauty for their own pleasure, and not to please men. To me, that felt liberating.

On the way to Colette's place, I stopped to pick up the wine. I decided to spring for a good bottle, a Juliénas, even though funds were low. I had dumped the job at Monsieur Vidal's place long ago, and the art classes where I modeled were just starting up again after the summer break. But it was worth it. This was a special occasion.

When I rang the bell, Colette greeted me as an old friend, kissing me on both cheeks. The room was packed, smoky and filled with low chatter. I felt I had stumbled into a meeting of conspirators plotting a new French revolution. And maybe I had. These women looked tough, especially Delilah, Colette's current lover. Several were in leather jackets. All were thin and most were in black. They observed me warily, but when Colette introduced me as a feminist from America they peppered me with questions and made me feel at home.

The meeting had been called to discuss plans for feminist actions in Paris throughout the autumn. Abortion had just been legalized, and with that victory behind them French women were in the streets demonstrating against everything from rape and police treatment of prostitutes to the incarceration of political prisoners in Franco's Spain.

The gathering went on for hours, fueled by a country-style buffet of salads, cold cuts, cheese and plenty of wine. By the time we got around to the Juliénas everyone was joking, laughing, bonded in a sisterhood of women who knew their moment in history had come.

As I poured myself another glass of the red, I succumbed to the intoxication of being at the epicenter of a movement that was going to shake the world. So much had changed for me in the year since I moved to Paris. Now, without Jacques but amid these women, I felt I had finally arrived.

WOMEN
1976

Without Jacques? It wasn't that easy. Our relationship seemed destined to move in cycles of attraction and separation. Was it merely passion that drew us back together, or was it some equally primal need – for the familiar, for companionship, for love? When it became clear in the autumn that I'd soon be leaving Paris, Jacques asked me to move back in with him. Then, in December, he flew east, to Southeast Asia, and I flew west, to the States, to write my Master's thesis. On New Year's Day of 1976, we were half a world apart.

As I began my re-entry to university life, I pined for my absent lover. We had agreed that Jacques would stop in Ithaca on his way back to France, after trekking through Thailand and Laos and visiting friends in L.A. But even as I longed to see him I feared his arrival, for I knew it would only bring a new separation. How was it possible, I asked myself, to be so maddeningly attracted to a man who practiced such a conditional form of love – but kept coming back to me?

By the time Jacques flew in, late that February, I had settled into a scholarly routine at Cornell and was reading everything I could by Marguerite Duras. I had found a feminist thesis adviser, a job waitressing at a trendy new café and a ground-floor apartment big enough for the two of us. Jacques had been in Southeast Asia with Jacqueline's brother, Antoine, also a sociologist. They had gone north and spent time with the region's mountain people – minorities like the Hmong, who were under pressure as the Indochina wars wound down. Some of them had cooperated first with the French and then with the Americans, and they were fleeing from Laos to avoid retaliation by that country's victorious Communists. The Vietnam War had finally ended the previous spring with the fall of Saigon in April 1975. Few researchers had yet ventured to the region. For two French intellectuals it was a fascinating expedition. Jacques left Southeast Asia with the aim of continuing to study its minority populations.

But life in an American university town proved nearly as interesting from a sociological point of view. It was Jacques' first visit to the States, and everything was new: the cold (20 below!), the snow (so deep!), the people (so open!), The New York Times on Sundays (four inches thick!), the Cornell libraries (so rich! so accessible!).

The fact that Jacques was the foreigner now, and not I, shifted the power dynamics of our relationship, but it didn't fundamentally change them. We resumed our life as a couple, going out and staying in. He struggled with English but managed to make himself understood. My friends found him quirkily charming. But Jacques' reserve appeared to have deepened during our time apart. The contrast between the poverty he had witnessed in Asia and the overabundance of American life proved hard for him to take. Did he somehow equate my natural exuberance with American excess? My needs and desires – for sex, for love, for bonding – he endeavored, most days, to keep at bay.

About a month into Jacques' visit, walking home from dinner as snow fell, we quarreled. It was the same old story – I wanted more commitment than he was willing to give. We entered the house through a pantry at the back where I grew some flowers and herbs. In daytime, light flooded in to warm the plants. Now the inky blackness outdoors formed a screen between us and the world. It was a private space, so private that the rules of comportment could break down.

Our dispute grew hotter as we faced off indoors, bundled against the cold, not bothering to remove our coats. Hurtful misunderstanding deepened with every verbal thrust. As Jacques stood there, countering me, it was as though a spirit entered my body. Mad with frustration, I picked up a flower pot and hurled it at the wall. It smashed into a cascade of clay splinters, dirt and crumpled leaves.

I picked up another as Jacques looked on in horror. And another. Smash! And another. Until, fury spent, I was through.

"Why do you always break the things you love?" Jacques muttered, brushing roughly past me into the kitchen.

The next day he took me out to dinner and made love to me. The day after that he called Air France and booked his ticket home.

But we couldn't escape the cycles. As soon as he left, Jacques allowed his longing for me to resurface. I felt devastated by the way he had departed but couldn't break my attachment. We wrote letters back and forth, aching letters of desire where the word "love" never appeared. He had flown home via Montreal on a round-trip ticket. In midsummer he was ready to come back – and I agreed to take him in, although by then my life had taken on new contours. I had finished the reading for my thesis. I had joined an Ithaca women's group. And I had a lover.

The connection was my job at the Café Dewitt. During the spring, my role had morphed from waitress to pastry chef, tasked three mornings a week with turning out lavishly decorated confections of sugar, chocolate, butter, jam, eggs, almonds, hazelnuts and whipped cream, not to mention a dozen loaves of whole-grain bread. This was a congenial development, for I loved to cook. The café was in the same mall as another popular new restaurant, Moosewood, a natural foods collective in the avant-garde of creative vegetarian cuisine. Every now and then, when Moosewood was short a cook, they would ask me to fill in. That's how I met Franklin, a lanky, bearded, bespectacled hippie who had found work as a chef at Moosewood.

Franklin convinced me to join him in the organizing committee for an anti-bicentennial march that would be held on July 4 in Philadelphia. Major hoopla was being planned in Washington to celebrate the 200th anniversary of the signing of the Declaration of Independence. To mark the occasion in a different way, a broad coalition of leftist groups planned to converge on Philly for a counterdemonstration.

One sunny June day, Franklin asked me to go to the countryside with him ahead of that evening's meeting of our committee. He was helping some friends build a wooden house in a particularly lovely spot west of Lake Cayuga. We drove out along country roads past sun-flecked fields and trees in tender bloom. Franklin parked his truck in a hayfield near the half-built house. As we set out on foot, the sweet odor of alfalfa rose up to greet us. Little butterflies danced around us. Wildflowers fluttered in the light breeze. It was so fine a moment that when Franklin took my hand it felt natural.

We stood beside each other for a while enjoying the magnificence of the day. When he drew me toward him, I let it happen. Our lips met, his rosy and smooth, mine warmed by the sun. A rush of desire shot through me. How can this be, I thought vaguely, as we stretched out amid the warm grasses and began undressing each other. I had never envisioned Franklin as a lover, but I was too aroused to care. He climbed on top and slipped inside me. A new rush of pleasure, immense, intense. It had been months since I'd made love, ever since Jacques left. When it was over, we lay looking at clouds for a long time, exhausted but exhilarated.

Jacques' arrival in mid-July made it harder to see Franklin, but I had become fond of my bearded friend and had no desire to abandon our dalliance. It seemed a fair trade. Jacques wanted a commitment-free relationship – he came and went as he pleased. Keeping Franklin as a lover would lend continuity to my life. When Jacques left Ithaca again, I wouldn't be completely alone. Although what I wanted most from Jacques was a wedding ring, literally or metaphorically speaking, it wasn't happening. He couldn't have it both ways, I told myself.

Jacques had been back about a week when I informed him that I wouldn't be sleeping at home every night. He tried to be cool, but looked shocked. Still, his principles meant he had to accept my decision. He kissed me goodbye as I went off to Franklin's place with my toothbrush.

Franklin was a superb vegetarian cook, so I merely did the peeling and chopping while he made dinner. We drank good wine as amazing scents wafted through the kitchen, or smoked grass when we had it. But the main thing was the sex. He took his time making love, letting the pleasure grow until it reached an almost unbearable intensity. After we came, we'd have a glass of water, maybe smoke a bit more, and start over.

The night I left Jacques to be with Franklin, a feeling of surreal detachment came over me during the act of love. It was like an out-of-body experience. I was in two places at once, having orgasmic sex with my number two lover while emotionally in intimate bondage with Jacques. Could I kiss one man while loving another? In the light of morning, I realized the answer was no.

"I'm so, so sorry," I told Jacques later that day when I found him on the steps of Smedley's, the new feminist bookshop in Ithaca. I hugged him and held him tight.

"Don't mention it," he said. And I never did.

A month into Jacques' summer visit we went to New York – his first trip there, and he loved it. We had plans to drive from there to Wisconsin with Roger and Françoise, who flew in, *sans* Maxim, on a sweltering August afternoon. Heading back into town from Kennedy, with me at the wheel, we were passing through a gritty neighborhood when Françoise spoke up.

"I'm dying of thirst," she said. "Could we please stop somewhere?"

Soon enough a McDonald's hove into view. We pulled over and I hopped out to accompany Françoise.

"Don't say anything at all," she instructed me. "I want to try out my English."

Petite, chic, quintessentially French, Françoise strode to the counter, where a tall, good-looking black attendant was taking orders. He perked up when he saw her.

"Hello, sir," she said in charmingly accented English. She flashed her ravishing smile. "If you please, a large cock."

A huge grin spread across the attendant's face.

"Sure, honey," he said. "Coming right up."

"A large Coke!" I said quickly. "She meant Coke!!"

Everyone in the place was laughing.

"What did I say?" Françoise stage-whispered in French.

Handing over her drink, the attendant tried hard to contain himself.

"Here you go, honey. Come again!"

A new collective roar erupted.

Françoise blushed to the roots of her frosted honey-blonde hair, grabbed the Coke and ran for the door. Back in the safety of the car, when I translated her faux pas to howls of laughter from Jacques and Roger, she swore she would never attempt English again.

But of course she did and we were all the better off for it, for Françoise had such natural elegance that her mistakes inevitably ended by winning the hearts of Americans all along our road trip.

Wisconsin should have been the high point. Ben was there, back from a year as an apprentice glass blower, his sense of humor saving the situation more than once when our mom got a little too personal with the guests. She and our dad treated their French visitors grandly, serving exotic American foods like corn on the cob and bratwurst grilled over charcoal. But despite – or perhaps because of – their hospitality, Jacques refused to play the role of putative son-in-law. He was terse to the point of brusqueness with my parents and, by extension, with me. By the time we left I was so relieved I didn't mind that we got lost in the middle of the night looking for Niagara and never found the falls. After we said goodbye to Roger and Françoise in New York, Jacques spent only a few more days with me before he, too, flew back to France.

At the end of August my lease expired. I asked around and heard about a woman who had a bedroom for rent in a house on Buffalo Street. She was someone I'd met and admired, a friend of a friend in my women's group. Her name was Madeleine and she looked like she had just stepped out of a pre-Raphaelite painting: long, wavy dun-colored hair, wide blue eyes and an ever so slightly crooked smile that could break the heart of the meanest man on earth.

Madeleine and her young son, Andy, were sharing their two-story wooden house with another single mother, Becky Lou, and her toddler, Susie. The two women were happy to have a housemate who would share the childcare. As for me, still longing for children, it seemed like a perfect situation, with friendly dinner-table conversation plus kids. When Madeleine came home one day with a present for Andy – a fluffy striped kitten named Fuzzy – my domestic satisfaction was complete, or as nearly complete as it could be in the absence of Jacques.

As it happened, it was also a feminist household. Madeleine had extricated herself from an unhappy marriage to a possessive husband who drank and ignored her until she finally packed up and left. She was dealing with it by immersing herself in a feminist collective she ran with two friends. Becky Lou had fled her marriage after being beaten by her husband. She was finished with men and had reinvented herself as gay, with cropped dark hair and a lot of attitude. But not nearly as much attitude as her lover, Portia, a militant dyke who dressed like a man and made her living fixing cars at a garage.

There was tension whenever Portia came over. She couldn't understand how Becky Lou could be friends with people like

Madeleine and me who consorted with the enemy – men. When winter came and Jacques returned to Ithaca for his third visit, he flirted with Madeleine and won over even Becky Lou with his Gallic charm. But in the morning at the breakfast table Portia wouldn't speak to Jacques – and Becky Lou, not daring to cross her, followed suit. That made for some pretty silent breakfasts. The tension persisted until one day Portia announced she would no longer speak to three-year-old Andy on the grounds that he was a potential man. Even Becky Lou had to laugh at that one.

Jacques had flown over in January, among other reasons in order to experience snow for a second time. There was tons of it, the heavy kind that forms eight-foot drifts along the roadside and just keeps coming. We decided to go off for a few days into the countryside, where I could work on my thesis and Jacques could read. We had a place to stay – the cabin I'd visited with Franklin six months earlier. It was finished now, and the owners had offered to lend it to us.

As we drove out, past snow so deep no plants could push through, we wondered how we would do at the cabin. There was no electricity. We would use kerosene lamps for lighting and a wood-fired stove for heat. We had stocked up on food and supplies before leaving Ithaca. I brought flour and yeast for making our own bread. It was like stepping back a century in time.

In the crisp cold silence of our first day at the cabin, I felt flooded with warmth and hope. Sun poured through the windows of our rough-hewn home, creating a cheery glow as we waited for the stove to heat up. We went outdoors to gather snow to melt for water. The sharpness of the cold made it hard to breathe. Glancing off the white mounds of snow, the sun sent glittering diamonds leaping like sparks against the deep blue of the sky.

Our cabin had a single room, with the cast-iron stove, a wooden table, a porcelain sink and a high double bed. After a dinner of soup, bread and cheese, Jacques and I stoked up the stove, brought the lamp to the bedside and snuggled in under a deep layer of covers. Snow was falling again, visible against the inky black of the night. There were no other houses in sight. We were alone in a magical universe – so magical that when we made love I imagined we were making a baby. We formed a perfect Platonic whole – two halves of the same being. In the flickering of the lamp, I observed my lover – high brow, intelligent eyes, still so attractive to me two years after we met. I was 27 now, the age of my mother when she gave birth to me. I wanted nothing more in that instant than to be pregnant, to bear his child. But that wasn't very likely, for I was wearing a diaphragm. I was still using birth control, at Jacques' insistence. An insistence I could have ignored but didn't.

In the spring when Jacques left for Paris, it was easier to concentrate on my thesis. I had chosen three novels by Marguerite Duras in which the same characters reappear in different guises. The books shared a theme: love and madness. I had to write in French, which had the advantage of giving me critical distance from my own text.

The plan was simple. I would wrap up the thesis in May and leave in June, joining Jacques in Paris in an apartment he was renting with Antoine and another friend. With my Master's degree, I could get a job teaching English at a French technical college. The job was golden because it would provide me with working papers, the essential first step toward a normal life.

But leaving Madeleine proved surprisingly difficult. We'd become close in our months together, as close as sisters. Madeleine's generosity of spirit, her quick irony and sharp tongue, her softness in the morning, the contentment she created around her, her firm sweetness in handling Andy, her commitment to her work, our conversations late into the night, our pleasure in seeing each other the next day – it added up to one of the happiest relationships I'd had.

"Too bad we can't be lovers," I teased Madeleine one morning. Neither of us was inclined to love women in a physical way. Still, I felt a pinch in my heart.

"I don't want you to go," she said as she threw her arms around me.

"Come to Paris," I said. She felt frail in my arms. "We'll pick up where we left off."

"Yes," she said quietly, "but it won't be the same."

She pulled back and looked at me with grave eyes.

"Think about it, Mona. We've been living together for nearly a year, sharing everything. Do you really want to give this up?"

When my leaving day came, Madeleine gathered everyone closest to her out on the lawn to see me off. They posed for a photo in the June sunshine – Andy waving his hands in the air, Becky Lou smiling at the lens through gritted teeth, Susie clinging to her mother's hand, Madeleine looking lovely in a cotton nightie. She was standing beside a former lover she had just started seeing again, Pete, who seemed to be a good man. A circle of love.

What would have happened if I had decided simply to throw away my plane ticket and stay there? Would Madeleine and I have continued to grow closer, becoming more like sisters every day? Would I have found a job in America and come to feel at home in my country of birth? Would I, too, in time, have found a good man?

I'd been back in France only a couple of days when I heard about a new Village Voice-style newspaper in English that had started up while I'd been in the States. Jacques mentioned it when I was wondering how I'd keep myself occupied over the summer while he was working.

"It's called The Paris Metro," he said. "I've heard it's pretty good. Why don't you take a look? Maybe you could write for them."

"What could a bunch of expat Americans know about Paris?" I replied, blithely dismissing his suggestion – and forgetting that I was an expat American myself.

When I finally saw the paper a month later, I was impressed. It had an edgy cover story, a hip cast of critics, a terrific back-page going-out guide and plenty of listings. But could I write for them? Jacques dared me to try.

August in Paris was gray that year, with one rainy day after another. A week or so into this gloom, remembering the dare, I slipped on my poncho and headed toward the Marais. The Metro's headquarters was on the Rue des Francs-Bourgeois, a 15-minute walk from Jacques' place. As the rain sluiced down I found myself in front of a 17th-century building that opened onto a cobblestone courtyard. Could this be it? I checked out the delapidated premises, evidently once a stately home, now coated in black soot. In the courtyard, a youngish man in a helmet was trying to get his motorcycle running. He looked like he could be American. I took a deep breath.

"Hi," I said, "is this The Paris Metro?" He looked up, irritated.

"Yeah. Why?"

"I think I want to write for them. Do you work there?"

"Yeah. I'm the editor."

He returned his attention to the bike.

"Oh, right." I tried to smile. "Well, um, my name is Mona Venture and I'd like to write for you."

"Yeah?" he said as the motorcycle again sputtered and died. "Do you know how to write?"

"Of course!"

"What do you write?"

"Letters."

"Letters?"

"Yes."

He looked up dubiously from beneath his helmet.

"Letters home, full of color. Long letters."

"Okay. You don't write. What do you read?"

"Um, books?" I said, fumbling for the right answer.

"No, no. What periodicals do you read?"

"I read Le Monde."

"What else?"

"Well, I read The New York Review of Books, and the International Herald Tribune when I can afford it."

"Do you read Harper's?"

"No."

"Do you read The Atlantic?"

"No."

"Do you read Esquire?"

"Certainly not!"

"Well then, what makes you think you can write for Metro?"

My heart was sinking faster than the Titanic.

"Well – I know Paris like the back of my hand. I'm completely fluent in French. People talk to me. And I think I can tell a good story."

"Yes, but you don't write…"

This was going nowhere. I was about to leave when a voice boomed down into the courtyard.

"Frank! Send her up to me!"

The deus ex machina was a curly-haired man leaning out of a top story window. He had apparently heard the entire conversation.

"Who's that?" I asked the motorcycle man.

"He's another editor. Isaac."

"Thanks!" I said gratefully, bounding into the building, up four winding flights of stairs and into a grubby corridor.

Isaac ushered me into his office and gave me a cup of coffee. Rain streamed off my poncho as I hung it on a bentwood coat rack. I caught my breath, but my heart was pounding.

"So what do you want to write?" he asked.

"I'm open to ideas. Please try me out. Suggest something. I swear you won't be disappointed."

"Well, we've been looking for someone to write a piece on where to find the best French bread in Paris. A survey piece. But I'd rather try you out on something simpler."

"No, no, I could do that!" I replied, excitement rising. "In fact, until I came back to Paris last month, I was working at a French-style café in the States where I had to bake 12 loaves a day. So I do know something about bread."

"Fine," said Isaac. "You can have 1,500 words. Bring me the story two weeks from today."

I left in a flutter. Where to begin? There were more than a thousand bakeries in Paris and I couldn't visit all of them. But I started asking around and soon I was wallowing in bread. The way to handle the situation, I decided, would be "*le taste test*".

The testers were the inhabitants of Jacques' place, a comfortable three-bedroom apartment not far from the Bastille. I brought home a few *baguettes* a day and chopped the long crusty loaves onto separate plates for blind tastings. Over uproarious dinners, our housemates graded the bread from 1 to 5.

Sometimes I went back to the same bakery a couple days in a row for quality control. It was fun, but it didn't solve the problem. I'd have to do more legwork.

At the French Bakers Confederation, housed in a magnificent quayside building on the Ile Saint-Louis, I learned that many bakers were now adding bean flour to their baguettes, which was legal but made the bread dry and tasteless. The best bakeries still used a sourdough-like yeast, which gave a moister, chewier consistency. Fine. It still wasn't enough for a story.

My next stop was Poilâne in the chic 6th arrondissement. It was famous for its huge delicious wheels of beige country bread. The boss, Lionel Poilâne, gave me a tour of his ancient stone cellar, where loaves were rising in linen-lined baskets and baking in wood-fired brick ovens. We went back upstairs to his office, where he showed me a curvy chandelier fashioned from bread dough. Intrigued, I followed him to the back office where Monsieur Poilâne opened the door to reveal an ornate four-poster bedstead that he had sculpted out of bread dough – for Salvador Dalí!

This is it, I said to myself, deciding on the spot to become a journalist. What profession could possibly be more amusing? Now all I had to do was write the story.

The "best bread in Paris" piece finally ran in October as a double-page spread with a teaser out front. Writing it had been harder work than I'd imagined, but Isaac was pleased with the result. Readers wrote in with their comments, I was given a new assignment and it felt like the start of something big.

That was the up-side of my life. The down-side was that Jacques was kicking me out again.

To be fair, he had always said it would be temporary – his housemates wanted no extra tenants.

"You knew it would only be for the summer," Jacques said one sun-splashed Sunday when we were lolling in bed. "You'll have to be out by September."

Suddenly I was wide awake.

"Yes, but what about us?" I replied. "When will we see each other? You'll be working outside of Paris, and so will I. It's crazy!"

My new teaching job was in Valenciennes, up near the Belgian border. Jacques would be working in Nantes, several hours west of Paris, where he had a new research project on the mental health of factory workers. I could group my hours over two consecutive days but Jacques would spend five days a week in Nantes. That meant we could be together only on weekends.

"Don't worry, we'll still see each other," Jacques said, planting a kiss on my forehead. "Now please get serious about finding a place of your own."

With a leaden heart I went to see a small apartment near the Place Daumesnil, seven metro stops away from Jacques' place. The building looked good – light brick with Art Deco ironwork, on the edge of a square with lions regally spouting in a fountain. Inside, the main room had a breezy feel, with a large window, light carpeting and a big double bed. There was a spacious bathroom with charming ceramic tiles. The main problem was the kitchen – it had no fridge and no stove. I knew the place would be unfurnished, but this was a bit extreme.

"It's not a problem, I assure you," said the owner. "Look!"

The kitchen window opened onto a small balcony loaded with pots and pans – there was even enameled Le Creuset cookware. She removed the bright orange lid of a huge Dutch oven to reveal a carton of eggs and a packet of butter inside.

"I use the balcony as a refrigerator," she said, "and to cook I use a camp stove."

On the kitchen counter was a small blue propane tank with a burner on top. She lit it and put some coffee on. I was impressed. If she had managed to live in this place, why couldn't I? My teaching salary would make the rent affordable, and I liked the improvisational aspect. As a bonanza, the owner was leaving me her cookware – she said it reminded her painfully of her late mother. Now all I needed was furniture.

Antoine gave me a dark blue trestle table to use as a desk. The owner left me her bed. I picked up a couple of chairs and a small table at the flea market. My books I stacked on the floor, and my clothes I would keep in my suitcase until I found a dresser. Still, the place felt empty.

Soon enough an ad in Libé provided the answer. Someone around the corner was giving away kittens. I chose Mathilde, a tiny black ball of fur with bright yellow eyes. She explored intrepidly, sniffing, hiding and leaping out at phantoms only she could see. When I gave her a bowl of milk she thanked me by jumping onto the bed and purring loudly. Now it felt like home.

Valenciennes turned out to be a largely charmless city, rebuilt in drab concrete after being flattened during World War II. My new colleagues tried to make me feel welcome, teaching me fragments of the local dialect, ch'timi, over endless glasses of strong local beer. Still, it was lonely. I went up on Mondays, taught all day, spent the night at an inexpensive hotel, taught Tuesday morning, took the train back to Paris and collapsed. Jacques didn't get back from Nantes until Friday evening, and he was tired too. So we rarely met up before Saturday night.

That left me with a lot of time on my hands. My Paris friends were rarely available – while I'd been back in the States, they had been starting families and careers. Ariel and Jacqueline now had a one-year-old son and were both working full time, which was possible in France due to the excellent state childcare system. Roger and Françoise, both doctors now, had moved with Maxim and his baby brother to the 18th arrondissement, which might as well have been another planet. Colette was teaching philosophy at a high school in Amiens, north of Paris. I spent my free days working on pieces for Metro and waiting for Jacques. And waiting.

One Saturday night, when we'd been to a party and had quite a lot to drink, Jacques brought me home to the Place Daumesnil in his father's car. It was wintry, and I was bundled up in a 1930s-vintage fur coat I'd acquired in Ithaca – one that Jacques found particularly fetching. As we sat parked outside my building, kissing like teenagers, I decided I'd waited long enough.

"Come upstairs," I said. "We can warm up better in bed."

Jacques locked the car and followed me into the hall, his gloved hand in mine. As we kissed in the elevator, my resolve grew firmer. It seemed everyone I knew was having babies. We stripped and fell into bed, hot with desire. Jacques was about to enter me when he stopped.

"Wait," he said. "Are you wearing your diaphragm?"

"No, I'm not."

"Well, go get it!"

"No," I said. "I'm through with that thing."

"What are you saying?" Jacques asked, languidly caressing my breasts. "I want you, Mona. Please go get it."

"No, Jacques. I want a baby. I'm 28 years old. I want to bear your child. If you're not ready for that, then birth control will be up to you from now on."

Jacques heaved a long sigh.

"Why are you springing this on me?" he asked. "I didn't bring any condoms."

"I didn't plan it this way," I replied. "It just happened."

The sexy spell was broken so I sat up in bed.

"I love you, Jacques," I said, "but I can't wait forever for you to make up your mind. I've been acting like a fool, taking precautions to ensure we don't have what I most desire – a child. It's crazy! I'm not going to do it anymore."

I didn't get pregnant that winter. Who could have imagined I would? We were seeing each other only on weekends, and Jacques never forgot the condoms. You hear about accidents when a condom splits, but ours stayed maddeningly intact. Still, I felt we were making progress toward a goal I didn't dare dream of: our baby, our little girl or little boy, our child of love.

In the absence of this child, I poured myself into work. On weekdays when I wasn't in Valenciennes, I went over to the Metro with a hungry look and every now and then they threw me a bone. The third man in the editorial troika was Josh, a witty Texan who ran the "Paris en Bref" section at the front of the book. I wrote a piece for him on the pre-Christmas bombing of the luxury food store Fauchon, an attack so spectacular that at least three groups claimed it as their work. The bombing caused more snickering than outrage among the French, many of whom were still infected with the irreverent spirit of May '68.

Now the country was entering 1978, an election year, and Metro was planning a special issue. Jacques worked with me on an article explaining the French electoral process. For the cover the editors chose a collective piece by Metro reporters who had asked various celebrities for whom they would vote. In an existentially perfect act,

Simone de Beauvoir hung up on them. The filmmaker Claude Chabrol said he was voting for the Communists even though they didn't have a chance in his wealthy suburb, Neuilly. The Communist writer Louis Aragon refused to confirm he'd vote Communist. The singer Georges Moustaki said, "Asking me whom I'm voting for is like asking me which woman I prefer." James Baldwin, who had been living in Paris for decades but as an American couldn't vote, said he expected the conservative party of President Valéry Giscard d'Estaing to win, adding, "I'm very melancholy about that."

By the time the election issue came out in mid-March, Jacques and I were already at work on the next special issue, "10 Years After: How May '68 Changed France." Jacques was golden for the Metro's editorial crew because he was French and had lived through the events. He interviewed Bernard Tricot, former secretary general to President Charles De Gaulle, who described how the wily De Gaulle had managed to defuse the protests – by dissolving the National Assembly and calling new elections, a vote that his party handily won.

I'd been assigned a different article, "Where Are They Now: Portrait of a Generation." Jacques helped me choose a dozen intelligent, amusing May '68 participants, most of whom declared with surprising candor that the events hadn't really changed anything. One was Annette Lévy-Willard, who was 21 in May '68 and had become a prominent journalist at Libération. She said:

In May, first and foremost, we had a really good time. I left my books,
I left a shitty relationship with a guy, and like lots of other people, I
think, I made love constantly. It was a kind of vast sexual liberation.

Jean-Jacques Lebel, a self-described "avant-garde artist with anarchist tendencies" and one of the leaders of the student uprising, had been 30 in May '68. Ten years later, he said:

The basic drive of history is hysteria; the movement had worked us up into such a state of intensity that we no longer saw what we were doing. But basically I think we were right. The idea must be to inject creative 'dadaism' into the stale political machinery.

Guy Hocquenghem had been a philosophy student in May 1968. Ten years later, he was an artist, writer and outspoken gay activist. When I interviewed him, he may already have contracted the AIDS virus that was to kill him 10 years later. But the world had not yet heard about HIV. In 1978, he said:

Now we're into doing artistic and literary things and there are all kinds of imbeciles who say we've been co-opted, that we should be working politically. Well that's just stupid because the fact of the matter is that working politically, in the sense of being a militant, is a much worse kind of co-optation than creating art objects, if those objects are scandalous or nonconventional. What I create is nonconventional, whether it's a movie, a book, whatever, and I think you can touch people much more deeply with a film or a book than with any political speech during a meeting.

Yes, I thought, and with a good read in a newspaper too.

By the time we wrapped up that issue, it was spring and Madeleine was coming to Paris. We'd been writing back and forth since I left nearly a year before, and my feelings had lost none of their power. Madeleine was special – my very special friend. As her visit neared, I wondered whether we could recreate the magic. Would I measure up? Would she still care for me?

Madeleine was leaving Andy at home with Pete, now her steady boyfriend. She was flying over with one of her sisters, Rose, and Rose's boyfriend, Hank. I went out to Roissy to meet their plane. Rose emerged first from customs control, laughing, waving, with Hank just behind, and then there was Madeleine – all fragility and strength, serenity and beauty. We hugged, and all felt right with the world.

On the RER express train into town we chattered nonstop. They'd never been to Paris before and their excitement was contagious.

"Oh my god!" said Rose in a loud stage whisper, pointing to a couple wrapped in a deep kiss. "There are people doing things in this metro that I wouldn't do in my bedroom."

The three of them were staying at a small hotel not far from my apartment. One evening after a dinner at my place with plenty of wine, Madeleine helped bring the dishes to the kitchen.

"We haven't had a chance to talk," she said. "If you don't have to get up too early, I think I'll stay on for a bit."

Rose and Hank were getting ready to leave.

"You go on ahead," Madeleine told them. "I'll have a last glass of wine with Mona. If it gets too late, I'll just spend the night here."

As the door closed behind them, we fell into each other's arms, hugging and laughing.

"I've been waiting for this moment," I confessed. "I'm so glad you came to Paris!"

"Me too," she said.

We sat on the carpet with our glasses of wine and brought each other up to date on the events of the last 11 months, all gravity dissolving in our tipsy good humor.

It was past one when we took the glasses to the kitchen. I gave Madeleine a T-shirt big enough to serve as a nightgown. I was fussing around trying to improvise a sleeping area on the floor when she took my hands and stopped me.

"I don't really want to sleep on the floor," she said.

I drew her to me.

"Let's go to bed," I said.

I was trembling. When we kissed, it felt so natural – and so strange. We sat together on the edge of the bed in our nightclothes, looking into each other's eyes, kissing again, not daring to touch. How far would we go with this folly? When we finally crawled under the quilt, I turned off the light. Although we'd seen each other nude many times before, I'd never gone to bed with a woman. Suddenly I felt shy. But she didn't. Madeleine surprised me. Before I knew what was happening she was removing my nightshirt, caressing my back, my neck, my breasts. In the darkness I explored her body. She had smooth, smooth skin and a softness that was totally disconcerting, so different from anything I'd experienced. I wanted to satisfy her but didn't know how. It felt odd not to feel a man's hardness between our bodies. We made love to each other after a fashion, we loved each other that night. But when it was over an unwanted pinpoint of light was pricking my consciousness. Through the fog of sex I could discern with utmost clarity the certain knowledge that my sexuality was and would always be hetero. Not just not gay. Not even bi.

We slept fitfully. In the morning I made strong black coffee, and we didn't talk about what had transpired. But I couldn't keep my eyes off Madeleine – my sweet friend, my heart-sister. I had loved her so much that I'd allowed myself the illusion that our closeness could translate into physical desire. In the cool light of a spring morning, I knew that had been wrong.

After coffee, Madeleine asked to take my picture. I was wearing a long robe of woven cotton with a hood in back. I still have that photo, me in the robe standing in front of my window, Paris in the background, my head turned wistfully, face bearing the shadows of the night before. It's in black-and-white, and I love it because it shows all the longing that can weigh on the heart of a 28-year-old woman.

Madeleine, Rose and Hank spent a couple more days in Paris. Their last night we went out to dinner at Le Procope, a centuries-old restaurant near Odéon. There's another photo, in color this time, that shows Madeleine and me at a prettily set table before a red wall adorned with gilt-framed mirrors. We look so happy there. And maybe we were.

But from the moment she left my apartment until their plane took off from Paris, we never spoke of our night together. We'd been friends, close friends, and we'd tried to get even closer, to give each other the deep pleasure we'd known with men. But it hadn't felt right, and afterwards we were farther apart than we'd ever been.

I sobbed when Madeleine left Paris. I longed for the wisdom, the comfort of her. I fantasized about being back in her arms, about the long conversations we'd have, about how we'd love each other. I refused to see Jacques for quite a few days. I wouldn't tell him what was wrong, and wouldn't let him come over. I didn't change the sheets – I wanted to keep the scent of Madeleine as long as possible.

But in the end, I came back to reality. I was in a relationship with a man – a man who drove me crazy sometimes with his warm-cold, love-you-love-you-not routine and his obsession with keeping a distance, but a man nonetheless, a man who made love to me in all his splendid hardness, who lifted me up and took me to that place where body and soul merge into fireworks and one senses the unity of all things on earth, that place where, if you're not a nun or a guru, you can feel closest to the eternal, to the idea of God.

Madeleine went back to Ithaca and resumed her life with Andy and Pete. I changed the sheets and brought Jacques back home to my bed. Madeleine and I exchanged letters sporadically for a while. It was a half-hearted effort. Our folly had thwarted our friendship. To my huge and lasting regret, we didn't see each other again.

As abruptly as Madeleine exited my life, another woman appeared.

Lucie phoned one summer day when I was at home working on a story for Metro about Parisian taxi drivers.

"*Allo?*" said a lilting voice. "Is this Mona?"

"Yes. Who's calling?"

"It's Lucie. I'm a friend of Jeanne's. I'm looking for someone who knows how to make poppyseed cake, and she suggested I phone you."

I did have a recipe, if I could find it. But how odd that Jeanne had thought of me.

"If you're friends with Jeanne, you must know Jacques," I told the caller. "You know, her former boyfriend. He's with me now."

"Of course," she said. "We're old friends. We were all together at Nanterre."

"Right," I said, wondering why I'd never heard about Lucie before. "Look, I'm pretty sure I can locate the recipe. Would you like to come over?"

Half an hour later I opened my door to find a striking woman around my age with black hair and deep brown eyes. She had a bearing that could have emanated from an Indian royal family – all that was missing was the sari. Instead she was wearing a flowery summer skirt with a simple tank top. Her warmth made her instantly likeable.

"Bonjour," she said, kissing me on both cheeks.

"Come in," I said. "I found the recipe. But why poppyseed cake?"

"I'm part of a collective – it's called La Cour des Noues. We have a counterculture bistro thing going and I'd like to try to make the poppyseed cake this weekend."

"A counterculture bistro?"

"Well, it's not exactly a bistro. It's a neighborhood center, with daycare for kids and workshops for adults during the week. It functions as a bistro on weekends."

"A bistro for kids?"

"No! Grownups only. We usually have a musical act of some sort, and we keep the prices down. It's *très parallèle* – you know, an alternative space."

"That sounds like so much fun," I said, handing over the card I'd pulled from my recipe box. "Here you go."

Lucie looked it over.

"You know," she said, "if you're free on Saturday maybe you could come to the bistro and cook with me. I'll take care of the main dish, and you can make the cake."

"For how many people?"

"Around 40. Then you can stay and have dinner with us."

She didn't have to ask twice. On Saturday I put on the purple houndstooth overalls I saved for special occasions and headed over to La Cour des Noues. Lucie was already there, cutting apart some chickens – removing the heads and feet and gutting them. We cooked all afternoon in what felt like a house for garden elves, with the daycare center's tiny tables and chairs scattered around. But as evening approached various shaggy-haired friends of Lucie's turned up to help convert the place into a bistro. I met her boyfriend, Charly, who struck up a flirtatious friendship at once. Tall and ironic with wire-rim glasses, a head of brown curls and a radiant smile, he'd been living with Lucie for years. He seemed so easygoing compared to Jacques that I envied her.

When evening came, the place filled up and chaos ensued as we served a three-course meal with wine for which our merry customers paid 30 francs each, or about $4.50. Even then it was incredibly cheap. Lucie cleared only a tiny profit, but she still paid me – and asked me to come help cook the next weekend too.

That was fine with me. La Cour des Noues was like a microcosm of hip post-'68 Paris. The people who came to our bistro were still riding high on the wave of revolt that had swept France ten years earlier – contesting the ordinary, seeking the extraordinary, engaged politically, hungry for life. It was the best crowd I'd run into since my student days in Madison. I felt incredibly lucky to be becoming part of that scene.

HEARTACHE
1978

Jacques and I were moving in together again. Of course I hesitated when he proposed it, but this time we were actually renting a place together, just the two of us. Had our relationship at last reached its cruising speed? Had we been through enough drama to settle down and enjoy each other without needing the adrenalin rush of conflict to keep things interesting? We'd been together on and off for three and a half years now, and I felt ready to try once again to live with Jacques. It was the closest I hoped to get to being married.

Our apartment was on the third floor of a turn-of-the-century building on Boulevard Voltaire, a tree-lined avenue in the 11th. We had a living room with oak parquet floors, a kitchen, and two bedrooms – one for us, and one for Jacques. He'd insisted on this. I thought he'd use the second bedroom as his study, but his first act was to install a mattress. He retreated there from time to time when he wanted to be alone, closing the door on me and Mathilde, my cat.

We spent our first couple of months peeling off ancient wallpaper and repainting the place. In the kitchen we had a real fridge and a real stove and a couple of pantry shelves under the window cooled by the air outdoors.

As the autumn deepened, Jacques bought a chunk of wild boar which he left marinating with juniper berries out there for nearly a week, until its edges were greenish. He roasted it and insisted I try it. One time only.

In Valenciennes, it was the second and final year of my teaching contract. I had a new set-up, renting a room one night a week from the school's librarian. It was cheaper than the hotel, and I enjoyed Paulette. She was well read and an interesting conversationalist. But even as we talked, I pitied her. Paulette had blonde hair that she wore in a braid. She had thick glasses that made her eyes look tiny and a visible fuzz over her lip. She could have been quite lovely had she let down her hair, bought contact lenses and waxed the fuzz. But I didn't dare broach the subject. She was lonely, she confided, and longed to be with a man. But at 26 she was still a virgin.

"She's bound to remain an old maid," I remarked to Jacques one evening, and instantly regretted it. Of all the abominable phrases that should be expunged from human parlance, that probably ranks at the top. "Old maid" – *vieille fille* in French. So derogatory, so debasing, and of course with no male equivalent. And yet Paulette, to my mind, was unlikely to escape that destiny. No husband, no children, not even a lover. That evening, as Jacques uncorked a bottle of wine, it never occurred to me that I might face the same fate one day.

By autumn I was cooking regularly on Saturdays with Lucie at the Cour des Noues. We had six hours to produce a meal for the lefty-intello thirtysomethings who turned up at our improvised bistro with the street chic young Parisians seem to acquire by breathing the air – or by shopping at Agnès B. We had no problem filling the place. The food was copious, the wine virtually free and we usually had an act after dinner, with regulars like Ben Zimet, a Yiddish singer, or a female rock band called Les Babouches ("The Moroccan Bedroom Slippers").

While Lucie and I cooked, we exchanged stories. Her mother had emigrated to France from St. Petersburg during the chaos that followed the Russian Revolution. Her older sister was born in Paris before World War II. When the Nazis invaded, the family survived thanks to the kindness of a family in the village of Lougratte in southwest France. Lucie came along a year after the war ended. When we met, she had recently lost her father. She wanted children and, at 31, she was feeling the pressure of time more keenly since he died. But Charly was dragging his feet. He already had a son from a previous relationship and wasn't ready to dive back into fatherhood.

"I know how you feel," I told her. "I want a kid too."

"You're a bambina – you're only 28!" she laughed. "You have time."

But I didn't. I was a year older than my mother had been when she had me, and I couldn't shed the feeling that I was running late. Even though getting pregnant seemed impossible thanks to Jacques and his blasted condoms, I kept hoping beyond hope that I would.

It wasn't an obsession, but I needed distraction. In free moments, when not teaching or cooking, I had The Paris Metro – but there were ominous and accelerating indications that the paper might fold. In November, under the headline *The Metro is Here to Stay*, the editors said that they had put together new financing "to pay not only for this current issue, but for many more to come." But they were wrong. That issue was the last.

We had a party a couple weeks later to mark the demise of what all associated with it agreed had been a great Paris institution. Jacques and I joined our colleagues at Bofinger, an elegant Alsatian-style brasserie near the Bastille with an oyster stall outside and a private room upstairs. The champagne flowed freely amid speeches, tears and much merriment. As the evening wore on, one of the paper's critics motioned for me to come with him. Sam had had his eye on me for a while. Curious, I excused myself and followed him to the restrooms. The door opened onto a tiled space with two stalls, one for men and one for women. Sam chose the women's and pulled me in with him. I was laughing and protesting.

"Shhh!" he ordered. "Sit down and be quiet."

There wasn't much space in there. I obediently lowered the toilet lid and sat while Sam rummaged in his pocket.

He pulled out a little silver case. Then he found a 50-franc bill and rolled it into a tube.

"Here," he said, tipping some white powder out of the silver box onto a small mirror, forming it into a line. "You go first."

"What is it?" I asked, leaning over for a better look.

"Are you kidding me?" said Sam. "It's…"

But the powder was tickling my nose. I sneezed and the line disappeared in a cloud of dust.

"Goddamn it, Mona," he said. "That was a hundred francs of cocaine!"

"I'm so sorry," I said, chagrined at my naïveté and trying not to laugh.

"Okay, okay," he grumbled. "Let's change places. I'll show you how it's done."

As I got up, Sam grabbed me and planted a big kiss on my mouth.

"No, no!" I protested. Jacques was out there, and besides, if I was attracted to Sam it was for his aura of fast living, not for his body.

As I was negotiating some distance between me and Sam, the door to the restrooms opened.

We froze as the handle of our women's stall turned. But we'd locked it.

"Come on," I whispered. "Let's go back out to the party."

"Shhh!" said Sam, carefully tipping a new line of coke onto the mirror. He inserted one end of the 50-franc tube, bowed his head, held one nostril closed and, with the other, sniffed. I watched, fascinated.

"What does it feel like?" I mouthed the words.

He raised his head and sniffed loudly.

"Hey, what's going on in there?" boomed a female voice. It sounded like Viola, the most sophisticated woman on the paper.

"Don't worry about it, honey," said Sam. "Just use the men's."

"Is that you, Hotdog?" the Viola voice said. "Who've you got in there? Whoever it is, watch out – he's a real pisser."

As soon as we heard the door of the men's stall lock, we made our exit.

"Where have you been?" said Jacques when I returned.

"Oh," I said, "I was just using the women's room."

It was around mid-December when Jeanne phoned to say she was arriving in Paris and we should buy some white wine. She turned up with a crate of oysters and, for me, a wood-handled kitchen knife as a belated birthday present. At 29, I had never had oysters – I couldn't get my mind around the idea that you ate them alive – but as Jeanne had hand-carried them on a train from Normandy, and as Jacques was opening them, I bowed to expectation and agreed to try one. Jacques demonstrated, taking an oyster on the half shell into his palm and squeezing a drop of lemon juice into it (to see whether it was still living – if it retracted its edges when touched by the acid, it was safe to eat). He then detached it from its shell with a sharp knife and, in one swift gesture, let the glistening gray morsel slip into his mouth with its transparent liquid. My turn. I copied what he'd done, closed my eyes and tipped the shell to my mouth. It was like swallowing a nutty salty mouthful of pure sea.

We must have each had two dozen oysters that day, and a lot of wine to go with them. As usual, being in the presence of Jeanne brought all kinds of emotions to the fore. I had managed to stash away my anger at her for what had happened at Floréal three years earlier. I was no longer (very) jealous of her relationship with Jacques. But I didn't feel I could trust her, although she presumably had no such qualms with me – for god's sake, she'd just given me a knife! Still, as the wine filled me with warmth, I let down my guard.

We talked about her life in the country – Thomas had left her, Brenda had gone to Holland, and Jeanne had moved to a village in Dordogne where she was bringing up Camille, now three, on her own. Jacques and I had seen them briefly there during the summer.

Thinking back to that visit now, to Jeanne's obvious delight in motherhood, I could feel my jealousy rising again. When Jeanne left, I took Jacques' hand and led him to our bedroom.

"Let's make love," I said. He didn't object.

Later, as evening fell and we tarried in bed, it felt like Jacques was reading my mind.

"I know you want kids," he said.

"Oh, Jacques!"

"But it's not a good idea."

"Why not? Let's not wait anymore. I mean, I don't even know if I'll be able to get pregnant."

"No, think about it, Mona," he said. "We argue all the time. It wouldn't be good for the child. We need to stabilize our relationship first."

"You're just scared," I said. "Scared of what?"

Jacques kissed my forehead, slipped his clothes on and went to clear up in the kitchen. Snuggling into the covers, I wondered whether I should tell him what I really thought: that starting a family would eliminate the source of the tensions between us. But if I argued with him, I realized, I would simply be proving his point. So I said nothing.

Later that night, when we crawled back into bed after a light supper, Jacques surprised me by reaching for me in the dark. He was aroused, and pressing to enter me.

"Wait!" I said, by habit or reflex. "You're not wearing a condom."

"I know," was all he replied.

When I flew to the States alone a week later I was in a state of agitated bliss. That may sound contradictory, but how else to describe the overwhelming feeling generated by my awareness that, for the first time in my life, I could be pregnant. We had made love without birth control. Now my period was one day overdue. The immensity of that thought filled my entire being as the Sabena jet's engines powered up at the Brussels airport. I had come up to Belgium with Jacques a day earlier to take advantage of the airline's Christmas deal. He took me to dinner at a mussels bistro with ceramic murals of fishermen on the walls, and kissed me sweetly when we parted in the morning. He wasn't coming to Wisconsin this time. It would be a Venture family Christmas.

Pressed back into my seat as the engines thrust the plane skyward, I was already counting the months until our child could be born. It was December now, which meant I would not yet be 30 when the due date arrived in September. It was so exciting – so terrifying! Was it real? I didn't dare hope. Should I say anything to my family when I got home? My mother was sure to raise the issue of grandchildren yet again. I could tantalize her by implying a baby might be in her future. But, no. I wouldn't tell her anything. Not yet. Nothing was sure yet. But Ben, now an established glass artist in the Bay Area, was flying in for the holiday. We weren't close, separated physically by a continent and an ocean, and psychologically by differences of character and outlook. Yet if I needed to confide in anyone, he was the one. I could trust my brother to keep the news to himself.

By the time the plane touched down in Chicago I was convinced I'd be having a baby. I could feel something deep inside my womb, tugging at me. I was sure of it. The exhilaration lasted through passport control and baggage collection. I was in such high spirits when my parents met me at the gate that they grew suspicious.

"Mona Venture – are you hiding something from us?" asked my mom as we headed north to Wisconsin in my dad's Oldsmobile sedan. "You're so bubbly, sweetie. Tell us! Has Jacques finally come to his senses and asked you to marry him?"

"No, no!" I laughed. "I'm just in a good mood. It's so great to see you both. Thanks for driving down to get me."

Snow was gusting across the highway, making it slow going. By the time we reached home night was falling. My father built a fire in the black marble fireplace that cast a cheery glow over the family room as we settled down to dinner at the white table, warm within our glass-walled house as drifts built up outdoors.

My father raised an eyebrow when I declined his offer of a glass of Margaux.

"Anything wrong?" he asked.

"I'm just tired," I smiled. "It's the jetlag."

When Ben flew in from California the next day, it was Christmas Eve and preparations were in full swing. Sure, we were Jewish, but we were American too, and the Christmas season was as American as, well, stuffed turkey. There was no question of calling our tree a Hanukah bush. We of course celebrated Hanukah every year, lighting the candles for eight consecutive nights and exchanging small gifts. But Christmas was Christmas, and this year my mother was pulling out all the stops. She had brought home a soaring Norwegian pine that we installed in the family room beside the TV, decking it out with candy canes, twinkling lights and some glass baubles Ben had made at his studio.

With the tree's piney scent filling the house, Christmas cookies baking in the oven, my mom humming along joyously to carols booming from the FM radio, memories of childhood engulfed me. It was in this house that I'd come of age, nurtured by the woman in the kitchen with flour on her apron and a song in her soul. She was my guardian angel, my tormentor, my best friend, my worst enemy. How hard it must be to be a parent, I mused. And now here I was, on the cusp of having a child.

Should I tell Ben my secret? I was tempted. My period was two days late, something that had never happened before, and it was harder and harder to push from my mind the certainty that I was pregnant. I wanted to share my excitement, to tell the world the good news. But I held back.

This turned out to be the right decision, for on Christmas morning my period came, complete with cramping so intense I went pale and had to lie down. To be honest, I wasn't really surprised. It would have been a miracle if Jacques and I had managed to create a new life the first time we hadn't put obstacles in nature's path.

Still, as I lay there on my childhood bed, trying to take it philosophically, my future felt as bleak as the snow-covered grass outside. No baby. No new life inside me. I didn't look forward to telling Jacques about it. There was every chance he'd heave a sigh of relief and start using condoms again

But I had no time to mope. We had company coming for Christmas lunch – my grandmother and a couple of my dad's medical students – and my mom wanted help in the kitchen. When we took our seats at the table, my father uncorked a Chassagne-Montrachet for the occasion. The roast turkey was succulent, Ben was cracking jokes, we had fruitcake for dessert, the students were telling stories over post-prandial cognac, and we were all in a relaxed mood when my grandmother spoke up.

I had mentioned earlier how much I regretted the demise of The Paris Metro.

"Monachka," she said. She always used a diminutive when addressing me, *ziskeit* ("sweetness") or *shayna punim* ("beautiful face") from Yiddish, or a Russian variant on my name.

"You know, Monachka, you have a cousin in journalism in Paris."

"I do?"

"Yes, of course. Milton Meyer of The Associated Press. My mother's brother was his grandfather. They came over on the same boat from the Ukraine, fleeing the Cossacks. That makes you second cousins once removed."

"Really!" At 83, my grandmother didn't miss a trick. No longer at the psychiatric "estate" where she'd been confined for more than a decade, she was now living in a Jewish home for the elderly and could visit her family on holidays, or whenever she liked. She may have been deemed crazy by society, including her own son and daughter-in-law, but to me she was simply a person too sensitive to bear the harsh realities of our world. Or maybe that's what crazy means.

"So what does this cousin do?" I asked her, wondering why my parents had never mentioned him.

"He's a reporter, *ziskeit*. He writes about France. I see his articles sometimes – he seems very talented. Why don't you give him a call?"

A door closes, a door opens.

When I got back to Paris and told Jacques I wasn't pregnant, he commiserated but seemed mightily relieved. He encouraged me to call my cousin without delay. My hands were trembling when I dialed the number, and so was my voice.

"May I please speak to Milton Meyer?"

"He's out now," said the secretary. "Who's calling?"

"It's his cousin, Mona Venture, but he doesn't know me," I said, instantly realizing how weird that sounded. I left my number, figuring he would probably never call back.

But late that afternoon the phone rang and it was Milton. He asked me to drop by in a couple of days. Simple as that.

I was nervous as a bumblebee when I entered the AP's Paris bureau on the Rue du Faubourg Saint-Honoré. The place was crawling with reporters, photographers, telex operators, secretaries, with used coffee cups and newspapers scattered about. Then Milton appeared. If I had formed a mental image of the foreign correspondent, he was a perfect fit. He was tall with wise eyes, a confident smile and a worldly air. After introducing me around the bureau as "the journalist Mona Venture," he took me to the inner sanctum – the office of the bureau chief.

If I had high hopes, they were dashed immediately. The bureau chief told me in the most cordial manner that he didn't have any jobs open that would suit me.

He threw me a bone, saying they'd keep my CV on file. Slight consolation.

"Don't look so disappointed," said Milton as he led me to his cubbyhole for coffee and a chat. "There's a lot of demand within the

AP for positions in Paris. That's understandable. But I may have something else for you."

"Oh?" I perked up.

"When I was bureau chief in New Delhi a few years ago, I got to be friends with a fellow named Philippe Cauchin. At the time he was Delhi bureau chief of Agence France-Presse."

"And?" I was holding my breath.

"And now he's head of AFP's English Desk. He phoned me the other day to say they were computerizing and needed seven new editors. He asked whether there was anyone I could recommend."

The three-day test at AFP was a breeze. I had to translate news dispatches and rewrite them in the style of the English-speaking press. I'd prepared for this by getting the International Herald Tribune and Le Figaro for a week and comparing their reports on the same event. Not just Le Figaro but the French press in general tended to use the "everything was going along well when..." approach, leading the reader suspensefully to the news. The American and English press, in contrast, tried to get the "who-what-when-where-why" into the top of the story.

For example, in 1963, on the day after JFK's assassination, the report in The New York Times read like this:

Dallas, Nov. 22 — President John Fitzgerald Kennedy was shot and killed by an assassin today.

He died of a wound in the brain caused by a rifle bullet that was fired at him as he was riding through downtown Dallas in a motorcade.

Vice President Lyndon Baines Johnson, who was riding in the third car behind Mr. Kennedy's, was sworn in as the 36th President of the United States 99 minutes after Mr. Kennedy's death.

Mr. Johnson is 55 years old; Mr. Kennedy was 46.

Shortly after the assassination, Lee H. Oswald, who once defected to the Soviet Union and who has been active in the Fair Play for Cuba Committee, was arrested by the Dallas police. Tonight he was accused of the killing.

The main report in Le Figaro read like this:

Washington, Nov. 22 – Assassinated like Abraham Lincoln, President Kennedy has just died of his wounds in a hospital in Dallas.

The first news of the attack reached here around 2 p.m. Details followed minute by minute.

Accompanied by his wife, Jacqueline, the governor of Texas, Mr. Connally, and the wife of the latter, Mr. Kennedy was going in an open car to a big hotel in the city where he was supposed to give a speech before 'the local council of citizens.' The population had warmly acclaimed him along the route. Suddenly, at the moment when the cortege was entering an underground passage beneath railway tracks, shots rang out and the president collapsed on the knees of his wife. Jacqueline was heard crying, 'Oh no.'

It seems that the assassin shot 'like at fish in a bowl' from a window on the fifth floor of a nearby building. A secret service agent had just the time to shout: 'Get down.'"

Although applicants to the AFP English Desk were supposed to have three years' experience in the press, this requirement was waived for me, ostensibly because my French was so fluent. But my cousin's friendship with Philippe Cauchin undoubtedly helped. So that was it. They hired me. I was – did I dare believe it? – becoming a full-time journalist.

But not right away. First I had to finish the school year in Valenciennes and jump through an impressive number of bureaucratic hoops for Agence France-Presse – like getting a fresh translation of my birth certificate, as though something had changed since the last translation. My new career would start only in June.

ò▲

While waiting for winter to end, we had a new distraction. Jacques had inherited some money and was hunting for a country house. He took me with him on his second foray.

We drove south in March when spring was not yet in the air, spent a frigid night in an unheated hotel in Brive-la-Gaillarde, then carried on to the Gers region where Jacques had found a promising real estate agency in the picturesque ancient town of... Condom. I insisted we go buy postcards before doing anything else. Why had the name of this pretty town been adopted in English as the term for the male protective sheath? Theories abound, but the reason is unknown – just as it's not known why the English use the term "French letters" for condoms, while the French call them *capotes anglaises*," or English hoodies. But given the cross-Channel rivalry between the two countries, it's not hard to guess.

It was so cold in Condom we could see our breath as we trod along medieval stone sidewalks to the agency, where a personable woman was waiting for us. She had already shown Jacques a property and he wanted me to take a look. Even in that weather the region was glorious. It was ancient Occitania, Armagnac country, the rolling land where d'Artagnan and the musketeers had rollicked in the stories by Alexandre Dumas, and it had hardly changed in centuries. The agent drove us through a medieval village and down a winding lane, past fields of bare plum trees and a charming chapel, until we reached what could only be described as a ruin.

The house, of pale stone, was falling to pieces. The roof had caved in, the walls were crumbling and a former duck pond along one side was stagnant and overgrown with brambles. But as the agent turned the key in the door, feeling Jacques' excitement growing, I tried to warm to the place. No hot water? We could fix that. No toilet or shower? It would just be temporary. The big hole in the roof? No problem, said Jacques, adding that he could get electricity installed within a few months, he was sure. The real problem, to his mind, was that the agent wanted to sell him not just the house but also the chapel – and the graveyard that went with it.

As for me, I could not imagine living in that house. The main room had dingy turquoise walls coated in soot, with prehistoric cobwebs hanging from the ceiling and a dark tile floor with a pool of water alongside one wall. There was no bathroom. On one side of the house was a former pigsty with a floor of beaten earth and walls made of mud and straw that Jacques wanted to convert into bedrooms. I kept my reservations to myself during the visit, but when we had thanked the agency woman and departed I gave Jacques a piece of my mind.

"What are you thinking about?" I fumed. "What if we have children? There's no way I'd bring a baby to this place."

"It's beautiful," said Jacques. "Okay, it needs some work. But just wait. You'll see. And let's not worry about a baby that doesn't exist yet."

True – no baby had yet taken hold in my womb. I tried not to worry about it too much. Sometimes we weren't together at the right time of the month, other times we quarreled and coitus was interruptus if at all. And did Jacques want a baby?

No way to tell, but he did want that house. He had a vision. He could picture it once the work was done. And it was cheap. When we got back to Paris, he phoned the agent, negotiated away the church and cemetery, and it was his. Most of the land around the house belonged to a farmer, but there were bits we could use as a garden. When we went back down to sign the deed, I spent a long time sweeping away cobwebs and planted some seeds. By late May, when we got the keys, flowers were blooming.

The headquarters of Agence France-Presse surges up along Place de la Bourse like an ocean liner of bronze-tinted glass and concrete. Standing in its shadow beneath the wispy clouds of a June morning, feeling very small, you can practically hear the sound of tomtoms beating out a message from some farflung outpost – a message that will make its way to AFP's nerve center in Paris and go sailing back out to newspapers, radio stations, television channels around the world. Even before you approach the door, your heart soars with the knowledge that you are about to begin an incredible voyage to parts unknown, joining those already on board as they ply their daily route through international waters, never knowing where their next port of call may be. You will ride the waves of war, peace, assassination, thievery high and low, blood, sweat and tears of joy as you contribute in your small way to the dissemination of what the world has agreed to call news.

On that June morning I emerged from the Metro feeling fluttery, made my way across the traffic-clogged Rue Réaumur and paused. As one of the Western world's four major news agencies, AFP was the big time, no doubt about it. I was scared and exhilarated at the same time. Would I make it? Was I good enough? Never mind. If I didn't hurry, I'd be late. I took a breath, buzzed and the guard let me in.

Moments later, Philippe Cauchin was introducing me around the English Desk, a long rectangle toward the back of the main newsroom, where a friendly assortment of English, Welsh, Scottish, Australian, Irish and American journalists greeted me briefly and got back to their typewriters.

It was hard not to feel overwhelmed in the newsroom, a vast space two stories high that felt as large as a football field. Halfway up, on a mezzanine, sat teleprinters spewing out dispatches from AFP correspondents and stringers around the world. At the editing desks, the journalists worked beneath a Rube Goldberg-esque track of pulleys and wires that had been installed halfway down from the ceiling. Clipped to the wires, bundles of dispatches zipped through the room until they reached the appropriate desk, where something triggered them to release and all the copy came crashing down a square glass chute. In one corner sat a half-dozen grizzled telex operators typing outgoing dispatches at high speed. From their machines emerged perforated white tapes identical to the ones being received in the newsrooms and bureaux of AFP subscribers around the world, and copies for the desks on more teleprinters.

At the English Desk, I was introduced to Matthew Street, a jovial Londoner who was that morning's head of desk. Seated at the column where the incoming dispatches arrived, he retrieved them from the bottom of the chute and looked them over, a process known as copy tasting. If they were deemed worthy of treatment, he distributed them to the copy editors, who were known at AFP as subeditors, or simply subs. Next thing I knew Matthew Street was handing me a report in French to translate and rework in English. I was given a typewriter and a "sandwich" – a six-ply sheaf of very thin yellow paper intersticed with carbons. When I was done, the dispatch went into a wire basket for the chief sub, whose job was to correct it and send it on to the telex operators – or, if it needed serious work, hand it back to me.

It was hard to concentrate in the atmosphere of that newsroom, where the banging of typewriters competed with the clattering of teleprinters and senior editors shouting orders to the subs in different languagues. The English Desk sat between the Spanish Desk, staffed by drop-dead-handsome South Americans, and the quiet, stolid German Desk. The French maintained dominion over the other desks – Foreign, France, French Overseas Territories, Politics, Business, Culture, and, if memory serves, Horseracing was there too (AFP sent the results of the races to cafés around the country, one of its most popular services). Off to one side was a glassed-in space called RedChef, where the agency's top editors, or *rédacteurs en chef*, kept an imperious collective eye on the proceedings. The heavily scented dark-tobacco smoke of Gitane and Gauloise cigarettes hung over the newsroom. Bells went off occasionally to signal the arrival of big news, which had to be turned around quickly to beat AFP's competitors: the AP, Reuters and UPI – or, as they were known in AFP's quaint internal parlance, Amélie, Rosalie and Ursule.

It was a relief when lunchtime came and a handful of subs were allowed to take a break. Like all large workplaces in France, AFP has a lunchroom with subsidized meals for its employees. But on that glorious June day, my new colleagues took me across the street to Le Vaudeville, a classic 24-hour-a-day Parisian brasserie. As we sat over sandwiches and wine, it was hard for me to follow the conversation. Greg Faraday, a ruddy-faced Yorkshireman, had an accent so thick I couldn't understand him. As he couldn't understand me either, we spoke to each other in French. But the problem of accents diminished the more wine we drank. Then it was back to work for a few hours.

By the time I left for home, I was exhausted but content. Most of my work had been approved by the chief sub, my colleagues were a genuinely likable lot and, even if I had not been entrusted with reports of earthshaking importance, I hadn't flubbed my debut in the business of international news.

My new job proved to be not just a crash course in international politics, but also an introduction into the way France handles news. We had a system of bells at AFP to signal the arrival of major breaking stories. An event deemed "urgent" received two bells and went out on the wire as a brief paragraph; three bells meant a "bulletin", with a single sentence of news; and four bells meant a "flash", usually just a subject, verb and source, for example, "KENNEDY SHOT – OFFICIAL."

When really big news broke, the clanging of bells would sometimes be followed by a voice booming out of a large loudspeaker down at our end of the room. This was the RedChef giving the newsroom instructions on how to handle the story – or, exceptionally, ordering us to kill the story, i.e. to throw the news in the wastebasket.

In my first few months at AFP, as we switched from typewriters to computers, one of the big stories concerned Jean-Bedel Bokassa, the self-proclaimed emperor of the Central African Republic, a former French colony. In September 1979, after Bokassa's troops massacred 100 students who were demonstrating against the high cost of school uniforms, and with rumors flying that the emperor practiced cannibalism, France sent a team of elite commando troops to overthrow the government in Bangui and install a more palatable president. But that was not the big story. What prompted the RedChef to get on the hooter was the revelation in October that the French president, Valéry Giscard d'Estaing, had accepted gifts of diamonds from Bokassa. It was a Tuesday afternoon when we heard the booming voice. AFP had received an advance copy of the weekly newspaper Le Canard Enchaîné, which had the diamonds story as an exclusive, and the French Desk had just put out a bulletin, which I was busily translating. When the kill order thundered forth the newsroom erupted in groans, but we had to obey. A short time later a new story was delivered quoting the Elysée Palace – Giscard's office – as saying,

> …exchanges of gifts of a traditional nature, notably during the visits of members of governments to foreign states, in no way have the character or the value mentioned in certain press organs with regard to Central African Republic.

That was what went out on the wire. Only a day later, when Le Canard was on the stands, did AFP's clients receive the real news.

There was no time at the English Desk to worry about the fact that Jacques was down in the Gers working on the house all summer while I was in Paris and therefore unlikely to get pregnant. As a new employee, I couldn't take vacation, but I did manage to go down for a long weekend in August. Jacques had made some progress but we still had to use a chamber pot and take showers outdoors under a hose with a sprayer. I made pickles from small cucumbers we got from the farmer next door and befriended his four-year-old daughter, whose presence only intensified my yearning for a child.

Throughout the fall I waited and hoped and pounded out dispatches on my newsroom computer. By the end of the year, Iranian revolutionary guards were holding 53 American hostages, the Soviet Union had invaded Afghanistan, I had turned 30, I still wasn't pregnant and Jacques and I were fighting again.

It hadn't helped the day when Jacques came home and announced that he was considering marrying Brenda – Brenda! – because, as an American, she was having a hard time getting working papers.

It was news to me that Jacques was even in contact with Brenda, Jeanne's co-counseling friend and my nemesis from the Cévennes.

"You have got to be kidding!" I said, sure that he must be.

"Don't worry, it will be a *mariage blanc*," Jacques persisted. "If I marry Brenda she can get citizenship, which will solve the problem. I'm just doing a favor for a friend."

"You're really funny," I said. "Forget about favors for Brenda. I'd like to remind you that we're living together. If you want to help an American get papers, why not marry me?"

The Brenda matter ended there. But when Lucie informed me she was pregnant, the news catapulted the tension with Jacques to a new level. I was happy for Lucie, of course, but it was hard seeing my best friend glowing with contentment when Jacques and I were failing month after month to conceive a child. We made love at the right time, halfway through my cycle, but nothing happened. Every month my periods grew more painful, until one wintry day Jacques found me on the floor beside the toilet. I had passed out from the intensity of the cramping.

It occurred to me at the time – after we'd undergone fertility testing and been found to be perfectly fine – that our quarrels might have something to do with the situation. It seemed that after the midway point of each month, just as I let a glimmer of hope enter my heart, Jacques picked a fight. To be honest, I contributed to those arguments. We repeated the same old script every month. It went like this:

Jacques *(coldly)*: "There's no way we should have a child together. The child would be too unhappy."

Mona (*distressed*): "How can you say that? I might be pregnant now!"

Jacques (*firmly*): "I hope not. It would be a disaster."

Mona (*throwing herself on the bed*): "Boo hoo, boo hoo."

My floods of tears did nothing to soften Jacques' attitude until the arrival of my period. Then he became charming again. We made love, and the cycle repeated itself – and with it the heartache. We were making love, but love itself was nowhere to be found.

Before spring came, Colette announced that she, too, was expecting a child. She had switched back to men and was seeing a former lover, Fernando, who had – effortlessly, it seemed – made her pregnant right after returning from a long stay in Portugal, his home country. Now my two best friends were approaching motherhood, and I was not taking it well. The arguments with Jacques grew more heated, we were making love less frequently and, as the days grew longer with the promise of summer, once again dishes flew.

Our apartment had a long corridor connecting our bedroom to the living room, a perfect venue, I found, for hurling plates against the wall when my frustration and unhappiness grew too much to bear. Unfortunately, as we discovered one evening when our downstairs neighbors appeared at our door, that corridor wasn't soundproof.

"If this continues, we're calling the police," glowered the husband as his wife stared with fascinated horror at the shards of china littering our hallway.

Jacques fended them off politely. But he turned on me when they left.

"This has gone on long enough," he said icily. "We can't continue living together."

"What do you mean?" I said, my world collapsing.

"I mean it's not working. We have to split up."

"No, Jacques!" I sobbed. "We can fix it. We..."

"We can't," he said, cutting me off. "Things have gone too far. I'm sorry, Mona, but we have to end this. You can look for a new place while I'm down in the Gers this summer. When I get back I want to be on my own."

"But this apartment is our place together," I protested. "You can't just throw me out."

"Okay," he said, "you can stay on here if you prefer. But this needs to be resolved by the end of summer. I'm warning you, Mona. You need to decide. If you don't move out, I will."

HOPE

1980

What shook my inner universe when Jacques walked out on me was not just the betrayal – of trust, of hope, of the illusion I still clung to that when a man and a woman lived together it was for life. What shook me was the fear. Fear of being alone, in so many senses.

Alone without a man, without the friendly camaraderie of a partner for meeting life's daily challenges, without sharing, without a companion for sexual loving, without love.

Alone without the distraction of a mate to form a shield between one's conscious self and one's usually repressed awareness that life will end – not so much fear of dying alone as fear of being alone to face one's knowledge that one ultimately must cease to be.

Alone, worst of all, without children. The fear that I would never get pregnant, that I would never find a partner for raising a child, that I would never experience the joy of a young voice calling to me in the morning, "Mama, get up and make my breakfast." Of a small person tumbling onto the bed and covering me with kisses. The joy of passing along to a child what little I know about life, of watching the child blossom, of being there for the triumphs and disasters, the laughter and the tears. The joy of being ready to see the child go off into the world in full knowledge that this young being will deliver the resonance of my heart into the future, will transfer my mind's meanderings to a new generation, will carry my soul's most intimate message forward when I die. Will, in the way children do, make me eternal.

It was September by the time I moved into my new apartment, on Avenue Ledru-Rollin, just a five-minute walk from my place with Jacques. He was still in the Gers. On moving day, I accepted the offer of a ride from one of those handsome South Americans from the Spanish Desk – an Argentinian who'd been pursuing me. Santiago had a small car in which he'd driven me home from work occasionally en route to the Paris suburb where he lived with his wife.

"I can help you set up your new place," he said. "We can take the boxes over there together and I'll help you unpack."

As I'd already made it clear that I wasn't about to start something with a married man, I saw no reason to refuse his offer. The move didn't take long – I wasn't taking furniture, only my clothes, some dishes and, of course, Mathilde – and Santiago, true to his word, helped me get settled. We went out for a glass of wine afterwards, and that was the end of it.

I spent the first few days buying a kitchen table and chairs and a sofa bed, and taking possession of items offered to me by friends, some of them quite wonderful, like a long dining table made of a single oak plank. I repainted the bathroom, made curtains for the bedroom, had wood delivered for the fireplace. When Jacques came back to Paris he brought over our bed, which we'd built together of sturdy pine boards that could easily be taken apart and reassembled.

Seeing him wasn't as hard as I'd feared. We'd been together for nearly six years, double the time I'd spent with Jake. Despite my sadness over the break-up, I also felt the kind of relief a boxer must feel when the fight is called against him and he can pick himself up, brush himself off and go home to a stiff drink. I'd gone as many rounds as I could with Jacques but it hadn't worked out. I'd tried to be the woman he wanted me to be, but that had proved impossible. I was flawed. Okay, who wasn't? The perpetual conflicts had suppressed a part of me I'd forgotten about. Would the real Mona Venture please stand up?

As I began to reassemble my life, work was a helpful distraction. In mid-September, strikes led by a shipyard worker named Lech Walesa gave birth to Solidarity, Poland's first independent trade union. Meantime, with his presidency at stake, Jimmy Carter was working frantically for the release of the Americans held hostage by Islamist militants in Iran. For Carter was facing a tough electoral contest in November against Ronald Reagan, the demon of the American left.

I so detested Reagan's radical right-wing positions, and was so sure he would be defeated in the primaries, that months before we split up I bet Jacques that if the star of "Bedtime for Bonzo" was elected president of the United States I would give up my American citizenship. The stake was a case of Champagne. By July, when Reagan won his party's nomination at the Republican National Convention, I was regretting the wager. The only way I could win was if a) Reagan was elected and b) I turned in my passport, something I would never do. But Jacques held me to it, gloating as opinion polls showed Reagan far outpacing President Carter. Even when we were no longer living together, Jacques would periodically remind me of my folly.

Voting day was November 4, and I was working the late shift at AFP. Santiago was there, too. When our shifts ended he proposed that we go to a late-night bar to follow the election results. He had never stopped pursuing me, and my resolve to resist him was fading. For one thing, over coffee that autumn, Santiago had informed me that he and his wife had an open marriage. She had had affairs, he said, and now it was his turn. For another, the chemistry between us was strong and getting stronger. He was tall with light brown hair, chocolate eyes, smooth golden skin and a boyish smile that lit up his bearded face. But that doesn't begin to convey the appeal of this sexy man, whose macho swagger was belied by the sweetness of his nature.

Santiago belonged to the generation of Argentinians who fled the military dictatorship of Jorge Rafael Videla in the late 1970s, at a time when leftist opponents were being kidnapped and tortured or murdered. He had sold kites in the form of birds outside the Pompidou Center before joining the Spanish Desk at AFP. At a time when I was still feeling fragile from the split with Jacques, Santiago was kind and never pushed too hard. So when he suggested an election night outing, I agreed.

We went to a bar in the Latin Quarter that had dancing downstairs. After a few drinks and a turn around the dance floor, I was starting to resign myself to the idea that Reagan might win. We went on to a quieter bar where a TV in the corner was beaming in results from America. It was after 2 a.m. – 8 p.m. on the East Coast – and exit polls showed that Reagan was demolishing Carter. As we sat slumped in overstuffed armchairs, the ice melting in our untouched Jack Daniels, I realized I'd had enough.

"This is painful to watch," I said. "Let's go."

In the car on the way to my house, Santiago put his hand on my knee, sending electric shivers through my body.

"Let me come upstairs with you," he said when we reached my building. In the two months I'd lived there, I hadn't been with a man. Now Santiago was beside me, wooing me in his soft Spanish accent. My resolve collapsed as we rode up in the antiquated elevator and he let his lips brush mine. I may have lost the bet with Jacques that night, but I'd won something I hadn't wagered on – a new lover, impassioned, tender, inventive, funny, who whispered sweet nothings into my ear after we made love and stayed nearly until dawn, when he left to go home to his wife.

His wife. I had seen her at a party once, short and slender with long wavy dark hair. She obviously adored Santiago. So what was I doing in bed with him? It was against my principles to sleep with married men. As someone who had wanted to wed for such a long time, I certainly didn't want to break up anyone else's marriage. As a feminist – no, as a woman – I didn't want to hurt another woman. But, but, but (and here I have to accept that Jacques was right, I am deeply flawed) Santiago was so seductive. He swore that his wife would not be upset if she found out – and also that there was no way she would find out. He desired me, as she had desired other men. Nonetheless, after that first illicit roll in the hay, I resolved there would not be a second one.

But there was no avoiding the fact that we saw each other at work every day. Every day, as I made my way through the newsroom to the English Desk, my belly tightened at the sight of Santiago typing away among his Latin American colleagues. We went out for coffee or wine together during our breaks, slipping off to small cafés on side streets where other journalists were unlikely to see us. We held hands. Santiago pressed me to let him come over again, but I resisted.

In a misguided effort to erase the memory of Santiago from my body, I agreed to go out to dinner with another AFP colleague, a Frenchman from the Foreign Desk who had flirted with me, and after our meal I invited him up for cognac. Marc was a Jewish intellectual who was determined to make a big name for himself as a journalist. He cringed when we entered my spartan apartment, which so clearly lacked the casual-chic charm that French women manage to create. But as the cognac warmed me I brushed his criticism from my mind, and in due course we made our way to bed. After a perfunctory bout in which he came almost immediately, as we lay side by side in the lamplight, Marc struck up a conversation about the Middle East. We were arguing about the relative merits of a Palestinian state when he popped the question.

"Would you ever sleep with an Arab?"

I had to laugh.

"I don't know," I replied. "Would you?"

"Absolutely not!" he said. "And I don't think I could stand to be with a woman who would. Especially a Jewish woman."

This entire experience was so different from the night I'd spent with Santiago that I couldn't help thinking of him, even while in bed with another man. Santiago, my one-time lover, who had refused to wear a condom because, he said, quoting his father, making love wearing a condom was like walking on the beach in socks. Santiago, my faux Latin lover, who had been born in Argentina but was not really Latin American because he was the son of an Irish mother and a Syrian father who had met in Buenos Aires. Santiago... A Syrian father...

"Come to think of it," I said, smiling sweetly at Marc. "I slept with an Arab last week. Well, he's actually only half Arab. His father is Syrian. You'd like him. He's a really great guy."

I might have said more but Marc had already jumped out of bed and grabbed his clothes. He dressed quickly in the living room and came back to take his leave. Standing over me as I lay there nude beneath the quilt, he could not disguise his contempt.

"I don't think this will work out," he said.

"Goodbye," I replied.

Although my parents were chain smokers, I had never smoked cigarettes – or maybe that was why. But once I joined AFP I was surrounded by smokers. Everyone, it seemed, worked within reach of a burning cigarette. A permanent pall of smoke hung over the newsroom as French editors puffed away on their Gitanes and Gauloises. The Latinos on the Spanish Desk preferred American blond tobacco. Santiago and his colleagues may have opposed the politics of the United States, but they saw no reason not to buy into the romance of Marlboro country.

After the incident with Marc, as I clung to my resolve to keep Santiago at bay, I surprised myself one day by going into a tobacco store and buying a pack of Gitanes. The blue box adorned with a gypsy woman appealed to me. I bought the kind with filters, took them home and lit up.

Coughing, spluttering after the first puff, I quickly put the cigarette out. But later that day I tried again, puffing lightly and making sure not to inhale. It was okay. I smoked the whole cigarette. This, I had convinced myself, would be my secret weapon. When I felt myself submerged with desire for Santiago, I would light up. That would give me a distraction until the feeling abated.

Unfortunately, beyond smoking's obvious drawbacks for health, this technique proved woefully inadequate for steeling my faltering will. A couple of weeks after our first night together, on a Saturday when Santiago and I had both been assigned to the early shift at AFP, he offered to drive me home after work. As it was mid-afternoon, the offer seemed tame enough. We hadn't been out dancing and drinking, the tender night had yet to fall. I could handle it. I invited him up for coffee.

We sat on the couch and chatted, a reasonable distance between us. When he moved closer, I lit a Gitane.

"Since when did you start smoking?" Santiago asked.

"Since a couple of days ago."

"Well, don't," he said, gently removing the cigarette from my hand and moving closer still.

Afternoon faded to night and by the time Santiago left my place our romantic entanglement had been consummated as more than a one-night stand. How to resist the overpowering desire we felt for each other, the deep sweet satisfaction we gave each other? As neither of us was going to leave AFP, we were doomed to meet daily. I was doomed each time I saw him to feel the sharp stab of longing that penetrated my body between my legs and rose straight through me, leaving me fluttery.

Through the rest of the autumn and into winter, Santiago came over as often as he could. We both had our jobs to do, of course. But in between dispatches we were in between the sheets. On Thanksgiving Day, when I was preparing dinner for a dozen friends, Santiago turned up and pitched in, helping me chop onions and celery and chestnuts for the stuffing, and teaching me a new trick – before stuffing the turkey, rub the cavity with brandy. When the bird was in the oven we had time to tryst only quickly, for he had to be out of there before the guests arrived. Our relationship was secret. Nobody at AFP could know. I had told only Lucie about Santiago – for the obvious reason that he wanted to "protect" his wife.

There is a certain perverse romance to having a secret affair, to seeing how far you can go without getting caught. Santiago pushed the limits on New Year's Eve when he insisted I come to a party at his place in the suburbs. After party-hopping in Paris with a handful of AFP friends, made brazen by alcohol, I didn't balk when one of Santiago's deskmates proposed driving us all out there in his minivan. On entering and seeing Santiago's wife, resplendent in her New Year finery, I realized my mistake. The party was roaring. It was nearly midnight, everyone was high. Face burning, I slipped off to an empty room, but Santiago followed me.

"Please call me a taxi," I said, turning away as he reached for me.

"Let me drive you back to Paris," he coaxed.

"No way," I said. "I've got to leave now. I'll see you tomorrow at work."

But matters didn't end there. Emboldened perhaps by his success at evading detection, Santiago proposed that we take a little trip together. We slipped away to Normandy one January weekend, walked the broad, empty stretches of sand with only seagulls for company, flirted over a three-tier seafood platter, tumbled into bed at a hotel facing the crashing waves of the steel-gray Channel. It was an exhausting, exhilarating 24 hours, the pounding of our hearts and the pounding of the sea distancing guilt to the far reaches of our consciousness as we bonded over and over, our desire fueled by the small packet of cocaine Santiago had brought along from Paris.

In February Santiago upped the ante. He had an Argentinian friend with a big apartment in Venice who had invited him to come for Carnevale, the pre-Lenten madness that invades the city when its reserved inhabitants don masks and let their spirits go free. Estrella was open-minded, he said, and wouldn't mind him bringing along a woman who wasn't his wife.

We left Paris by train in late February. We had a sleeper compartment to ourselves. I was wearing a colorful striped mohair sweater I'd knitted, but it was cold in the compartment and we snuggled to keep warm. When we awoke in the morning the frosty golden light of an Italian winter was beaming into the train, beckoning us to the world's most magical city.

Estrella's place was on a small square not far from the Piazza San Marco. She gave us a room under the eaves where we could have some privacy. Other friends from Argentina would be arriving to occupy the guest rooms below. It was several days before the Carnival started, and Venice was still fairly quiet. Steam rose from the canals in the morning, casting a mysterious haze over the ancient stone streets. When we went inside the Accademia to see works by Venetian masters, I was startled to see people in the centuries-old paintings who looked just like those we had passed moments earlier outdoors.

One morning we went by boat to the glass-blowing island of Murano, where an artist friend of Estrella's bestowed on me a clear glass bowl with a fine black spiral spun through it, its beauty enhanced by its extreme fragility. In the afternoons, Estrella's neighbors performed the ritual known as the *passegiata*, strolling around the piazza beneath her window and saluting each other. It could have been the year 1600.

In this ambiance I felt transported, and not just because Santiago and I could be with each other 24 hours a day. As Carnival neared and the Venetians began making their daily stroll masked and in costume, an anything-can-happen buzz permeated the city. Two nights before we had to go back to Paris we managed to get tickets to Teatro La Fenice. Nearly everyone in the audience was wearing a mask. Magical! Then it was our last night and we were having a party. Masks were de rigueur, but we hadn't brought any.

"It's not a problem," I told Santiago. "I've got lots of makeup. I'll design your face as a mask."

As we sat in Estrella's kitchen that afternoon, I worked as though in a trance. It felt like some external creative force was guiding my hand. At the end of it Santiago's face was white with a black line down the middle. One side was jovial, the other diabolical. The effect was spooky, but Santiago liked it. I powdered my face white, sprinkled on some glitter, put on my sexiest outfit and awaited the guests. That night, as we danced and drank glass after glass of bubbly Prosecco, the partying grew wild. Was it the masks that allowed people to cast off their inhibitions? Or was it the cocaine being snorted in the kitchen?

In the wee hours, as we sat at the kitchen table, Santiago suddenly switched gears.

"Mona, you have bewitched me," he growled.

"What are you talking about?" I said, thinking it was a joke. But he shot a black glance my way. It was as though the duality of his mask had released the conflicts of his soul.

"I can't go on with this double life anymore," he muttered. "It's put my marriage at stake."

As he looked dangerously upset, I kept quiet. But I couldn't help thinking back over his long seduction of me, the months he spent pursuing me before I finally capitulated. And now I was being accused of bewitching him! Unfair.

On the train back to Paris the next morning, drained and sober, we had to face the reality that our Venetian adventure had taken us too far afield. I still hoped Santiago would change his mind. It was natural he was on edge, I told myself.

For a week we crossed paths only at work as he resumed his marital life. By then I was smoking Gitanes easily, half a pack a day, but that did nothing to ease my longing. When Santiago finally came over to my place, it was to say goodbye. We sat on the couch, but he kept his distance. He told me he needed to cast off his double persona and regain his oneness, his peace with himself. If our passion for each other was to be a casualty of our Venetian folly, so be it. And so it was.

Serendipity, according to Webster's, is "the faculty of finding valuable or agreeable things not sought for." When I returned home from Venice, I found a letter waiting from the husband of a second cousin on my father's side. His 12-year-old daughter was approaching her bat mitzvah, he wrote, and as a gift she had asked to know her family's origins. It was March 1981, and Alex Haley's magisterial "Roots: The Saga of An American Family," published five years earlier, was still having a profound effect on the national psyche. If an African American like Haley could trace his family's roots back through slavery to Gambia, my young cousin reasoned, why could our Jewish family, too, not know our history?

Enclosed in the letter was a one-page account of the ancestry of my father's father's mother, the matriarch of the Venture family, going back through Russia and Poland – and here I have to say the coincidence astounded me – to the Venice of the 16th century. It began by saying that she had always claimed to be descended from a long line of scholars and rabbis, but that nobody had believed her. However, research had now established that this was true. One of our forebears, Rabbi Saul Katzenellenbogen Wahl, had become famous as Poland's legendary "king for one night" when nobles met to elect a new sovereign in 1587 but couldn't decide. His father, Samuel Judah Katzenellenbogen, had been elected Rabbi of Venice in 1566, the heydey of the Jewish community there, and had walked the very streets I'd just visited.

At a time when I was suffering from the loss of Santiago, this letter had a surprisingly soothing effect. It linked me genetically to the city where he and I had just experienced such an exquisite high before crashing to earth. Was this family connection to Renaissance Venice why everything had seemed both strange and familiar during our visit? Why I'd picked up the vernacular as though breathing the air? Why people on the street had approached me to ask directions, as though I belonged to the city?

If I'd had doubts previously about my decision to leave the States for Europe – to *return* to Europe, as it turned out – these doubts vanished with the realization that I had not run away from the New World. No, when I crossed the Atlantic in 1974, I hadn't fled. Rather, in choosing Europe, I had moved toward reconnecting with my family's past. In an odd way, I'd come home.

Despite everything I somehow remained confident enough – or reckless enough – to present the image of a woman with an open persona. At 31, I was at the peak of vitality. Wavy-haired, with sculpted cheeks and laugh lines starting to form around my eyes and mouth, I literally bounced down the streets in my little heels, black leather Agnès B. coat, sheer black tights and the size 10 blue velours minidress I shared with Lucie. At AFP, the attentions of my male colleagues were a welcome distraction from the pain of losing first Jacques, now Santiago. I had women colleagues, too, and a few became good friends. But we were in the minority. The vast majority of journalists in that era were still men. There were the Brits on the English Desk – tall, witty, understated, sexy. And then there was the rest of the newsroom – good-looking Frenchmen as far as the eye could see. Even those who were married flirted with abandon. After all, it was the national sport.

"But it's a romantic hothouse over there!" Lucie teased as I sought to find my bearings after the Santiago fiasco. "Darling, you have everything it takes to please a man. I don't understand why someone's not snatching you up."

Lucie had given birth to Natasha six months earlier, just as I was packing up my things and leaving Jacques. She'd been through a couple of difficult months with Charly. As the birth neared, he had grown nervous and distant. But now, with his tiny daughter's shrieks of joy filling the house, Charly had fallen in love with his new progeny. As for Lucie, she was in a state of postpartum bliss. They formed a happy trio.

I still aspired to the same kind of happiness, of course – I always had – but at that time it felt light-years beyond my reach. I'd been hurt by my relationship with Jacques, so deeply hurt that I didn't want to repeat the experience by making myself vulnerable again – by falling in love. These thoughts were much with me as I looked back over the few months I'd spent with Santiago. The fact that he was married, I realized after the fact, had been one of the most attractive things about him. With Santiago I may have let myself get swept up in an infatuation, but the gate to the garden of paradise was locked. He was taken. We could only go so far. And that, I reasoned, made me less vulnerable.

Until the next unattached man came calling.

Patrick was a young filmmaker, friend of a friend. I ran into him at a party in February 1981, just before the trip to Venice with Santiago. Dashing even by French standards, he had light blue eyes, sandy hair, chiseled features and a movie-star smile. He surprised me the day after the party by phoning me at AFP to ask me out for coffee – right away.

"I can be there in 15 minutes," he said.

Bundled into my 1930s-vintage brown fur coat, I went down to the Vaudeville during my break and found Patrick waiting at a table beside the bar. He flashed a shy smile, took my gloved hand in his and kissed me on both cheeks. As we talked, he looked longingly into my eyes and wanted to make a date, but I told him I was seeing someone. He said he'd wait.

A month later, as the emotional waves from the Venice trip began subsiding, I remembered that Patrick had written his number on a scrap of paper. As soon as I called we began seeing each other – going out, staying in, his place, my place. We went to the movies a lot and he showed me his first short film. The sex was fine. He had nicknamed his member Bayard after a 15th century French soldier known as "the knight without fear and beyond reproach." He thought my pussy needed a name too. That was easy – Mathilde. As for birth control, I pooh-poohed Patrick's concerns. I had failed to get pregnant during years of unprotected sex with Jacques and a few more months with Santiago. This, I assured him, meant there was no problem.

Although Patrick had appeared besotted with me when we first met, it emerged during our courtship that there was another woman in his life. She had moved back to her homeland, Chile, after several years in Paris. They had recently resumed writing to each other and talking on the phone. Patrick said they were just friends. Still, he planned to go visit her during the summer. Was this a good thing or a bad thing? I chafed against it even while realizing that – as with Santiago – the limits on our relationship could protect me. If Patrick had been truly unattached it would have been far easier to fantasize about a possible future, replete with the holy grail of marriage and children. After everything that had happened with Jacques, I wasn't ready to reconnect with that fantasy.

In the spring, when Patrick and I had been seeing each for about a month, we took a trip to Normandy, where Lucie and Charly had part-ownership of an old stone house. They were bringing little Natasha. Colette would also be there with her new baby daughter, Rebecca. We would eat shellfish and homegrown lettuce from the garden and walk along the dunes of Cotentin, Normandy's sandy westernmost shore.

We left in high spirits in Patrick's car on a glorious sunswept morning. As we sped along the motorway, he asked for a blow job.

"What if somebody sees us?" I protested.

Patrick smiled encouragingly.

"Don't worry, no one will notice."

He was so unperturbed I had to wonder whether he'd done this before.

"Everyone's in a rush to get to the shore," he said. "They're not looking into other people's cars."

Gingerly I bent over and unzipped his pants, trying not to interfere with the steering wheel. As I reached in and extricated Bayard, Patrick kept his eyes on the road. Gingerly I stroked Bayard until he had reached a height beyond reproach. I tried to look out the window to make sure no one was watching, but Patrick pressed my head right down again. I took Bayard in my mouth.

"Wait!" said Patrick, a note of urgency invading his voice.

"Why?"

"We haven't reached the toll booths yet! The idea is to come at the very instant the coins hit the bin."

Geez, where did he get this scenario?

Laughing, I slowed down until Patrick told me he could see the toll booths ahead. Then I tightened my lips. Bayard was without fear, ready for action. Patrick was driving fast, then slowing, slowing, slowing... I didn't let up, going at it for all I was worth and praying that nobody saw. As the car slowed to a crawl, I heard the coins go clink into the bin and Patrick floored it.

"Ah ah ah ah ahhhhhhhhhhhhhhhhhh," he sighed as the car thrust forward.

When I extricated myself, Patrick was roaring down the motorway oblivious to the 80-mile-an-hour speed limit.

"That was fantastic!" he grinned. "The best!!"

Still aroused, I stroked his jeans. I waited, but the feeling lingered. My hand on his knee, looking straight ahead at the traffic, I had to ask: "And what about Mathilde?"

We drove off the motorway and into a little town where we rented a hotel room just for the afternoon. Patrick undressed me and examined my body with his filmmaker's eye. He wanted to film me, but I wasn't sure.

"Let's see later," I said, drawing him to me.

We reached our destination late that afternoon. When we found the house and were settled in the back garden, surrounded by babies and happy mothers, the memory of sex still hot inside me, I couldn't suppress the desire that had haunted me for so many years. I wanted a child. We were sitting around a picnic table, me in my red corduroy jacket, Patrick beside me, his hair swept back by the wind. It was brisk but not cold, a perfect Normandy evening. Colette was breast-feeding Rebecca, Lucie was preparing her daughter's soup. As the sunset lingered and I fed little spoons of soup to Natasha in her high chair, I wondered how long it would take for me, too, to become a mother. How long would it take for me to get over my distrust of men enough to travel that road? But even with Patrick beside me, there was no point in musing much on the subject. He was leaving for Chile soon.

France had been led by conservatives ever since Charles de Gaulle founded the Fifth Republic in 1958, but now it looked like a Socialist might have a shot at the presidency. On election day, May 10, 1981, I was working the afternoon shift at AFP. As the day wore on and our colleagues in the Political Service received the first embargoed exit polls, intimations that President Valéry Giscard d'Estaing might have lost were buzzing around the newsroom. I rushed home to be there when the news was announced at 8. I'd been to New York in April and had picked up a string with RKO radio, which wanted live coverage of the event.

I switched on my big black-and-white TV and waited for the official announcement. When the call from RKO came through at 7:59 p.m., I was ready.

"This is Mona Venture broadcasting live from Paris, where we are about to hear the name of the next president of France."

The TV's musical prelude to the news came on, and seconds later there it was, from the mouth of the anchorman:

"François Mitterrand has been elected President of the Republic with more than 51 percent of the vote."

As I translated the historic words for my American radio audience a huge roar went up outdoors. People were pouring into the streets, shouting, laughing, chanting. I held the phone out the window to capture the sound. Honking cars were converging on the avenue below as a human wave unfurled down Rue de la Roquette toward the big square nearby where an infamous prison once stood. Everyone was trying to get to the Socialists' election night bash. My broadcast ended with the joyful sounds of Parisian revelers en route to storm the party at the Place de la Bastille.

Yes, in a way it was a new revolution. Not the bloody kind that toppled the French monarchy in 1789, but a revolution by a populace fed up with abuses of the Giscard-Bokassa variety, a nation that treasured its motto of "Liberté Egalité Fraternité" and wanted a leader who could restore the balance among those ideals. As a Socialist, Mitterrand had campaigned for freedom of the press, equality for women, and brotherhood via reforms to narrow the gap between rich and poor. The majority had just demonstrated that they stood behind him.

For the '68 generation – my generation – the election of François Mitterrand marked a major victory. Thirteen long Mays after French students and workers battled police in the streets to demand a more just society, we were partying in the streets to celebrate the triumph of a man we felt embodied our ideals. The festivities went on all night, with live music and lots of champagne. The next day we awoke to a new France.

When Patrick returned from Chile in September we took up where we had left off, although the fire between us had cooled. After he and his ex spent two months traveling together through the Andes, he could tell me whatever he liked – it was obvious their friendship was more than platonic. When I pressed the matter one afternoon, Patrick admitted that, yes, they had made love. And why not? They were good friends.

"And me?" I wanted to know. "Where do I stand in all this? Have things changed for you since we met?"

"You remember that first day in the Vaudeville?" he replied. "I was overwhelmed by desire for you. When we touched hands it was electric, even through our gloves."

"Go on," I said, moved by this tender memory.

"If you had agreed to start something right then," he added, "everything would have been different."

I looked at him blankly.

"What do you mean?" I said. "I phoned you less than a month later. What had changed? I was the same person."

"It wasn't that you were less attractive or anything like that," he said. "It's just that the moment had passed."

Put off by his casual cruelty, I lowered my expectations of Patrick. We still saw each other, but less often now. For one thing, I was busy. I'd been promoted at AFP and was working the news slot – monitoring incoming copy and deciding which stories to handle. Sometimes it was unbearably intense, like the day when Anwar Sadat was assassinated in Egypt, October 6, 1981. Urgents and bulletins flew in to the English Desk from all over the world in reaction to the fourth shooting of a major world figure in less than a year: John Lennon had been gunned down in New York the previous December, President Reagan was shot in Washington in March, and Pope John Paul II was critically wounded by bullets in St. Peter's Square in May. With major breaking stories like that we had to work twice as fast as our competitors at "Amélie" and "Rosalie" because we were not just turning the news around but translating as well. In my new job on the English Desk, beating the competition had become my responsibility.

At the same time, in hopes of eventually moving on from AFP, I had begun writing freelance articles for the International Herald Tribune. The second of these features, about shifting attitudes in the French Jewish community since the bombing of a Paris synagogue a year earlier, came out not long before my parents arrived in Paris for my 32nd birthday, and they were suitably impressed. We were going down to Lyon on the TGV, France's brand new high-speed train.

As we left for this celebration, I realized my period was late. I wasn't really worried about it. Still, when we got off the train in Lyon, I slipped away to a pharmacy to buy a pregnancy test.

That evening my parents took me out to dinner at a superb bistro. They were charming, regaling me with stories about events back in Wisconsin, but I couldn't concentrate on the food. As soon as I got back to the privacy of my hotel room, I opened up the test.

Did I or didn't I want to be pregnant? The awesomeness of the moment rushed over me. Patrick as the father of my child? No. It didn't compute. We weren't in love. I couldn't imagine him marrying me. But but but... Pregnant! After so many months of failing to conceive a child. If the test was positive, it would mean I wasn't sterile. I could have a baby!

The instructions said to urinate on a strip of paper. If two pink lines appeared within a few minutes, the result was positive. If only one pink line appeared, it was negative. I did as instructed and, holding my breath, took a look.

There were two pink lines.

No, I thought. This must be a mistake. I can't be pregnant. Not now. Not with Patrick! How will I tell him? What will I tell my parents?

I took another look at the two pink lines. Let's not get excited, I told myself. Maybe this test is wrong. I'd heard that happened a lot.

But what if it's right? That would mean... No. Not possible. It can't be. But maybe it is. And if it is... Yes. It is! It could be. It makes sense. If it is, then... I'm... No. It's unbelievable, it can't be right. If it was, then I'd be... Pregnant! A child within me.

My eyes welled up. Can it be? How can it be? I hugged myself, trying to contain my excitement. My heart was pounding.

"It's a miracle," I whispered, trying to keep my cool. "It's a miracle," I said aloud, alone in my hotel room. "It's a miracle," I sobbed as the emotion powered through me. "I'm pregnant!" I laughed, tears streaming down my face. "I can be a mother. Thank you! Thank you!!"

It was hard finding sleep that night. When I awoke, before meeting my parents for breakfast, I phoned Patrick from my room.

"We'll be back in Paris by mid-afternoon," I said. "I need to see you. Could you meet me around 4 at that café downstairs from my place where we always go?"

He was sitting there at the appointed time. Before I was able to say anything at all, he spoke up.

"Mona, I warned you this could happen," he said sternly.

"What are you talking about?" I asked, lowering myself into a chair.

"You're pregnant, aren't you?"

Patrick's gaze was as cold as his heart. I merely nodded.

"I was late so I took a test," I said. "I should probably take another one to confirm the results. But I'm already sure. I can feel something inside me. It's like a tightness. And I've been feeling nauseous the last few mornings."

"Why did I listen to you?" Patrick moaned. "We should have used birth control."

But as my tears began to drop onto the table, he softened his tone.

"Look, I'm sorry," he said. "It's just that I'm not ready to have a kid yet. But I also can't stand the thought of a woman aborting my child. This is so huge. Let's think it over for a few days."

"Okay," I said. I'd been expecting that we'd talk some more, and that maybe he'd join me and my parents for dinner. But he was rising and paying the check.

"I have to go now," he said. "I'll call you."

My parents left the next morning, and I bought another test. The results were not as clear this time – there was merely the shadow of a second pink line. It seemed odd, but I didn't have time to worry about it as I rushed off to work. All day I waited for Patrick to call. When I got home, there was no message from him. I made myself a simple supper and went to bed.

A few hours later I was awakened by severe abdominal cramping. I had suffered for years from menstrual cramps, but this pain was excruciating, like nothing I'd experienced before. Bent over, unable to stand, I made my way to the toilet. Blood was gushing from my womb, with huge dark glistening clots. Frightened, I cleaned myself up as best I could and crawled back to the bed. The phone was right beside it. I picked up the receiver and called Jacques.

"Can you come over?" I whispered, trying not to cry. "I think I'm having a miscarriage."

Jacques was there a few minutes later. He sat beside me and held my hand while I waited for the cramping and blood loss to subside. It took several hours, and when it was over I knew I wasn't pregnant anymore.

When I phoned Patrick the next day, he took the news with aplomb.

"Let me take you out to dinner," he said.

"No thanks," I replied. "I'm not feeling so well right now."

I took the day off work and went to see my friend Jacqueline, now a practicing gynecologist. She confirmed that it had been an early-pregnancy miscarriage – so early, in fact, that I wouldn't need a curetage.

"Go home, make yourself a pot of tea and curl up with a good book," she advised. "You'll feel much better by tomorrow. And you know, very many women miscarry the first time they become pregnant. The good news, for you, is that this proves you can conceive a child."

She kissed me on both cheeks and showed me to the door.

I wept a lot that afternoon, grieving for the tiny being who had existed for an instant deep within me. But as I sipped my tea, I remembered Jacqueline's hopeful words.

Yes, I consoled myself, in a way it was good news. My fears that I could never become pregnant were unfounded. Yes, in time, it might happen again. Yes. I could have a child.

BETRAYAL
1982

Who was at fault for the pregnancy? I tried not to blame myself. I knew we'd been irresponsible, but the origin of life is inevitably irrational – the primeval urge to reproduce dominating even the most rational humans so completely that responsibility can fly away like so many dandelion seeds in the wind. As I got past the initial shock of the miscarriage, the realization that a new life had ever so briefly taken hold in my womb came to the fore. I was a woman. I was a woman with the power to create life. An unfathomable power, the most sublime calling of our time here on earth. I'd become pregnant at age 31. Was that irresponsible? One might as well call an amoeba irresponsible for dividing in two.

The immediate result of the pregnancy was the end of my relationship with Patrick. We didn't discuss the matter. It was just over. The experience left me wondering yet again where I was going in life.

On the positive side, there was my job. Almost by accident, I'd been propelled from the confusion of my student days into a career in international news. Even at my lowly level of translating dispatches, I was little by little turning into a competent professional. But working with material filed by others was ultimately less than satisfying. There were few writing opportunities at AFP for staffers who were not

French. If I wanted to be a reporter – to go out in the field and grapple first-hand with the news – I'd have to find a way to move on.

On the negative side, there was my personal life. After the twin fiascos of Santiago and Patrick and the debacle with Jacques, I had to face facts. I was officially a member of a club I didn't want to belong to – the club of single women over the age of 30. What had gone wrong? Was I failing at sex or love or both? And by the way, how did things get so complicated? Most of the men I knew were either gay or married. At 32, I wondered, had I already missed the boat?

Sometimes it felt like news was taking over my life, but maybe that was a good thing. It was December 1981, and I'd been assigned to work the late shift on Christmas Eve. I dreaded the prospect, but at least I'd be with colleagues. I wouldn't be spending the evening alone.

A few days before Christmas one of Lucie's friends mentioned that she knew someone at AFP and asked whether we'd met.

"Alexandre's a good guy," she said. "Smart, funny, all that. You should look him up. But let me warn you – he's not available. He's been living with his girlfriend for years."

"That's a point in his favor," I replied. "I wonder why we haven't crossed paths. What does he look like?"

"He's blond," she said. "A bit younger than us. I think he's on the Foreign Desk. Should I give him your number?"

"No thanks," I said. "But I'll keep an eye out for him."

I didn't have to look hard, for the next day as I was typing away at the English Desk I felt a hand on my shoulder.

"You must be Mona."

The blond man standing over me was wearing a black leather motorcycle jacket and a mischievous grin.

"Are you Alexandre?" I said. "Hello."

"My friends call me Alex," he said. "Do you have time for coffee? I'm on my way to the Vaudeville."

"Okay," I replied. "I can be there in 10 minutes."

Long enough to consider whether I should keep the date or, as the

French say, "leave him a rabbit," i.e. stand him up. Girlfriend or no girlfriend, it was clear that Alex was hitting on me. Everything about him spoke seduction: the casual way he laid his hand on my shoulder, the way his light gray eyes crinkled when he smiled, the way he wore his blond mane swept back off his wide forehead. He was the spitting image of a lion – all he needed to do was roar.

Curiosity got the better of me and I kept the date. We chatted over coffee and went our separate directions. For the next week we nodded to each other in the newsroom. Then it was Christmas Eve.

Working the late shift meant I would miss the lighting of the Christmas tree candles at Lucie's for little Natasha. I was musing distractedly on the cruel fate of journalists when the in-house phone at my elbow buzzed.

"Hey baby," a French voice purred. "What are you doing tonight?"

"Who is this?" I laughed.

"Aha!" said the voice. "You don't recognize me."

"No," I said, "and I'm going to hang up unless you tell me."

"No, wait!" said the voice. "Will you be free later?"

"Okay, time's up."

I put the phone down and went back to my work. Right away it rang again.

"Mona! It's me, Alex," said the voice. "Look, I'm right back here."

I stood and glanced around the newsroom. He was there in the back, waving at me with a silly grin.

I returned to my work, but next thing I knew Alex was beside me, hiking himself up to sit on the English Desk.

"Hey, I've got a story to finish," I protested.

"These friends of mine are having a party," Alex said. "They live near the Bois de Vincennes. If you can get out of here by 11:30, we can hop on my motorcycle and make it over there by midnight. It'll be a blast. Come with me!"

"Wait – what about Céline?" I asked.

He had told me about his girlfriend the other day at the Vaudeville.

"She's down in the south with her parents," he said. "So I need a date, and I'd like to take you."

I was tempted.

"Just as friends?" I asked.

"Of course," he replied. "Just as friends."

When I finished my shift he was waiting out front with his bike. It was a cold crisp night. Alex handed me a helmet and off we sped. A light snow began falling. He was a good driver, fast with no false moves. As I gripped his waist the motor hummed between my legs.

The party was in full swing when we arrived, a couple dozen people crammed into a cozy apartment smoking joints and drinking champagne. I hadn't seen so much grass since arriving in Paris. Jacques never touched it, nor did my other French friends – the main difference between their '60s and ours back in the States.

But this group was a bit younger and had clearly embraced it. Offered a puff – *une taffe*, they said – I was only too happy to accept. Alex introduced me as a colleague. We stayed till around 2 when I said I had to go.

"Let me walk you up," said Alex when we reached my place. The fatal words.

"Okay," I said, yawning. This night would end at my door.

But Alex insisted on coming inside.

"I've got something I'd like to share with you," he said.

We sat on the living room couch and he removed a small silver box from his pocket.

"I scored some coke," he smiled, spilling some onto a record cover and drawing a couple of lines.

"Fine, but I'm kind of tired. I think I'll pass." I didn't want to be uncool, but all I could think about was sleep.

"This will wake you up," said Alex. "Come on! The night is young."

Christmas Eve – actually Christmas morning now – and a velvet calm had descended on the city. For once there were no cars beneath my window, no lights shining. Just us in the room together, Alex and me, on the couch, "just as friends."

Alex found a banknote, rolled it into a thin tube, inserted it into a line and sniffed deeply.

"Here," he said, handing the tube to me.

I hesitated.

"Mona," said Alex, "it's Christmas. Give yourself a present."

The high was instantaneous. A tickling in my nose, a tight buzz in my head.

"Don't fight it, just let it come over you," said Alex.

He had moved closer to me and – was I imagining things? – he was slipping his hands inside my sweater. Was it the coke? It felt fabulous. Now he was kissing my neck.

"Wait a minute!" I said, fighting my impulse to succumb. "Céline. You're living together."

"Yes, but our relationship's on the rocks," he said. "She's having some psychological problems. I think we're going to separate."

"But you're still together. We shouldn't be doing this."

"Just tonight," he whispered, unhooking my bra. "Just as friends."

We made love right there on the couch, had some more coke, then drifted into the bedroom. I didn't feel like sleeping anymore. Alex's leonine looks carried over into his style as a lover. When we awoke it was past noon on Christmas day.

"Let's go out to lunch," said Alex. Back on the bike, he took me to Lipp on the Boulevard Saint Germain for oysters and white wine. I could still feel the cocaine. It took another day to wear off completely. Unfortunately by then I was hooked – not on the coke, but on Alex.

When we'd been seeing each other a couple of weeks, Alex informed me that he had split up with Céline. Or rather she left him when she found out he was fooling around. His friends deserted him, calling him a traitor for leaving his long-time lover. But he insisted he didn't mind. Céline was psychologically unstable, he said, and had refused to get help. He couldn't live with it anymore. I accepted this explanation, but didn't fall in love. It felt too risky.

Within three months I was pregnant. We hadn't bothered with birth control given my history, and his – he and Céline had tried to conceive a child for many months but hadn't succeeded. And all my years of trying to get pregnant with Jacques had convinced me I had a problem, not to mention the recent miscarriage. I was so sure there must be some mistake when I missed my period that I didn't tell Alex about it. I wanted to take the test first.

This time the result was unequivocal, but any elation I may have felt at being proven to be fertile was tempered by the terrifying question of how to proceed. Alex and I were lovers, but we weren't in love. We had no plans to marry. I tried but failed to conjure up an image of him as a lifetime partner. Even though we each wanted children, the situation didn't feel right.

At the same time, there it was. The miracle. It was as though some hidden barrier had lifted – as though not being in love with a man was the key I needed to open the door to conception. Or maybe the key was the absence of the kind of conflict that had poisoned my relationship with Jacques.

"I see," Alex said when I delivered the news. "We'll have to think this through." We'd been out to dinner and were lying in my bed together. He kissed me on the cheek and rolled over. We didn't make love that night.

After work the next day Alex drove me home on his motorbike. We sat on my living room couch like we had the first night. He took both of my hands in his. I didn't know what to expect. Would he want to keep the baby, or not?

"Mona – you know Céline is unwell," he began. "She's been in a depression for years. I didn't tell you about this sooner because I didn't want to upset you, but a couple weeks ago she went into a clinic for the mentally disturbed where she's finally getting some help. It seems to be going well, and I'm happy about that. Even though we're separated, I still have feelings for her. I don't want to hurt her."

A little late for that, I thought skeptically. I steeled myself for what I now knew was coming.

"So Mona – dear Mona – I have to ask you to make an exceptional gesture. Think of it as an act of mercy. Oh, god! This is so difficult for me!!"

He looked as though he might cry.

"Believe me," Alex went on, "this pains me as much as it pains you. But there is no other choice. I want you to abort."

There. He'd come out with it. To my surprise, I felt nothing. His words couldn't hurt me. I was in shock.

"You know how much I want children, so this wasn't an easy decision," Alex rumbled on. "But Céline is so unstable. If she finds out I'm having a child with another woman, it'll kill her. I mean, she'll kill herself. Literally! I couldn't live with that on my conscience."

It made sense. I didn't want Céline to die. Of course I had to abort. I merely nodded.

"So you'll do it?" Alex asked.

I nodded again.

"Thank you," he said, covering me with kisses. "Thank you, thank you."

"Please go now," I said. "I need to be alone."

How could I have agreed so reaily to such a major decision? Even now, looking back, I believe I made the right choice. I wanted to have a child, yes, but not on my own. When I tried to imagine such a scenario, I simply panicked. It was too far removed from the image I'd never cast off of myself as part of a happy family, as wife and mother. I wanted a man beside me to love the child, and to support me – not just financially but also in the wonderful and momentous job of raising the child, of teaching the child how to live as a happy person in our complex world. And then there was the question of how to tell my parents. I dreaded their reaction to this news. An unwed mother? It would bring shame on our family. Their desire for a grandchild, which they had voiced over and over, simply did not extend to what they would inevitably view as an illegitimate child – a bastard.

And there was something else. I was young, just 32, and felt there was plenty of time. Now that I knew I could get pregnant, I wanted to wait until the circumstances were right. Until a man who loved me wanted me to bear his child. Alex had made it perfectly clear that he was not that man. I didn't blame him for my pregnancy – I was just as responsible as he was. And I wanted to assume responsibility for our moment of carelessness in bed. For the first time in history, women were able to make such choices. Unlike our mothers and grandmothers and all the women going back to prehistory, we had the power to decide when and how to bear children. We could use birth control, and if that failed we could choose to abort. In France, abortion had been legal since 1975. A woman's right to choose had become law. For better or for worse, we were empowered. Although I didn't realize it at the time, my decision to use that power was the act of an independent woman.

I went to see Jacqueline the next morning. As feminist gynecologists, she and her two partners practiced a type of early abortion that could be performed right in the office, without a general anaesthetic. The pregnancy had to be less than a month old. There was no counseling to go through and no waiting period.

It was a matter-of-fact procedure. I was given a Valium to relax me, then clamps were inserted to open my cervix so that a small vacuum tube could suck out the contents of my uterus. The pain was bearable. It took no more than five minutes.

Afterwards, when I stood, I nearly passed out. They gave me a glass of sugar water and had me lie down for a bit. Then I rose, dressed, walked the short distance to my place and crawled into bed. The phone was right beside me.

"It's over," I said when Alex rang.

"My shift finishes at 3:30," he said. "I'm coming to see you."

"No, don't," I said. "I need to sleep."

But he came anyway, bearing a gift. It was a first edition of a book of poetry by Paul Eluard, a surrealist whose work I'd read many years earlier as a student in Avignon. The book bore an inscription to Alex's mother, who had known the poet. She had since died of cancer, leaving the book to her son.

"I want you to have this," Alex said. "It's a family treasure, and now it's yours. I'm so grateful for what you've done. You have no idea."

He stayed a short while, sitting on the edge of my bed with his coat on as I wept. When he left, it was easy to sleep.

Alex and I crossed paths only at work for a couple of weeks, but then we started sleeping together again. Impossible? No, for the heart works in mysterious ways – and, as I discovered uncomfortably, the end of my pregnancy did not mean the end of desire. We were seeing each other less regularly now. But with the approach of spring, Alex surprised me by suggesting we take a trip.

"Let's go to Morocco," he said. "I have some friends in Rabat. We can stay with them."

The friends were a couple who had chosen to enter the government's overseas cooperation program in lieu of military service at a time when France had not yet abolished the draft. They had a small flat in the historic center of the Moroccan capital and were paid enough to maintain a beach house up the coast as well. In exchange they worked in a literacy training program.

We flew down in mid-June, just as Britain was about to claim victory in the Falklands War with Argentina. Not an ideal moment to leave the English Desk, but a glorious time of year in Morocco. Everything was in flower. It was hot at midday and cool in the evenings. We went carpet shopping at the souk in Rabat, had a fabulous lamb tagine at a local restaurant and spent a weekend at the Kenitra beach house with Alex's friends, drinking beer and playing tarot, a French card game. The cards, with images like the Magician, the Lovers, the Priestess and Death, are the same as those used in fortune-telling – and I might have saved myself some trouble had I called on their divinatory powers.

A few days into our stay, all four of us piled into a car and drove north almost all the way to Tangier. We stopped at a small seaside town and found lodging at a dilapidated café with rooms for rent. We couldn't get wine with dinner because the Muslim fasting month of Ramadan was approaching and the whole country had gone dry. But Alex's friends had brought along plenty of hashish, so getting high wasn't a problem. Our second day there, we found a spectacular beach that unfortunately offered no shade. With my freckles and fair skin, I had to take shelter in the tiny pool of shade cast by the car.

The ride back down to Rabat the next day was painful. My skin had turned an almost neon shade of red – I could feel every bump in the road, and there were many. And Alex had gone quiet.

We had barely brought our travel bags upstairs to his friends' apartment when Alex took me aside.

"We have to talk," he said.

I sat down.

"This trip was a mistake." He was pacing around our small bedroom. "I can't get Céline out of my mind. I feel so guilty about leaving her. As soon as I get back to Paris, I'm going to ask her to move back in with me."

Given my track record with men, this shouldn't have come as a shock, but it did. Waves of pain engulfed me. Why did this keep happening? Why didn't I have the kind of self-protective reflex that kept other women from getting hurt so often? I was not unintelligent – for goodness sake, I'd been a Phi Beta Kappa – and yet I clearly lacked the emotional intelligence needed to make relationships work in our era of redefined sexual politics. It was as though early images from my childhood had imprinted themselves so deeply that I couldn't cast them off.

I remembered my parents, the way my mother dropped what she

was doing and ran to the door to embrace my father when he came home from work – every day, just like in the movies. They may not have had a perfect marriage, but they created the image of being an invulnerable unit, unbreakable, unsinkable. They had taken a vow to love, to honor and to cherish each other, and they stuck to it. That was my model of how couples should operate. And despite all evidence to the contrary, I still clung to that myth. Nothing kicked in to prevent me from opening myself to the sort of betrayal I kept experiencing. Feminism may have taught the women around me to question the balance of power in their relationships. I knew the theory by heart, but somehow couldn't put it into practice.

As soon as Alex left the room I called Air France and bought a ticket for the next flight out, the following morning. Trying desperately to keep my composure, I phoned Jacques in Paris and asked him to come pick me up at Orly.

He was there when I flew in, waiting at the wheel of his father's car. On the drive into Paris, as I recounted my latest sentimental disaster, Jacques listened compassionately. He was reliable that way. And I could confide in another friend when I got home – Rita, who was visiting from New York and had been looking after my cat.

Rita was wired, wiry, smart and smart-mouthed, with a strong Brooklyn accent and a sense of humor to match. We had been friends since the early '70s, when she was creating her persona as a lesbian feminist intellectual who had scratched her way up from red-diaper beginnings. She was salt-of-the-earth – I trusted her completely. It had worked out well for both of us to have her housesit.

Rita heard me out as I unleashed my tale of woe, describing the trip, the perfidy, my foolishness at being taken for a ride by yet another man. It took me a while to notice her packed suitcases in the living room.

"Are you going somewhere?" I asked.

"Actually," she said, "I'm moving to Jacques' place."

Rita was gathering up her things to leave. I looked at her blankly.

"You'll find out anyway, so I might as well tell you now," she said. "Jacques and I started seeing each other while you were away. We weren't expecting to. It just happened."

Oh! Now I got it.

Rita and Jacques were having an affair.

While I was getting jilted in Morocco, she had been sleeping with my former lover.

In my bed.

"I thought you were gay," I said.

"Yeah," she smiled. "Most of the time."

Before leaving for Morocco I had begun scouting around for a new job. I was acquiring a significant file of clips: I'd written for the International Herald Tribune and Libération on subjects from French feminism to the Mitterrand government's secret nuclear dealings with South Africa. AFP sent me out occasionally – to Omaha Beach to cover Nancy Reagan's visit for the 38th anniversary of D-Day, for example – but these reporting assignments were rare. I felt ready to move on.

My dream job would have been a full-time writing position at the International Herald Tribune, which was conveniently based in Paris. But the paper's co-owners, The New York Times and The Washington Post, already had plenty of reporters. The IHT had only a handful of staff writers, mainly big-name columnists. Clearly I wasn't qualified. And there weren't many other places in town offering positions to English-language reporters.

For a couple of months after the break-up with Alex, I was too busy trying to reglue the pieces of my shattered psyche to worry about job-hunting. Then one day I heard through the grapevine that Reuters wanted to hire a journalist locally to report for its Paris bureau. I applied at once, and in short order was summoned to an interview. The bureau was right down the street from AFP.

"So you're Mona Venture," said the bureau chief, James Roberts, when I entered his office. He was a soft-spoken Englishman with the penetrating eyes of a seasoned observer.

"You speak Russian, do you?" he asked, glancing at my CV. "It says here that you did two years of it at the University of Wisconsin."

"To be honest I've forgotten most of it," I smiled. "But does that matter? I thought I was applying for a job here in Paris."

"You are," he said. "But don't forget, my dear, that Reuters is an international news agency, and we are always on the lookout for Russian speakers. I'm a former Moscow hand myself – I was bureau chief there before coming to Paris."

"Does this mean you're considering me for Moscow?" I asked, trying not to squeak.

"No, not immediately. But you are of course in competition with other candidates for the job here in Paris. Your foreign-language knowledge could help you get a foot in the door."

"*Spasibo*," I said, reluctantly dredging up the Russian for "thank you." I had no desire to move to Moscow. It was the reporting job in Paris I wanted. It would be so great to escape AFP, where I still crossed paths with Alex and Santiago quite regularly – and where I had no hope of pursuing an actual writing career.

"Do you have a lot of candidates?" I asked.

"We do have one particularly strong one," James Roberts replied. "But your CV looks good also."

He said he'd call me. There was nothing I could do but wait.

Sobered by two unplanned pregnancies in less than a year, I went back to Jacqueline to get a prescription for the pill. No more unprotected sex. I thought back to the many times I had failed to take precautions. And now, in addition, we were just finding out about AIDS.

The subject came up with Rita one afternoon over iced tea at a sidewalk café. She and I were back on good terms – her flirtation with Jacques had proved less important to me than keeping the friendship of a woman I found very special in a quirky way. As we sat there chatting on the sunsplashed terrace, it emerged that we had both read a recent article in The New York Review of Books about Kaposi's Sarcoma, a new plague affecting gay men. The disease was so little understood in the summer of 1982 that it had only just been named. As part of New York's gay community, Rita was aware of HIV. When the first articles about it came out I'd discussed it with my father, for he was deeply involved in immunology at the time.

"It's not going to stay confined to the gay community," he'd warned, and I passed that thought along to Rita.

And just how contagious was the disease, we wondered? I'd had bisexual lovers. Could they have passed the virus on to me?

Like so many people of my generation who had enjoyed the wild ride of the sexual revolution, I had to rethink my behavior. It was a defining moment – the moment, perhaps, when the '60s ended and we collectively had to grow up. Of course the act of love had always carried devastatingly powerful risks for the human heart – risks the birth control pill merely obscured. Many of us, myself included, had suffered emotionally as a result of thinking we could indulge in carnal pleasures with impunity. But now the physical risks had returned to the fore. If sex could kill, then we'd have to be more careful. I knew I would be.

At summer's end James Roberts phoned to say that Reuters wanted to send me to London for a two-day tryout. They flew me over and booked me into a decent hotel not far from the agency's headquarters at 85 Fleet Street.

As I stood outside the venerable building's massive doors, daring myself to go through, I felt like I was about to walk into history. Then it was up to the World Desk, at the far end of another vast newsroom, where the editor in charge gave me some stories to edit. Afterwards some of the editors took me out for beer at the Old Bell, the pub around the corner, apparently to check out the drinking bona fides of any possible newcomer to Reuters.

A couple weeks later I got another call from James Roberts.

"You're hired," he said. "How soon can you start?"

Even today, I cannot describe the jubilation I felt at that moment. And yet, at the same time, I panicked. I wasn't sure I'd be capable of meeting the new challenge before me, even though this was without doubt a great leap forward. I was joining a major English-language news agency, not as a translator/editor but as a full-time reporter. In fact, I was becoming a foreign correspondent. I'd be out on the front lines of the news. My reports for Reuters would be carried by papers and broadcast media all over the world. And that was the problem.

Could I, Mona Venture, handle the task and not be found out as a fraud? Or, more precisely, as the fraud I feared I was? One side of me, the feminist, ready-for-anything side, tried to sweep these doubts into the dustbin. Of course I could handle it – this was the kind of job I'd longed for, the chance to do something that mattered. By reporting the news I'd be making a contribution to the weft and warp of history as it's been woven through recorded time by the narrators of world events. A very small contribution, but a contribution nonetheless. And maybe one day, when I'd honed my skills, my reporting could make a difference for readers trying to understand a complex world. Maybe my work could help them in the same way that the reporters of the Watergate break-in had helped the public reach informed opinions during the Nixon presidency. That was my dream.

Yes, but. The other side of me struggled to push the doubts away. After James Roberts called, I spent a few days wondering whether to answer an ad I'd seen in Libé. A Paris rock band was looking for a female lead singer. I had no qualifications for such a job, but for a brief while it felt infinitely more appealing than putting my name at the top of articles that would be read by thousands – sometimes hundreds of thousands – of people. What if I made mistakes? What if there were consequences? As I sang along full blast to the latest album by Blondie, imagining myself on stage before a surging crowd of rock fans, I mused on the irony of the situation. Why was I, a woman who'd come a long way since leaving Wisconsin, fantasizing about becoming a rock star when I had the chance of a lifetime before me? As Debbie Harry launched into Track 1, Side 2, a song called "Die Young Stay Pretty," I came to my senses. I didn't want to die young, and didn't really care if I stayed pretty. What I wanted was a man and a family, but that clearly wasn't happening. I'd failed at that. What worked for me was work.

Leonid Brezhnev died on November 10, 1982 – by chance, my last working day at AFP. The death of the Kremlin leader, who had presided over the economic ruin of his country and stoked the Cold War, lent a ding-dong-end-of-an-era feeling to the newsroom as I packed up my things and prepared to move down the street.

By early December, I was learning the ropes at Reuters, where within moments I found myself staffing the news slot on my own. This entailed monitoring French radio and television newscasts as well as the press, and writing up everything of international import. Any lapse of attention could result in a "rocket" – a message from London berating the bureau for missing a news item caught by one of our competitor agencies, most often the AP.

For my colleagues, entrusting the slot to the low person on the totem pole was a long and valued tradition. It left them free to write leisurely features about France and indulge in one of the country's most convivial practices – the two-hour lunch. Led by Colin Hornsby, the buff and hearty news editor, they would depart in jovial camaraderie and return flushed and happy from red wine.

We all worked for James Roberts, but direct oversight of my work fell to his senior reporters: our chief correspondent, Rory Fraser, a dashing but irascible Scot; Magnus Logan, a moody Glaswegian with elegant prose and an impenetrable accent; and Colin, who as news editor drew up the "rota" – the work schedule that had me arriving at the bureau most mornings before dawn. These British lads were a genial lot, admirable journalists all, but not beneath assigning stories nobody wanted to do to a newcomer. I was, after all, American and, worse, a woman. Why shouldn't I be saddled with a boring update on the latest refurbishment of the Eiffel Tower? Not even Gerald, the 22-year-old trainee, would touch that one.

As it turned out, the reporting was a lark and the story virtually wrote itself.

"Renovators are taking longer to give the Eiffel Tower a facelift than Gustave Eiffel took to build his ironwork masterpiece almost a century ago," my piece began. It was picked up by papers around the world, including, to my amazement, the prestigious Financial Times.

"How did you do that?" groused Colin. "Nobody from Reuters gets a byline in the FT."

"Don't start getting big ideas," Magnus warned me. "It's just beginner's luck."

Ensconced in earphones to monitor the 1 p.m. television news, I tried to keep from smiling too hard. To my surprise, when the newscast ended, no one had left for lunch. The lads appeared to be waiting for something.

"Come on, then!" said Rory. He was hovering over my desk with my coat.

"But I can't leave the slot," I said.

"Don't be daft, girl!" said Colin. "Gerald can fill in for you. Put your coat on! We're taking you out to lunch."

In that first month at Reuters, I wrote dozens of pieces – on politics, floods, a bombing, the so-called "new poor," anything that came my way. When these articles were published around the world and the clips came winging their way back to Paris, it was thrilling to see my work in print. Now I was reporting not just from time to time after scrambling to get assignments – I was out there every day. I felt, professionally at least, that I had turned a page.

At the same time, my love life had gone into a cold spell. There was no time for male companionship. In the dreariness of a Paris December, I rarely saw the light of day. It was dark when I left for work, and dark when I got home at night, too exhausted for anything but sleep. So I was surprised one evening when my doorbell rang and there stood Alex, my erstwhile lover.

"I could tell you were home," he said. "I was passing by on my bike and could see the lights on up here."

"Come in," I said reluctantly. "What's up?"

"Nothing much," he said as he entered, brushing past me into the living room.

"How's Céline doing?" I asked. It might have sounded like provocation, but I actually wanted to know.

"Oh, she's a bit better now," Alex said distractedly. He didn't take off his motorcycle jacket.

What can he want with me, I was wondering, when he blurted out an answer.

"You remember that book I gave you last spring?"

"The poems by Paul Eluard? Sure."

"It was given by the poet to my mother. I'd like it back."

"Are you kidding?" I said, as all the resentment I felt toward Alex sliced through me. "That book was a present. You gave it to me the day I aborted. You can't just give it and then take it away. I won't agree to it."

"Mona, I'm not asking you to give it back. I'm telling you – I'm taking it with me today. It's part of my family heritage. Now, where is it?"

Dressed in leather and jeans, looming over me, he planted his feet in a menacing way. Resisting seemed futile. What did it matter anyway? It was just a book, and every time I saw it I was reminded of one of the worst days of my life.

"Here," I said, taking it from the shelf and handing it over. "Now get out, and don't come back."

RISK
1983

In my first few months at Reuters, as I struggled to transform myself
from news translator to bona fide reporter, I scarcely noticed Magnus
Logan. Only gradually did a vision of the man himself emerge. Not the
cool-headed journalist. No, the other Magnus, he of the misty eyes,
deep as the gloaming of a cool dawn over the heath. He of the high
color in his cheek when he angered, of the sensual downward curve of
his lip, all hinting at the passionate nature that lurked, I was sure,
beneath his starched exterior.

Magnus was a classic Reuters newsman – sharp, accurate, witty,
fast. He had an ex-wife and small daughter living in London. Well, not
a wife actually, as they had never married, but they had been as good
as wed until they split when he moved to Paris. And were as good as
divorced, or so I understood. But such musings vanished when he
growled at me in his Glasgow burr.

"Mona Venture," he'd say, "when are you turning in that copy? Do
you plan to take all day?" He always addressed me by my full name,
never just Mona.

It was hard to tell, but in these gruff admonishments I thought I
could detect... what? He seemed to respond to my presence in the
bureau. I was conscious of the inflection of his attention when he
strode to my desk to see how I was getting on. I invited him out for

coffee a couple of times to check my impression that, in some convoluted Scottish way, he was hitting on me. But it was impossible to tell.

The tension between us built up little by little. It had hardly begun when Grace came along in January – Grace MacIntosh, elfin and grave, or at least so it seemed until she let loose with the wackiest sense of humor I'd encountered this side of the Rockies. The arrival of a second woman changed the balance of our news team, even if she was – again – a Scot.

Grace quickly befriended Marcel, the bureau's archivist and collective memory, an odd little Frenchman with bug eyes that only served to emphasize his acute sense of irony, especially concerning French politics. Marcel had worked as a reporter for many years before taking on the titanic job of organizing our bureau's clip files. He was full of helpful hints.

"If you want to understand what's going on," he would snarl in heavily accented English, "just read the last paragraph of any article in Le Monde."

Magnus and Grace were around in February during the computer training incident. London had sent over a team of techies to rewire our office for new PCs. We each got an individual training session in the back of the bureau on what we were told was a closed circuit in Paris. When it was my turn, the trainer suggested I write a fake urgent.

The idea of inventing a story with bells on it made me nervous.

"Are you quite certain that my dispatch will stay in this office?" I asked him.

"Don't worry, love," he said. "We've been training people here for nearly a week. It's watertight."

I wrote my fictional dispatch. It looked like this:

URGENT ⏷⏷⏷ GUNMAN FIRES AT MITTERRAND'S CAR
PARIS, Feb. 24 – A gunman fired several shots at President

François Mitterrand's car today as the French leader was leaving the Elysée Palace, eyewitnesses said.

It was not immediately known whether Mitterrand was injured.
MORE

I pushed the "Send" button and started writing the next dispatch.

BULLETIN 🔔🔔🔔 🔔🔔🔔 MITTERRAND SHOT: WITNESSES

PARIS, Feb. 24 – President François Mitterrand was wounded today when a gunman fired at his car, witnesses said. MORE

I was about to push the "Send" button again when Gerald, the trainee, shouted over to me from the newsdesk.

"Mona, somebody in London wants to talk to you."

"Not now, I'm busy," I said.

"He says it's important!" Gerald was waving the phone at me.

"Okay, I'm coming." I left the bulletin on the screen and went to answer the phone.

"Hi Mona. Langford here." The tense voice was emantating from a very senior editor. "That urgent about Mitterrand. We don't see it on the other wires. Could you confirm?"

"No no no, don't use it!" I cried. "It's fake, it's..."

But before I could finish my sentence, Steve Langford was barking orders to the World Desk.

"Kill! Kill! Kill!" he shouted. "Kill the Mitterrand story from Paris! Get it out of the system. This is a kill!"

He caught his breath and, trying to keep his cool, returned to me on the phone.

"So Mona, could you kindly explain what's going on over there? Is something sinister happening, or was this just a fuck-up?"

"The... the... the story shouldn't have reached you," I stammered, beckoning madly to the computer instructor. "We were in a training session, and the dispatches were meant to stay in a closed-circuit system in Paris. I'm so sorry! Here..." and I handed the phone to the red-faced instructor.

"Yes, I'm afraid that's right, sir," he told Langford, one of the select team of top editors known within Reuters as The Four Horsemen. "Must be a question of crossed wires. Ever so sorry, sir. Won't happen again, I can assure you."

Magnus and Grace were following events with consternation – or was it amusement?

"Looks like your career at Reuters will be rather short, Mona Venture," said Magnus. "I suggest you start packing up your things."

"No, no," I protested. "It really wasn't my fault."

I was shaking as I returned to wipe out the fake bulletin I'd prepared. I collapsed into my chair and laid my head on the desk.

A moment later Magnus was by my side.

"Don't take it so hard," he said. "You just need to be a bit more careful when you're killing off presidents. Come on, we'll buy you a glass of wine. You look like you need it."

It was one of those days when April makes a mockery of the notion that it could be the cruelest month – robin's egg blue sky, daffodils on sale at street corners, the warmth of the sun stirring awareness of summer heat to come. It was still bright when I left the bureau after my shift. Something had been vaguely troubling me all day. When I went out to the Rue Réaumur and felt the caress of the mild breeze, that troubling feeling shimmered through me.

I decided to walk home. By the time I reached the Rue de Bretagne, I knew what it was. Magnus. As my body heat rose, I couldn't wait to make it back to my apartment. For months we'd bantered in the office, ignoring the subtext. For months I'd pretended nothing was happening. But now my desire for Magnus Logan rose in me like sap in a budding tree. I felt electrically charged. His image, his voice. I wafted down Boulevard Voltaire, borne by an erotic force strong enough to carry me home.

Should I call him? It wasn't even a question. I found his home number in my datebook and went straight to the phone.

"What's up, Mona Venture?" he said.

"Well, ah, it's such a beautiful evening, I was thinking maybe we could meet up for dinner."

"I'm afraid not," he said. "Not tonight. I've got some matters to take care of here at home."

"Magnus," I said, "couldn't that wait? You don't want to miss the most glorious moment of spring! Everything's in bloom, the air's all violet, it's gorgeous. Besides, I need your advice on a story. We could meet at 8. That gives you an hour. I'll come to your neighborhood. What do you say?"

I held my breath.

"Well, Mona Venture, you drive a hard bargain. I'll see you at my place, then, at 8."

Impossible to sit still. I ran downstairs and bought some daffodils, filling my apartment with bursts of yellow. I took a bath, dressed carefully and checked myself in the mirror: blue velours minidress, bright scarf. I put on some lipstick, brushed my hair and bounded back out of the house.

On the metro I tried not to muse on what might transpire with this intriguing man. He was so reserved that reaching out to him felt like attempting Everest. I had taken all the initiative, something I rarely did. And yet.

I was sure, I felt it, there was something going on between the two of us. And not even the disaster of my relationship with Alex could stop me from risking an adventure with another man.

Magnus's place was small but nicely furnished with a great stereo system. He was, I learned, deeply knowledgeable about classical music. We chatted briefly over wine and then were off to a bistro. During dinner the ambiance turned sultry. He offered to walk me home and, as we retraced my steps down the Boulevard Voltaire, he took my hand.

"What is it, Mona Venture?" he asked as we neared my place. "Are you chilly? Your teeth are chattering."

I was embarrassed.

"I'm fine," I lied.

When he walked me upstairs I invited him in for a last glass, but we never got around to that. Inside my apartment, Magnus took my hands and drew me close to him. Then, as though dancing with me, he moved me gently backwards toward the wall, leaned down and brushed my lips with his.

"More please," I said as he pressed himself into me.

"Let's go to bed," he said after a while. "Take off that blue velvet sack so I can see you."

I closed the bedroom curtains and removed the offending garment to reveal black lacy underwear.

"You've got a lovely figure," he said. "Why do you always hide it? You should wear dresses that show it off. Come here."

He removed the rest of my clothes and his own. As he drew me down to the bed, the longing that had pervaded me all day was so overpowering I could hardly contain it. But our foreplay was mercifully brief. As he entered me I surrendered to pleasure of an intensity never before known to this woman.

We had both experienced office affairs before and were determined to keep this one quiet. Not difficult, as all Magnus had to do was to maintain his cool exterior – and all I had to do was to avoid looking at him. We didn't see each other every evening, far from it. Magnus had part-time responsibility for his two-year-old daughter, Diana, who was brought over to Paris by her mother some weekends and dropped off at his place. And then, for both of us, there was work.

In March, before this all started, Magnus had sent me to Marseille, where Gaston Defferre, the French interior minister and longtime Socialist mayor, was facing a rightist challenge in municipal elections. My first trip for Reuters, it hadn't been a total success.

"Where's the bloody copy?" Magnus thundered down the phone as I sat before a blank page in my hotel room overlooking the magnificent port. "Come on, Mona Venture. Send it over!"

I had plenty of material, but couldn't figure out how to explain that the wily mayor was virtually sure to win because of the way he had recut the voting districts in Marseille. This was borne out on voting day when Defferre received fewer votes than his challenger, but was re-elected anyway.

Now it was May, and Colin Hornsby announced he was sending me to cover Roland Garros, the French Open tennis tournament. As I knew nothing about tennis he organized a short course for me, and off I went to the clay courts at the edge of the Bois de Boulogne, where I interviewed an unknown teen named Steffi Graf, new to the women's circuit, and inadvertently sparred with Martina Navratilova in her post-set Q&A.

The assignment removed me from the orbit of Magnus Logan for a couple of weeks. When it finally ended, he invited me to dinner at his place. I arrived early. By the time we dined, it was past midnight. Magnus put Rossini's "Stabat Mater" on the stereo while he was cooking. Maybe it was the music, maybe the wine, or maybe the level of physical abandon we'd reached making love to each other. We were beyond close – or so it felt.

The next day it was hard to leave. This is it, I told myself. Despite differences of culture and personality we had much in common, not least our Scorpio sexuality. Our birthdays were only a day apart. Magnus was smart, he was funny, he was tender and passionate. We could raise a family together, I mused. He could be a good father – he had already proved it. Yes, I felt. This is it. This is a man I could love.

I kept these thoughts to myself, even as it became harder and harder to maintain the appearance of normalcy in the bureau. I hoped we'd soon be able to relive the magical evening we'd spent at his place. But the gods of destiny proved fickle. In early June, Magnus was notified by

London that he was being posted to Warsaw to run the bureau there.

At that point Poland had been under emergency rule for a year and a half and the country was in crisis, both economic and spiritual. Lech Walesa had been released from prison, but many other dissidents were still jailed under a crackdown ordered by General Wojciech Jaruzelski. The rules of martial law – literally a "state of war" – had put Poland under military command.

Magnus was told to get ready to move to Warsaw in the fall. He needed to learn Polish and study East-West relations, which were seething against the backdrop of the nuclear arms race. Yuri Andropov, Brezhnev's successor in the Kremlin, was being challenged by President Reagan, who had denounced the USSR as an "evil empire" and gone on to unveil his Strategic Defense Initiative for basing American weapons in space. Reagan's "Star Wars" plan was being furiously assailed by not just the Soviet propaganda machine but also by Western critics who said it would undermine the policy of deterrence appropriately known as MAD – Mutually Assured Destruction – that had helped prevent nuclear armageddon for 40 years. At the same time, stirrings for democracy in East Bloc countries like Poland also had the Kremlin on edge.

There was no way Magnus would turn down such a posting. As he launched into intensive Polish lessons, I consulted an astrologist, desperate for clues about the future. As if that could help. While fond of me, Magnus never suggested I go with him to Warsaw. And not only that. As I learned while we were dallying in bed one morning, he would be spending his monthlong summer vacation with Diana, his young daughter – and her mother, Emma, his ex.

"Will you sleep with Emma?" I asked quietly. The green-eyed monster had shadowed me all my life, and now here it was in my bedroom.

"I suspect so," Magnus said with aplomb.

"I don't think I can handle that," I said.

"Sure you can," he replied briskly. "Don't worry so much, Mona

Venture. We'll see each other before I leave. And once I'm settled, I'd like you to visit me in Warsaw."

La fuite en avant. I dealt with the situation by fleeing. Lucie and Charly had rented a place in Corsica for August and, aware of my predicament, they invited me down.

I had never been to the Isle of Beauty, as it's known in France, and was unprepared for its intoxicating assault on the senses. The hot scent of the parasol pines, the rugged mountains and stately ancient villages, the chirping of the cicadas at midday, the pristine clarity of the pale blue sea – it was enough to make me (almost) forget about Magnus. Our cottage was 40 minutes up a steep winding road from L'Ile Rousse, not an island but a town on Corsica's northern coast. We avoided the town's groomed beaches in favor of unsupervised sandy pockets along the shore where Charly and Lucie could sunbathe naked. I played happily with little Natasha under a parasol, taking frequent dips in the sea when it got too hot. Nina, a friend from La Cour des Noues, was vacationing nearby with her boyfriend, and they joined us more than once equipped with snorkels and a trident for spearing sea urchins. We lunched barefoot at a beach shack set up as a restaurant amid the dunes. They would prepare the day's catch for us and serve it with Coriscan rosé wine. It was as close to paradise as I could get – without a lover.

When I flew back to Paris, Magnus was packing for Warsaw. We had time only for a brief goodbye dinner and he was off.

"Don't forget to come see me," he said. As if I could.

Magnus was not the only member of our bureau to leave at the end of summer. As he flew off to Poland, Reuters posted Rory Fraser to Moscow to serve as bureau chief. Replacing Rory as chief correspondent in Paris was the outgoing Moscow bureau chief, Malcolm Crombie. They had simply swapped jobs.

Malcolm was still arranging his desk on September 1 when a series of urgents started coming across the Reuter wire. I was in the slot. Hearing the bells, Malcolm came over to see what was happening. The first urgents reported that a Korean passenger jet en route from Anchorage to Seoul had dropped off air traffic control screens while flying near the USSR's Sakhalin Island. Officials in Moscow denied knowing anything about it. Only much later did they admit that flight KAL 007 had been shot down by Soviet fighters after straying into prohibited Soviet airspace. All 269 people aboard were killed. The Kremlin claimed the flight had been on a spying mission, which Washington and the South Koreans vehemently denied.

This incident sent East-West tensions into the stratosphere. Questions were being fired off from all sides. How could the Russians have shot down a civilian passenger plane? Why did it enter Soviet airspace? And what ironic god in the life-imitates-art department had seen fit to have this happen to a flight numbered double-0-7?

Malcolm supervised my handling of the French reaction to the incident. Calm under pressure, he played the chief correspondent role well, and looked the part: dark hair, neatly trimmed beard, eyebrows that lifted at each small burst of his droll sense of humor. Although we were the same age, he had a fatherly air in the bureau – not surprising, perhaps, as he had arrived from Moscow with his wife, Julia, and their two small sons.

When Malcolm brought Julia to dinner at my place a few weeks later, I discovered a remarkably well-read woman with opinions on just about everything. She matched her erudite husband's ability to tell a good yarn, especially about their years among the Russians. We quickly struck up a friendship.

It was November and I was finally going to Poland to see Magnus. It had been a rush getting ready and now the anticipation was maddening – the end of the wait approaching, repressed desire rekindling, two lives about to be remingled. My nerves were so brittle heading out to the airport in a taxi that I spent the drive fantasizing about the huge

Jack Daniels I'd indulge in once my Air France jet lifted off.

"Run," said the pretty Air France clerk after checking in my bag. "The gate is at the far end of the corridor. You can just make it."

I raced to Gate 48 but could see no sleek Air France plane, only a smallish Lot aircraft from some other decade. Shit – a flight share. Flying on a Polish plane was the last thing I wanted on my first trip behind the Iron Curtain. In the boarding queue, stout fatalists in heavy overcoats carried plastic shopping bags overstuffed with rare gifts from the West – oranges, bananas, pineapples, coconuts. I found a seat near the front of the plane. There were no overhead baggage compartments, just a shelf overflowing with everyone's bulky offerings. So what? With the command in Polish to fasten our seatbelts, the thrill of travel sliced through me and I prepared to relax into a big whisky. Mistake. The rickety old airliner had only Bulgarian wine on board. It also had no doors on the overhead shelf, only netting that gave way every time the plane banked. Oranges and pineapples were flying all over the cabin. This must be a Polish joke, I thought, as martial air hostesses patroled the aisles, collecting the wayward fruit and scowling at passengers.

By the time we landed I was nervous, thirsty and starving. In my hurry to get to the airport, I'd skipped lunch. Cold air hit with a shock as we left the plane and were herded into the air terminal, the arriving passengers partitioned by glass from a big crowd on the other side, the aura of the free and foreign world we'd come from still clinging to our garments. Passport, baggage, customs, interminable queues. But then there was Magnus, waving, smiling, his navy wool scarf warm against my face, his tweed jacket beside me, his arm around me, my heart beating wildly. We were together again.

"I have to go back to the office to finish a story," Magnus said, taking my bag. "Then we'll go get dinner."

It was already dark when we left the airport in Magnus's black BMW. There were no streetlamps, no illuminated storefronts to brighten the night. As though a metaphor for Poland's political situation, the city was enveloped in murky dimness, hunkered down for winter. Jaruzelski had lifted martial law during the summer, and Lech Walesa had just been awarded the Nobel Peace Prize, but Solidarity was still banned, paramilitary police were on patrol and the future felt as bleak as the frigid wind off the icy Vistula River.

When we reached the Reuters bureau, up three flights of stairs decorated with photos of tractors, a Polish translator/assistant offered me cheesecake with green jello on top. As Magnus typed away on his computer, the bureau's ancient wooden telex machine rattled into life.

"Go see what that is, would you please?" he said, not lifting his eyes from his work.

I wandered over to the telex. It looked like a message from Emma:

PLEASE ASK FORNMIN EXPEDITE OUR VISAS FOR ARRIVAL 28/11. LOVE, E.

It can't be, I thought as I read the message again. That's the day after I go! Why is she coming so soon? This just can't be.

Magnus was at his computer, seeing nothing, oblivious to the somersaults inside me. I sat down and lit a cigarette to try to calm my nerves. Maybe there's a reason, I thought. Can't fathom it, though. What am I doing here?

Magnus finished his story and rose.

"Are you hungry?" he asked. "Shall we go to dinner?"

We drove to an expensive hotel restaurant where Magnus did his best to amuse me, as did the waiter who offered to sell us caviar "on the left," i.e. under the table. Then it was home to Magnus's sprawling apartment, a warren of rooms in the style of a hunting lodge. We fell into bed and made love, but my heart wasn't in it. Only the next morning, when Magnus appeared at the bedside with two steaming mugs of Nescafé, did I mention the telex.

"Is Emma coming to visit you?" I asked.

"Yes, and she was not pleased to hear that you were coming here first!" Magnus replied. He seemed to find that funny.

"But it looks like she's arriving the day after I leave," I protested. "Are you sharing your bed with her too?"

"Of course," was all he said.

"Explain this to me, please. I need to know. Why are you still sleeping with your ex? How do you feel about her?"

"Emma is my connection to Diana," he said. "She is therefore part of my life."

End of discussion.

Magnus had to go to the office even though it was Saturday. As he dressed for work, I opened the curtains. Outdoors everything was covered in whiteness, the snow swirling down. My first daylight view of Poland – cold, bleak, white. Magnus left quickly, saying he'd be back for lunch. And so, alone and unnerved, I began the process of settling in. For I would be staying for two whole weeks.

Over the weekend Magnus showed me around a city of which I knew little beyond accounts of the destruction of the Warsaw ghetto during the war. He drove me past the Palace of Culture, Stalin's postwar gift to the Polish people, its 42 stories a monument to Communist pretentiousness and inhumanity, its gray stone structure erected by people who had no food and no money to rebuild their economy. We visited the Stare Miasto – the Old Town – where historic shell-pocked buildings had been only partially restored in the 38 years since the war. We strolled past narrow houses from a bygone era, their decoration reflecting the trades and lifestyle of a Middle Europe so foreign now to the Communist culture of Poland.

One afternoon as night was falling, our jackets covered in white from huge feathery snowflakes, we made our way down a stone embankment to the edge of the leaden Vistula, watching its gray-black water move sluggishly past, looking out across the river to black trees lining the other side, their bare branches reaching upward into the graying sky. Later, in the central marketplace, a vast expanse framed by quaint little buildings, we stopped in at what looked to be a bar.

"*Nie ma piwa*," said the man behind the counter. We tried a few other places, and the refrain was always the same. I had learned my first phrase in Polish. "We have no beer."

Back at home, our love life seemed to be dying, apparently killed off by my questions about Emma. Magnus was unfailingly polite, but distant. My efforts to cheer him up weren't working – when he was home, that is. Most of the time he was at the bureau. Lonely and more than a little depressed by the situation, I needed distraction.

Shortly before I left Paris, Jacques had sent a Polish friend to see me with a package for delivery in Warsaw. The Pole, Leon Engel, had been in France a few months in hopes of making money in his field, computers. This had been impossible in Poland – where he had left a wife and two small children, as well as his father and sister. I wondered whether Leon had been blocked because there was no work or because he was Jewish. His relatives were among the few Jews remaining in Poland following the extermination of a Jewish community of 3 million souls during World War II.

My third day in Warsaw, deciding the time had come to deliver the package, I phoned Leon's father, Felix Engel.

"Yes, of course, you may come over," a gravelly voice said in near-perfect French. "Come right away – come this afternoon."

Using Warsaw's antiquated bus and trolley system was not as difficult as I'd feared, and I arrived quickly at my destination. The tall, slightly stooped man who opened the door had sparse gray hair combed back and bright intelligent eyes. Ushering me in to his spartan but immaculate apartment, he served me tea, putting aside the package from Leon to examine later, when I'd gone. He appeared every bit the simple pensioner that he was. But appearances are deceiving.

Felix Engel, I knew from Jacques, had been a Communist as a young man in Poland. As anti-semitism gained strength in neighboring

Germany he had fled to France in the 1930s, joined the International Brigades in Spain to fight Franco's forces, then returned to France and joined the resistance during World War II, becoming an expert forger of documents. When the war ended, Felix Engel could have settled down in Paris like his friend Marek Rosenblum, Jacques' father. But with a Soviet-installed government in place in Warsaw, Felix and his wife, still Communist true believers, had returned to Poland "to help build socialism," as he put it. He went into politics, rising to become a senior government minister, a post he held until the late 1960s — when he and other Jews in positions of power were purged in a so-called anti-Zionist campaign. His wife, Leon's beloved mother, had succumbed to cancer a few years earlier. Now he lived alone.

"What would you like to do?" asked Felix, who appeared happy to have some company.

"Please show me your Warsaw," I said. "I have plenty of free time."

That afternoon we commenced our tour of a once proud city that was still trying to hold its own despite decades of repression. We started with the Jewish Historical Institute, where I wanted to check my family's ancestry, and also visited the Jewish cemetery, a sprawling snow-covered collection of gravestones dating back nearly 200 years that spoke eloquently of the vibrancy of the Jewish community that once held so prominent a place in Poland. Felix proved a remarkable tour guide, with a deep knowledge of history and a witty sardonic patter. He introduced me to his daughter, and she in turn to a friend with whom she taught at the university. They were active in the political underground, and I was proud when I got home one evening to be able to give Magnus a small scoop for Reuters.

When the weekend came and Magnus had time for me, we visited the riverside flea market, mingling with swindlers and thieves, and took a drive into the snowbound countryside. But nothing was as it had been. When we got lost on a dead-end road it felt like a metaphor for our relationship. I had no choice but to recognize it was over.

❧

Back in Paris, deeply sad, I could see nothing clearly. My life felt enveloped in fog. It wasn't just that things hadn't worked out with Magnus. It was my consummate failure, by the age of 33, to find a suitable man and forge a lasting relationship. So, with a heavy heart, I decided to seek help. Via Jacques I was introduced to Georges Cabanès, a soft-spoken psychoanalyst. He practiced on Boulevard St-Germain with a team of "anti-psychiatrists" who saw private patients when they weren't out at La Borde, the asylum run by Félix Guattari.

In the security of the office of Doctor Cabanès, little by little, we retraced the chapters that had brought me to his couch. My Wisconsin childhood in a loving household, my break with America, my self-imposed exile, my many laughable and less laughable loves. If the word pain was ever mentioned, I don't remember it. What I do remember is how, as I lay there twice a week, Lucie's words floated in my head, taunting me.

"Darling, you have everything it takes to please a man. I don't understand why someone's not snatching you up."

It would be months before I would feel strong enough to walk out of this new psychoanalytic relationship, leaving Doctor Cabanès's comfortable office behind. Nothing specific happened. There was no "Aha!" moment, no flash of inspiration to illuminate the source of my difficulties. But along the way my battered sense of self-confidence began to revive. I'd been so frightened to lose love, I slowly realized, that I'd been unable to insist that a man respect who I was – a woman who wanted commitment and children – and to walk away if he couldn't. With the help of Doctor Cabanès, I came to understand that my fear of taking that risk was undermining my relations with men.

This didn't mean that I was ready to take the risk. But at least I was ready to be aware of it, if ever again I took the fearless-mindless plunge into that sweet intense insanity called love. That folly, that *folie à deux*, that crazy melding of souls that meant the sound of a voice could send the blood rushing to your head, that hot hot desire that could madden you with the urgent necessity to merge your lips with his, to feel his tongue caress you, to drink in his kisses like a baby drinks mother's milk, to feel the thump thump of his heartbeat as he moves his hands down your body and finds the place where in a short while your two selves will become one. That sweet sweet sadness that follows the act of love, that tender complicity that forms between the lovers, that hope beyond hope that it can go on and on, that lives once separate can intertwine and create a whole greater than its parts. That state of high tension, the feeling of life lived at the edge, the pangs for the absent lover, the untenable yearning, the longing, the waiting, the anticipation, the thrill of meeting anew, the joy of rediscovery, the deep deep physical pleasure, the shared intimacies, renewed over and over, until once again two souls must separate. Sometimes forever. No, while seeing Doctor Cabanès, I was not ready to take that risk.

But nonetheless life went on.

Suddenly it was 1984, auspicious date, and with the new year Reuters began making serious noises about sending me to Russia. It was James Roberts who broached the subject.

"We'll be needing a qualified Number Two for Moscow within the next couple of years," he said. "That gives you time to refresh your Russian. You'll need to spend some time in London first to change your status from 'French local hire' to 'international staff.'"

Given what I had seen in Poland, I was far from thrilled with the idea of living on the other side of the Iron Curtain. Dark, depressing, joyless is how I remembered Warsaw. On the other hand, I'd grown up in America's heartland in the depths of the Cold War, with nuclear-tipped Nike missiles stationed at a launch site 10 minutes from home, right beside the Wisconsin freeway my father took to his medical research lab every day. In our grade school during the Cuban Missile Crisis in 1962, we had been taught at the sound of a bell to assemble in the main corridor and sit on the floor with our arms folded over our heads, as if that could protect us from a Soviet nuclear strike. Riding home in a yellow school bus, I would scan the skies anxiously to see whether a Russian missile might be hurtling our way. Everyone was frightened of the Communist behemoth on the other side of the ocean. Neighbors were buying canned goods and building bomb shelters. Nuclear annihilation was just a touch of the button away.

With my Cold War upbringing, Russia felt like a vast dark fortress, a secret place to which few had access. And that was its seductive power. Not everyone found it frightening. Malcolm and Julia Crombie, for example, spent hours regaling me with stories about life on the other side. They had lived in Moscow for nearly six years, modern-day explorers who had dared set sail into the unknown. Could I do that? Why not? I was part Russian, after all, wasn't I?

James Roberts was waiting for an answer.

"I'll think about it," I said.

And so, in the Orwellian spring of 1984, shortly after another geriatric changing of the guard in Moscow, with the ailing Konstantin Chernenko succeeding the late Yuri Andropov in the Kremlin, I dug out the Russian books I'd kept from my days at Madison and began reviewing the declensions and conjugations of that rich and convoluted language.

The president of the United States was coming to France. The Queen was arriving on the royal yacht Britannia. It was the 40th anniversary of D-Day, and the Allied powers were pulling out all the stops. This would be the biggest world media event since the wedding of Charles and Diana, and for some reason Reuters had entrusted its coverage to Grace and me. She was in charge of the Brits and I was covering my old nemesis, Ronald Reagan, whose wife I'd followed at the D-Day beaches two years earlier. TV teams were flying in to Normandy from around the world for the June 6 commemoration, creating a logistical nightmare. All the hotels in the area were booked. But Marcel said he knew someone who could lodge us at Arromanches, not far from

Omaha Beach, a Frenchwoman who had been stringing for Reuters since the war. He set it up, Grace and I rented a car and off we drove, armed with Tandys – primitive portable computers that plugged into a phone line. To prepare, I'd read Cornelius Ryan's "The Longest Day" for a second time, and Grace had printed out reams of background material. But we were hardly prepared for what we found when we rolled into Arromanches on a cold gray day in early June.

Madame Yvette, Marcel's friend, was waiting for us in her house a block back from the sea. It was so dark inside it was hard to say which was more decrepit, Madame Yvette or the house. Cobwebs hung from the ceilings, a thick layer of dust covered the furniture and the clutter was so dense it looked like nothing that entered the place had been removed since D-Day. Madame Yvette could have passed for a French version of Bette Davis in "Whatever Happened to Baby Jane," minus the makeup. When she escorted us upstairs, the stacks of old magazines piled high along the steps made it nearly impossible to climb them. Worse, there appeared to be no beds in the bedroom. Grace and I tried not to laugh. It was obvious we couldn't stay there. Then Grace had a moment of inspiration.

"Would you be so kind as to show us the phone lines?" she asked Madame Yvette, who rummaged around behind a stack of old books and finally located a telephone socket.

"Thank you," said Grace. "That'll do for one. What about the other?"

"I don't really use the telephone much," said Madame Yvette. "I only have just the one."

"Oh well, then," Grace replied, "it's a pity but I don't think we can stay here. We need to send our stories urgently, so we definitely need two lines. I'm ever so sorry."

Madame Yvette protested but we made our getaway, promising we'd make sure she got paid for the room nonetheless. She looked like she needed the money, if only to buy a broom.

Uncertain what to do next, we went down to the sea.

Arromanches lies more or less halfway between Deauville and Cherbourg on the stretch of sand that the Allies named Gold Beach. It was the middle of the five invasion beaches where 160,000 men stormed ashore on June 6, 1944, in a desperate effort to defeat Nazi rule over Europe. To the far west lay Utah Beach, where American paratroopers who landed during the night had prepared the terrain for the infantry, making for a relatively easy landing at dawn. Next came Omaha Beach where American troops suffered terrible casualties at the hands of the Germans in the first few hours of the invasion. To the east of Gold lay Juno Beach, where Canadians faced fierce resistance from Hitler Youth Panzer divisions but managed to make their way further inland than any other force. Farthest east lay Sword Beach, where British and Free French commandos had come ashore.

The British troops who landed at Gold Beach had been tasked with establishing a beachhead and linking up with the Americans to the west and the Canadians to the east. By midnight on the first day, the British had brought 50,000 men ashore and captured Arromanches under heavy German fire.

Now, as a light rain spattered down, hulking concrete remnants of a Mulberry harbor loomed out of the gray water, a stark reminder of the ingenuity that had gone into Operation Overlord. The harbor had been built in England, its pieces towed across the Channel under cover of night to be assembled off the Normandy coast as wave after wave of soldiers made their way ashore. As Grace and I pondered our options, the harbor seemed to mock us. In the mist we could almost feel the ghosts of the men who had died on the beach in their fight to end the four-year Nazi occupation of France and ensure that we, the future generations, could live in freedom. The enormity of their courage and sacrifice felt overwhelming, everything else trivial.

And yet we needed a place to stay.

It was raining harder now. What to do? Just up the beach a bit, a bar beckoned. A cold glass of the white and a half-pint of beer were called for. As the wine warmed me, I recalled I'd once stayed at a country house not far away owned by the parents of a Parisian friend. We used the bar's phone to make the call.

"No, I'm sorry, our place is fully booked," said Madame Martin. "But I have a friend with an old farmhouse who sometimes rents out rooms. She may still have space."

No GPS, no cell phones – they didn't exist yet – but we did have a good map. Down a winding country lane bordered by hedges, so narrow only one car could pass, we made our way to a rambling farmhouse with chickens pecking in the courtyard. Rustic, yes, but the place was impeccable, with dark antique furniture polished to a high sheen and fresh flowers in gleaming porcelain pitchers. We were given adjoining rooms, each with a telephone socket. I tried out my Tandy, sending a quick dispatch to Paris with our new whereabouts. Everything worked.

The next day Grace was covering Prince Charles and I went off to Sainte-Mère-Eglise for a jump by American and British paratroopers re-enacting the dramatic airborne drop that launched Operation Overlord. I hadn't expected this to be a life-threatening assignment, but as I stood in the field with my notebook high winds pushed some of the men off course. A few landed in trees, just as their heroic forebears had done when dropping into unknown territory to face Hitler's forces, and I had to run for cover when one paratrooper just missed hitting the knot of reporters where I was standing.

Finally it was June 6. Grace was with the Queen, while I was covering President Reagan's speech at Pointe du Hoc, the bleak promontory where U.S. Rangers landed in the early hours of D-Day and struggled up sheer cliffs to destroy a battery of German guns. His audience included 62 gray-haired survivors from that force of Rangers, some of whom wept as he spoke.

"Here the Allies stood and fought against tyranny in a giant undertaking unparalleled in human history," Reagan said. "In seizing these cliffs, they began to seize back the continent of Europe."

He turned to the veterans.

"You risked everything here," he said. "Why? Why did you do it?"

Answering for them, he said simply that some things, like democracy, are worth dying for.

Along with other reporters, I'd received an advance copy of Reagan's speech and had already written most of the story I'd file as soon as he finished. Yet, in the presence of this man I had detested, the words had a different ring. It was remarkably moving to hear the president speak out for the values I'd treasured in my youth, before Vietnam led an entire generation to question the foundations of American politics.

Ending his speech, Reagan paid tribute to "the great losses also suffered by the Russian people" during World War II.

"Twenty million perished," he said, "a terrible price that testifies to all the world to the necessity of ending war."

He had spoken bitterly of the continued presence of Soviet troops in European cities like Warsaw and Berlin. But now he added, "In truth, there is no reconciliation we would welcome more than a reconciliation with the Soviet Union so, together, we can lessen the risks of war, now and forever."

And in words that would come to seem almost prophetic, Ronald Reagan declared that the United States was looking for "some sign from the Soviet Union" that change was coming.

With Moscow stuck in a tar pit of stagnation, with fears of an arms race in space fueling Soviet animosity toward the West, it was hard on that brisk June day to imagine change in the USSR coming anytime soon.

Nonetheless, said Reagan, standing before a stark granite stele commemorating the Rangers, "We will pray forever that some day that changing will come."

LONDON
1984

When Julia Crombie and I flew into Moscow a month later, in
midsummer of 1984, Konstantin Chernenko was in power in the
Kremlin and it seemed that rigid old men would be running the place
forever. In the no-man's-land of Sheremetyevo International Airport,
grim border guards tested the mettle of arriving passengers with
interminable waiting in the visa control lines. I felt jumpy as a flea, as
eager to try out my Russian as I was nervous at the prospect of
emerging into the daylight of a Soviet July afternoon and actually
being among the Russians.

The trip had been Julia's idea. She wanted to celebrate her 35th
birthday with friends in Moscow. Malcolm couldn't go with her – he
had to run the Paris bureau in July – so she asked me to come along.
During our four-hour flight from London, she had briefed me on what
to expect.

Rory Fraser, now the Moscow bureau chief, was lending us his
apartment in exchange for cat-sitting. He lived and worked at a place
called Sad Sam, the same foreigners-only building where Julia and
Malcolm had lived. She said she'd introduce me to her Russian
friends, which could be useful later if I was actually posted to
Moscow.

"Do you really want to work in Russia?" Julia asked as our British

Airways jet hummed along above the clouds. "Judging from Malcolm's experience, it can get rather intense."

"I don't know," I replied. "I'll see how it feels once we've landed. But in principle, yes, definitely. What could be more exciting than reporting from Moscow?"

"I thought you wanted children," Julia said tartly. "You obviously can't do both."

I had too much respect for Julia to give her a piece of my mind, but this was over the top. Maybe she'd been on the road so much with Malcolm that she'd managed to miss the women's movement.

"Hold on," I said. "There are plenty of women today who combine family and a career. Childcare does exist, you know."

She did know, as Julia and Malcolm had enjoyed the services of both a nanny and a housekeeper while bringing up their two little boys in Moscow, even though Julia wasn't working outside the home.

What she didn't know was that an old friend from AFP days had flown into Paris from the Middle East a week earlier and had managed to upset me with his comments on the subject of children. Tom had been after me for years but I'd declined his advances because he was married. Now, he informed me, he was estranged from his wife.

"The biological clock is ticking, Mona," he remarked. "Don't you think you ought to do something about it?"

I tried to dismiss Tom's words as meaning simply, "Let's go to bed," but they still bothered me. Of course he knew nothing of my two failed pregnancies. Nor did Julia.

"You have to face facts," Julia said. "Look at the timing. You're 34 now. By the time Reuters gets you from Paris to London to Moscow you'll be at least 36, and postings last a minimum of two years. Of course people do fall in love in Moscow, but don't forget it's practically impossible to have a relationship with a Russian. As a Westerner you will be watched by the KGB, and if you get too close to anyone the authorities can create problems for them or their families. Very few Russians are willing to risk that."

This conversation was echoing in my head as we at last reached the front of the visa line. The biological clock. Would moving to Moscow for Reuters mean I couldn't have children? The guard in the drab brown uniform sternly studied my passport, looked me up and down, checked the visa, studied me again, and waved me through. Julia was already on the other side.

We'd made it. I was in Soviet Russia.

Soaring pines and birches lined the groomed road out of the airport, lending a poetic Mother Russia feeling, but as soon as we hit the main highway the ambiance changed. We had been picked up by Boris, the Reuters driver, a slight, dapper man with a courtly manner who beamed at Julia as he escorted us to his Zhiguli sedan. Now we were out on the thoroughfare, where rickety trucks of all shapes competed with passenger cars speeding along. In the center was an empty lane reserved for sleek black Zils carrying senior government officials – clearly this was a some-are-more-equal-than-others country.

On our right, a huge rusty sculpture loomed up.

"I think those are meant to be tank traps," Julia said.

"It's a monument to our heroic Soviet forces who stopped Hitler's troops here in 1941," said Boris, his gruff passion conveying how strongly Russians still felt about the war.

Along the road small wooden houses quickly gave way to massive concrete apartment blocks. As we neared the center of town, we could see the soaring neo-Gothic towers built under Stalin that defined the Moscow horizon. We turned left onto the so-called Garden Ring, a 12-lane thoroughfare with no greenery in sight.

"We're nearly there," said Julia, excitement mounting in her voice. We swung up a small hill to the right and drove slowly past a guard box through a large archway.

So this is Sad Sam, I thought, looking around as Boris unloaded our bags. The property, home to so many storied correspondents, was separated by a high wall from the Russians next door. I'd heard so much lore about the venerable building I couldn't wait to go inside.

Rory and his tiny striped kitten were there to greet us when we rang the bell.

"Meet Chut-Chut," Rory said.

"'Chut-chut' means 'little bit' in Russian," Julia said, laughing. It was an appropriate name. I had never seen a skinnier cat.

"She eats only fresh fish," said Rory. "Just ask Sonya" – his KGB-assigned maid – "to get some each day at the market."

And with that Rory was off on his summer vacation, leaving us to get acquainted with our surroundings. The flat was huge for a single man, with a master bedroom, guest room, spacious living room, generous dining room, big kitchen with a walk-in pantry, sizable bath and separate loo. The floors were of oak, the ceilings decorated with sculptured moldings. Everything felt solid – unsurprisingly, Julia said, because the building had been constructed not by Soviet workers of the "they-pretend-to-pay-us-and-we-pretend-to-work" variety but rather by German craftsmen taken prisoner during the war.

Sad Sam was named not for a person but for Sadovo Samotechnaya, the traffic-clogged stretch of the misbranded Garden Ring running beneath Rory's windows. The building was the most legendary of several Moscow apartment complexes that served as ghettos for foreigners. The militiaman who stood guard outside was theoretically there for the residents' protection, but in fact served to screen and intimidate Russian visitors. Downstairs were three separate entrances to the building, each with its own elevator to the eighth floor. To the ninth, actually, but the elevator button for that floor was permanently pressed in, making it impossible to go there.

"That's where the KGB listeners sit," Julia told me. "At least that's what we've always assumed."

"Did you ever see them?" I asked.

"No," she said. "I think they use the service stairs, or else they must go up while we're still sleeping."

I looked around our flat for listening devices, but could see none. I knew they were there, however, because of the many apocryphal stories I'd heard or read about the listeners. Like the time a dozen correspondents were celebrating New Year's Eve at Sad Sam. As midnight neared, the story goes, one of the guests raised his glass and proposed a toast.

"Here's to those poor bastards upstairs," he said. "Just think — we're down here having a party, and they have to work tonight."

On the stroke of midnight the telephone rang. When the host answered, there was no voice on the other end — just the sound of a Champagne cork popping.

Over the next few days I met Julia's friends, an eclectic mix of intellectuals and artists who were willing to take the risk of welcoming foreigners into their homes, even though they knew they could be reported by neighbors to the police. The fear of denunciation was palpable in Moscow at a time when any behavior deemed anti-Soviet could land citizens in Lubyanka, the KGB prison — or, worse, in a psychiatric hospital. If approached by a foreigner, Russians in the street would hurry off in another direction. Yet a certain number of Soviet citizens in those days had made the decision to live as normally as possible despite the political repression. Julia's friends clearly viewed her as an interesting person, not as a dangerous foreigner. Despite the low standard of living in Communist Russia, they produced fabulous spreads for us no matter when we arrived. We found ourselves at tables laden with delicious salads, fresh herbs, pickled garlic, sliced sausage, tangy black bread and sometimes caviar, accompanied by very drinkable wine from Soviet Georgia.

I was able to try out my textbook Russian in these settings, but it was hard going as Julia chattered away. I needed to set out on my own. I'd heard there was good Soviet jazz to be found in Moscow, and my dad loved jazz. So one day, determined to buy my father a present, I went off to GUM, the massive, musty department store on Red Square. Julia — who disliked both jazz and GUM — stayed home.

I can't remember when I noticed the Russian in the faded jean jacket. He was dark haired, slightly balding, fit, with hazel eyes and a voluptuous mouth, and he was standing beside me, sorting through records in the jazz department. Somehow we struck up a conversation. For me, it was a chance to speak Russian, for him a rare opportunity to chat with a Westerner.

"My name is Kolya," the man said quietly. "You're not Russian, are you? Where are you from?"

"I'm Mona, and I'm actually American – but nobody's perfect," I replied.

He got the joke – a point in his favor – once he got over the shock of hearing he was beside a bona fide American.

Kolya helped me select "Moskovsky Dixieland" and introduced me to GUM's arcane system of shopping, which entailed waiting in three separate lines: once to get a bill, again to pay, and finally to collect the purchase. All this time we chatted, and afterwards he invited me to have a Pepsi at one of the umbrella tables lining the dusty boulevards. It felt safe enough, so I agreed. We peppered each other with questions about our alien worlds. I couldn't hear enough about his life in Moscow – his childhood, his family, the way he lived.

"My room is small," he said.

"How small?"

"Four square meters," just big enough for a bed and a little space around it. He felt lucky to have even that much space to himself in a *comunalka* – a communal apartment. When I had to leave, Kolya asked if he could see me again and we agreed to meet the following evening. I was going to the theater with Julia. Kolya would meet us afterwards in the street outside. We quickly went our separate ways.

When I got back, Julia and I spent a while considering whether my meeting with Kolya had been a set-up. We assumed omniscience on the part of the Soviet authorities – they must have known that a Moscow posting was in my future. Had they somehow sent him to meet me? On the other hand, Kolya had been critical of the regime when we spoke and seemed about as far from a KGB-nik as I could imagine, especially considering his straitened lifestyle. And we were only there for four more days. What could happen?

When I saw Kolya outside the theater the next night, he took my hand and a tingle of pleasure rose through me. Julia had brought a Russian friend, Valya, to the performance. The four of us walked back to Rory's flat together. The first problem was getting our Russian guests past the militiaman, in fact a KGB officer in disguise. Valya and Kolya uncomfortably signed in. Then there was the matter of two Russians who hadn't met before eyeing each other suspiciously and largely refusing to talk. Julia and I brought out some wine and snacks, and eventually the chill lifted. We chatted about everything and nothing, knowing we were being listened to. After a few drinks Valya said she had to leave, but Kolya lingered. The moment he'd taken my hand outdoors, I'd known he'd be staying the night.

The guestroom at Rory's apartment had a single bed. Kolya and I squeezed in together and hid beneath the sheets, laughing, in case the walls held eyes as well as ears. He proved to be more than an adequate lover, making up in vigor for what he lacked in French-style savoir-faire. We slept little and in the morning arose tired but content.

When he left, Julia lectured me.

"Don't get involved with that guy," she warned. "It could lead to trouble for him, and for you."

But Kolya and I had agreed to meet again that night, this time at his place. Julia and I were flying out in a couple of days, and I couldn't imagine leaving Moscow without spending one more night with him.

I went to dinner with Julia before taking the Moscow metro out to the city's edge, so it was nearly dark when I reached what I hoped was Kolya's building. He had given me precise instructions. He had to, because there were no accurate street maps in Moscow at that time – by order of the KGB all Soviet maps contained distortions, allegedly to protect state secrets. As I made my way into a large apartment complex, wild roses growing over the path scratched my arms. I tried to find the right entrance – the complex had several. Taking a breath, I chose one, climbed to the third floor and knocked timidly on the door on the left, where Kolya's room was supposed to be. An unshaven Russian in a sleeveless T-shirt and shorts came to the door.

"*Vam chevo?*" he growled. "What do you want?"

Visions of Lubyanka sped through my brain as I apologized and crept away, heart racing. Now what? Each staircase of this apartment complex had a front entrance and they all looked alike. I couldn't call Kolya because he didn't have a phone. In the dark, I edged toward the next entrance and softly called his name. Nothing. Then the next. Still nothing. Suddenly I noticed a crack in the step leading to the next entrance. That's what he'd told me to look for! In my fear, I had forgotten. I climbed three flights and tapped on the door on the left. Kolya swept me into his arms.

"I thought you weren't coming," he said. We collapsed onto his army-style cot and made love long into the night.

The next morning we exchanged addresses and I promised to write, telling him I would most likely be back at some point – I just didn't know when. He promised to write back to me. We knew we would be read by the KGB's mail censors, but that didn't matter. We just hoped we'd see each other again.

Reporting from France was tame compared to our Moscow adventures but it was never boring. In July, before the Russia trip, Malcolm sent me to Corsica, where separatists were trying to drive out the mainland French through a series of deadly bombings. The man in charge of fighting the separatists was Police Commissioner Robert Broussard, who a few years earlier had notoriously ended the career of France's public enemy number one in a hail of bullets. After I interviewed Broussard, he offered me a lift across the island in his unmarked police sedan. A cheap thrill, maybe, but it was a Lionel Poilâne moment – one that made me remember why I had gone into journalism in the first place.

From Corsica, Malcolm sent me to the Fondation Maeght in Saint-Paul-de-Vence, outside Nice, to view a birthday retrospective of Marc Chagall's paintings in company of the artist and his wife. As we toured the paintings, Chagall, still bright-eyed and lucid at 97, kept stopping and pointing excitedly at his early works.

"I remember that!" he exclaimed each time he came across a painting that had never before left the Soviet Union. Chagall had emigrated to France after World War I – he hadn't seen some of these canvases in more than six decades. Contemplating his work, he seemed briefly to reincarnate as the young Chagall of Vitebsk, the Russian-Jewish city of his youth that he immortalized in his paintings. Again, a thrill. Again, an immense sense of gratitude that I had fallen almost by chance into the world's greatest profession.

That had been back in July. Now it was August – the dead season for news. Few took notice when a French freighter sank in the North Sea off Belgium on August 25 after colliding with a West German ferry. I was alone in the bureau the next day, a lazy Saturday, when it emerged that the freighter, the Mont Louis, bound for the Soviet port of Riga, had been carrying 375 tons of uranium hexafluoride, which can be enriched and used to make nuclear fuel. I wrote up a brief report on the incident. But matters didn't end there.

When I returned to the bureau from lunch a few days later, Colin was waiting for me.

"How would you like to go on a cruise?" he asked.

"Sure," I replied, imagining turquoise waters.

But Colin was smiling a little too smugly, and the rest of the newsroom was watching.

"Wait," I said, "what kind of a cruise?"

Everybody laughed.

"A nuclear cruise," said Colin. "Greenpeace phoned while you were out. They're going to the North Sea to monitor the Mont Louis and want to take some reporters along. I told them you'd be on board."

On my way to the Greenpeace office that afternoon, I read clips provided by Marcel. The uranium hexafluoride aboard the Mont Louis, while only mildly radioactive, was highly toxic. If one of the 30 sunken containers of it was damaged, poison could seep into the sea. The authorities of both France and Belgium had been playing down the danger. Greenpeace fitted me out with credentials and told me to be in Amsterdam by noon the next day to board the Sirius, the ship that was conducting the mission. We would leave from there in mid-afternoon.

I was so sleepy at Air France check-in early the next morning that I didn't notice the man standing beside me until he spoke up.

"Mona, what are you doing here?" he asked, eying my portable typewriter and waterproof slicker. "Don't tell me you're on the Greenpeace mission too?"

It was Robert Gauvain, a writer I knew through friends, and I was happy as a sailor on shore leave to have him as a traveling companion. Robert knew Amsterdam well and was an experienced sea voyager, having toured the world on a freighter for one of his books.

When we landed in Amsterdam, Robert took me to a seedy hole-in-the-wall bistro near the port for a fabulous Indonesian lunch. Then we made our way to the quay where our vessel was being readied to go to sea. A converted pilot ship, the Sirius bore the rainbow colors of Greenpeace on its hull.

By the time we arrived all the bunks had been taken except for two next to the engine room. We'd be sleeping amid ferocious noise and the pervasive sickening odor of diesel fuel. But I was so exhausted I didn't mind these conditions.

We soon began moving through the North Sea Canal, a journey so smooth that I wondered at dinner why the tables were bolted to the floor. I finished my meal quickly and fell into bed.

When I awoke at dawn Robert was sound asleep in the upper bunk. It was early but I was hungry, so I quietly rose. The ship was pitching and heaving so much I could hardly keep my balance. In the corridors there was no one about. I decided to go up to the bridge to look for the captain, a Dutchman.

"Where is everyone?" I asked.

The captain eyed me strangely.

"Where were you last night?" he asked in return. "I don't remember seeing you when we hit rough seas."

A tempest had struck when the ship left the canal for the North Sea, the captain informed me, and most of the people aboard had been violently ill.

"I don't get seasick," he said. "What about you?"

"I don't know," I replied nervously. "So far so good."

"If you go to the cafeteria, you can find some bread and coffee."

I was sitting at one of the bolted tables with my breakfast when the first wave of nausea hit. The ship was lurching so hard I barely made it to the loo in time. When I emerged, hungry no longer, a few crew members were up. They had no instant remedy.

"You'll just have to stick it out," said the Greenpeace press person, whose face was a delicate shade of green.

By the time Robert emerged I was starting to get the hang of moving about a ship buffeted by gale-force winds and 20-foot waves. The night before, he told me, when the ship left the safety of the canal for the surging sea, the BBC man had had to interrupt his live broadcast to go heave over the side of the ship. Robert decided to skip breakfast. In any event, as we were approaching the site where the Mont Louis went down, it was time to start reporting.

Various other ships were at the site when we arrived – a tug, a minesweeper and some warships. There appeared to be an oilslick on the surface. A couple of Greenpeace monitors boarded a Zodiac inflatable craft with a Geiger counter to take a reading closer to the wreck. An official of Britain's National Union of Seamen, Jim Slater, came aboard to speak to the press about the need to ban hazardous shipments like the one carried by the Mont Louis. When I'd typed up my notes into a story I got on the radio-phone to Paris. After dictating the dispatch to Colin, I told him about the shipboard conditions.

"I wouldn't worry about a little seasickness," Colin replied. "It may get worse. We expect you to come back glowing in the dark."

The storm didn't let up, meaning we couldn't do much reporting, and the next day Colin reluctantly said I could head home.

The Sirius was stationed about 12 miles offshore, and every day a couple of Greenpeace staffers went across in the Zodiac for supplies. I could leave with them. The only problem was how to board the rubber dingy as it bobbed and swayed in waves the height of a two-story building.

My knapsack on my back, clutching my typewriter, I hesitated at the top of the ladder that led down the side of the Sirius. The Zodiac was swinging madly up to the foot of the ladder and back out to sea.

"Come on, Mona," the Zodiac's skipper cried impatiently, straining to make his voice heard over the wind.

As the rolling waves frothed and churned beneath the ladder, I went down a few rungs.

"What should I do?" I cried, trying to put off the moment of truth.

"You have to jump!"

"What if I miss?" I shouted.

"You get wet."

Over the roar of the sea, I could hear another roar. Up on deck, the crew of the Sirius was laughing at me.

Desperate to get back to dry land, my honor at stake, it seemed I had no choice. I went down another rung and, as the Zodiac surged forward, I jumped.

Was it luck or divine intervention? I didn't get wet.

Back in Paris, *la rentrée* was in full swing. The September season known as "the return" means not just back to school but back to normal life after the August hiatus. Back to work, back to commuting, back to trysts with your lover. Theaters reopen, shops display new collections, the city seems briefly to whirr with the anything-can-happen excitement you feel every day in New York. In my case, *la rentrée* meant Reuters was getting ready to move me to a new posting. I would soon be sent to the London World Desk, James Roberts informed me, adding that he had arranged for me to begin taking Russian lessons.

"When will I go on to Moscow?" I asked.

"Hard to say," he replied. "It could be soon, or not for a few years. I may well be back as bureau chief by then."

"Really? What about Rory?"

"He'll surely be there for a while," said James. "But I've been in Paris a long time now and feel ready for a new tour in the *rodina*" – the hallowed motherland.

I wondered about James Roberts, and in fact about all the Moscow hands I'd encountered at Reuters. James, Rory, Malcolm. Did they have some subterranean *coco* connection – *coco* being French argot for Communist? Were they fellow travelers, who beneath the veneer of journalistic objectivity secretly endorsed the Soviet Union's take on Marxism-Leninism? Or did they simply relish aspects of Soviet life? I knew that Malcolm and Julia disdained the system even as they admired the generosity of the Russian people, their reverence for poets and love of the arts, the way friendship really mattered in a country where individual rights were so limited.

These thoughts were on my mind as I dived into my last *rentrée* for the foreseeable future. I'd been in Paris 10 years – rich, exhilarating, agonizing years. With London looming, I was determined to make the most of my time in what to me was the world's most romantic city.

Part of the romance of Paris was living among intellectuals who generated the kind of excitement usually reserved for sports heroes or rock stars. Writers like Simone de Beauvoir, whose provocative thesis sparked the modern feminist movement.

"One is not born, but becomes, a woman," Beauvoir famously wrote in her magisterial philosophical work "The Second Sex."

In October 1984, I met Beauvoir at a news conference about a television production marking the 35th anniversary of that work.

"Many things have changed," Beauvoir said, citing the legalization of contraception and abortion. "But many things still remain to be achieved. Equal pay for equal work may be legal on paper but it is easy for employers to cheat. The chances for girls and boys are not the same. Many careers are still closed to women."

What would Beauvoir think if she saw how women in France and other Western countries were faring today? Does anyone seriously believe that women have achieved equal pay for equal work? Equal career opportunities? Even enterprising women in the vanguard of feminism who are ready to fight for their rights? In my personal experience, and the experience of the women closest to me, such equality has not yet arrived.

A few days before I moved to London, my cat died. The vet said it was diabetes, but I was convinced that Mathilde died of heartache. We well-read, computer-literate modern-day humans may have lost the sixth sense that earlier people possessed, but the same cannot be said for cats. Mathilde had an uncanny ability to feel what was going on in our household. When I was sad, she would comfort me, coming to sit on my lap. When I was glad, she would frolic about the house, chasing imaginary mice. Now that I was leaving for England, the plan had been to leave her with Leon Engel so she wouldn't be put in quarantine, and then come pick her up when I was posted to Moscow. About a month before I was due to leave Paris, Mathilde stopped eating. As she grew steadily more rundown, the vet prescribed insulin. She seemed to perk up a bit, but one morning she couldn't get off the couch. Ill or merely disconsolate, she died that afternoon.

The next day the movers came and packed up my things – the few things that remained. I had given most of my larger possessions away, for Reuters was providing me with a furnished flat. When the movers left I went outdoors with my camera to immortalize the unmatchable Parisian faces and places of my neighborhood. The fruit and vegetable lady, her lips painted into a perpetual bowlike smile. The bird lady, who freed her pets from their cages to sing with them. The man who sold wood, coal and sausages from his Auvergnat café, proudly posing for me in his ancient doorway. The fish stand, my lens capturing *colin, cabillaud, lieu noir, congre, carrelet, daurade, truite de rivière, truite de mer, langoustines, colinot, raie, saumon frais, colinot friture, lotte entière* — and this was only a portion of its abundance. Going back upstairs one last time, I wandered briefly through the apartment, now empty of everything but the memories inscribed in its walls. And then it was time to go.

I stayed at Lucie's place on my last night in Paris. The morning of my departure, she invited some friends over for going-away drinks followed by a Mexican brunch. This event is immortalized in another photo — Lucie and Charly, Jacques, Malcolm and Julia with their two boys, and Leon, all smilingly expectantly at me, the photographer. All of us wondering what lay in store as I embarked on a new adventure.

The margaritas had worn off by the time my British Airways jet touched down in London. A cab took me to my new lodgings, a depressing apartment-hotel in South Kensington. The next day I went to work at Reuters while at the same time beginning my search for a better place, ultimately finding an apartment across town in Islington, just a 15-minute bus ride from Fleet Street. The apartment, the bottom half of a four-story house, had a living room with fireplace and master bedroom upstairs, a large kitchen/dining space and guest room downstairs, and out the back, to my delight, a garden. It was owned by an architect and charmingly furnished, the nicest place I'd lived in since leaving my parents' glass house.

Solving the housing problem did not, however, solve the problem of how to live in London, a place far more foreign to me than Paris had ever been. It wasn't just fear of being run over by a red double-decker bus trundling down the left-hand side of the road, or of failing to recognize somebody's class by their accent, a serious faux pas. I couldn't even order a drink. Asking for a beer, I found, won't get you anywhere. You need to say "a half of lager" – pronounced *hahf a lah-gah* – and I couldn't seem to get it right.

As for work, the editors on the World Desk were impressive. The professionalism, the camaraderie, the dry British sense of humor made for a fine working environment. But here, too, I faced communication problems, especially with some of my older colleagues.

I had been on the desk for only a couple of months when a senior editor named John Black, a rather old-fashioned fellow, wandered over to my computer for a chat.

"I hear you live in Islington," he said.

"I do," I smiled. "On Florence Street."

"Well then," said John, "I live quite close to you. One of these days I'll come over and knock you up."

Excuse me?

British English, it transpired, for "I'll stop by."

Working on Fleet Street was a thrill that didn't wear off. Each time I entered the historic Reuters building, across the street from The Daily Telegraph and a stone's throw from the Daily Express, I felt the same frisson. How many great correspondents had arrived from afar to pass through these doors, sometimes after risking their lives to get a story? I felt proud to be in the company of these professionals, whose work could bring to light important hidden truths.

For the moment, my job was hardly the glorious work of a correspondent. As a subeditor, I was editing breaking news arriving from Reuters correspondents and stringers around the world. The edited dispatches were then sent back out to clients worldwide. Reuters put a premium on accuracy, but there was always a tension between accuracy and speed, for we had to get the news out quickly enough to beat the competition – mainly the AP.

In March 1985, my first full month on the World Desk, Konstantin Chernenko died in Moscow – the third septuagenarian

Kremlin leader to succumb in just over two years – and was succeeded by a relative youngster, Mikhail Gorbachev, 54. A few months earlier, as a rising star in the Politburo, Gorbachev had sparked curiosity in the West when Margaret Thatcher declared after meeting him, "We can do business together." Now the world's eyes were on him as he began the herculean task of trying to right the shipwrecked Soviet economy.

In the months that followed, I did my best to keep tabs on Gorby while handling copy from around the globe. Standards of professionalism were higher at Reuters than they had been at AFP, and the company prized its reputation for objectivity. Sometimes, however, it was hard to remain objective on the World Desk. Amid the daily flood of impersonal news dispatches, an event could touch even the most objective journalist in a personal way.

On July 10, 1985, the Greenpeace ship Rainbow Warrior, sister ship of the Sirius, went down in port at Auckland, New Zealand, when two mines exploded 10 minutes apart. A friendly young man I'd met aboard the Sirius lost his life in the bombing. He was Fernando Pereira, the Greenpeace photographer, who evacuated the Rainbow Warrior when the first mine went off but then went back below deck to rescue his cameras. As the urgents from New Zealand flew in to the World Desk, I was overwhelmed to learn that this sunny individual had lost his life on a peaceful anti-nuclear mission. Weeks later, it emerged that the sinking, at first thought to be the work of terrorists, had actually been carried out by French agents working for the Socialist government of President Mitterrand. For the Rainbow Warrior had been due to go on a protest mission to Mururoa, the Pacific atoll where France was conducting underground nuclear tests. A lesson in the cynicism of realpolitik.

Six months later, I was at work on the World Desk during the launching of the space shuttle Challenger from the Kennedy Space Center in Florida. The launch had been delayed for about a week by weather and technical problems. It was finally cleared for takeoff at 11:38 a.m. Eastern Standard Time on January 28, 1986 – 4:38 p.m.

in London. We had a TV that was tuned to CNN for live coverage of such events. As usual, we prepared a bulletin on the launch in advance so we could just push the "send" button as the shuttle departed. This was such a routine event that few editors were actually watching the broadcast when the Challenger, with a crew of seven, blasted off into the clear Florida skies. The winged shuttle was clearly visible against its booster rocket as the launch began normally. We sent the bulletin and someone began writing an urgent giving a few more details about what we had just seen. Our stringer in Florida would file more fully in due course.

"The 25th space shuttle mission is now on the way after more delays than NASA cares to count," said the CNN newsman. He was still talking 73 seconds into the flight when a massive explosion was visible on the screen.

"Look at that!" shouted the chief sub. "What was that?"

Now everyone's eyes were glued to the TV. We watched transfixed as the shuttle's trajectory split into two separate trails of white exhaust trailing out and downwards against the deep blue of the sky.

"Hold the urgent! Write a flash! Write a flash!" the duty editor bellowed.

The CNN newsman, as bewildered as we were, kept talking calmly as though broadcasting a sports event.

"Looks like a couple of the solid rocket boosters blew away from the side of the shuttle in an explosion," he said as a huge white cloud formed where the shuttle should have been.

"Flight controllers here looking very carefully at the situation," he said, adding, with impressive understatement, "Obviously a major malfunction."

On the ground, families of the seven crew members watched in shock as the Challenger plummeted downward. The parents of Christa McAuliffe, the first school teacher ever to blast off in a space shuttle, scanned the skies anxiously, their faces crumpling when it was announced from the flight control center that the Challenger had exploded.

As this human drama unfolded we were madly writing bulletins and urgents and putting them out on the wire. We may have felt like weeping as we banged out the copy, but no emotion went on display. It wouldn't have been right. After all, Reuters was British.

During my months in London my life was inevitably colored by the fact that I'd be leaving, sooner or later, for Moscow. There was no sense of permanence, no real possibility of engagement. Was I still desperate to be a housewife? Something had shifted. As much as I longed to find happiness in a family setting, my work as a journalist was intense enough most days to blunt the yearning. Yes, the biological clock was ticking. Yes, I was 35 and it was time to have a baby. But yes, I was also in training to go to Moscow – studying Soviet politics at the London School of Economics, refreshing my Russian in a conversation group that met once a week at a pub. I was being groomed to do something that really mattered. It felt like my life was taking on new contours. I was engaged in something bigger than myself. The rest, I assumed, would follow.

How soon I could go to Moscow was uncertain. A different reporter had just been sent in as Rory's number two. It was a logical move. Steve Saint Leger had already served in Moscow as a Reuters trainee, while I was still getting to know the World Desk. As his posting would last a minimum of two years, I resigned myself to a long wait. But fate intervened.

In mid-September 1985, six months after Steve and his family moved into Sad Sam, London expelled 25 Soviet nationals, effectively accusing them of spying. Moscow retaliated tit for tat: 25 Britons were summarily declared persona non grata. Among them was Steve Saint Leger, who found himself catapulted back to London, never mind that he wasn't a spy. For a brief moment it looked like I would be sent in to replace him. But it was impossible to organize my arrival on such short notice. Reuters assigned a former Moscow hand to serve temporarily as Rory's number two – until I could get up to speed in Russian and be accredited as a correspondent.

It was around this time that a Russian man came into my life – not a boyfriend, just a friend with whom I dined from time to time.

Grisha was a scientist I'd met while in Moscow with Julia. After some considerable waiting, he had managed to get out of the Soviet Union thanks to his British wife, Tessa. They and their three daughters were now living outside London, where Tessa had a job. But Grisha, who couldn't find work there, came up to London occasionally in hopes of better luck in the big city. Sometimes he came to my place for dinner and stayed over in the guest room to avoid the long journey home and back. I enjoyed these evenings, which allowed me to practice my Russian in company of a spirited, intelligent man – who always brought along his backgammon set, and was patiently teaching me the game.

One evening, as we studied the backgammon board after dinner, Grisha spoke up.

"I have problem," he said.

"Yes? Tell me."

"It concerns Nani. You remember her, right?"

Of course I did. Nani was Julia's wild-haired Georgian friend – as in Soviet Georgia, the romantic, mountainous land of wine, warriors and poetry lying south of Russia along the Black Sea. A marine biologist, she was in Moscow without her husband, Vanya, who was away working in the Russian provinces. Nani was a fabulous cook, and Julia and I saw her more than once, taking advantage of her wonderful hospitality. She lived far from the center of Moscow in one room of a communal apartment, which is where she told us she was expecting a baby. On one of our visits her husband was in town. They seemed an odd couple. Vanya was as mousy as Nani was extravagant. But he beamed with pleasure every time somebody mentioned the baby.

"What's the problem?" I asked Grisha.

"Well," he said cautiously, "as you probably know, Nani had a son."

"Yes. He's called Sese, right? I heard about it. How's he doing?"

"Fine. But she wants to take him out of Soviet Union. She wants to move to the West."

"What about her husband?"

"They're actually no longer married," said Grisha. "In fact they were colleagues from work who mainly got married so that Nani could get residency papers in Moscow. But now they've divorced."

"That's incredible," I said. "They seemed so happy. She wants to take the baby and leave for good?"

"Yes," said Grisha, "that's why I need your help. I was wondering whether you knew anyone who might be willing to marry Nani – a Westerner, I mean – because that is her only hope for escape. She feels like prisoner in Russia, and she wants better future for her son."

"Wait, this is going too fast for me," I said. "She just got divorced, and now she wants to get married again?"

"It would be – how do you call it? – a *mariage blanc*, just for papers. Once she has residency in the West, they would divorce. She can't really afford to pay. It would have to be someone willing merely to do good deed."

"Let me sleep on it," I said. "If I think of anybody who might be crazy enough to do this, I'll let you know."

It was a couple days later when the solution came to me. Jacques. After all, he had considered marrying Brenda so she could get French working papers. He was a romantic at heart. And he didn't believe in marrying for love, at least that's what he said.

I got on the phone to Paris.

"I don't know," Jacques said when I'd explained the situation. "Maybe. Give me Grisha's number, and I'll call him."

A few days later Grisha came for dinner again, excited and upbeat, for Jacques had agreed to consider marrying Nani. But after we finished eating Grisha's mood turned somber.

"There's something I need to tell you," he said. "I wasn't perfectly frank when we spoke last time."

"Yes?" I said warily.

"The thing is, Nani and I are in love."

"You're joking," I said. "What about Tessa?"

"She doesn't know," said Grisha. "Nani and I worked together at biology lab for years, we all became friends, then this just happened. It's stronger than either of us. I'm going crazy without her."

"But you have a family," I protested. "Your daughters."

"I don't intend to leave them," said Grisha. "But now I have son, too."

"You don't mean to say that Sese is your baby?"

"Of course," he said. "Nani's marriage to Vanya was pure fiction."

"He didn't seem to know that!"

"He didn't. He thought it was his child. But now she's told him everything. And I want to be reunited with my son."

I didn't know what to say. I was fond of Tessa, Grisha's wife. Now I found myself in the hugely uncomfortable situation of arranging a *mariage blanc* for another woman who, it turned out, was Tessa's husband's lover. On the other hand, Nani and Sese existed. If they didn't leave the USSR, they would never see Grisha again, for he had exited on a one-way ticket out. There would be no return visa for him unless he moved back there permanently.

"Don't think about it too hard," said Grisha, seeing my confusion. "Call Jacques. Tell him. Let him decide."

The next morning, I once again got on the phone to Paris.

"So she'd be marrying not just for papers, but for love of her child's father? That makes it so much easier," said Jacques. "I will call Grisha and arrange to meet him in London in the next couple of weeks."

Like I said, he was a romantic at heart.

In early 1986, with my posting looking more imminent, Reuters assigned me a Russian tutor who came by a couple times a week, challenging me to read works like Pushkin's "The Bronze Horseman" about Peter the Great and the city he founded, Saint Petersburg. Kolya and I had been writing back and forth, and in the spring I informed him that I'd soon be returning to Moscow. Reuters sent my passport to the Soviet Embassy with a request for a journalist's visa valid from early May. But again, fate intervened.

As my leaving date approached, I was detached from the World Desk and assigned to other Reuters departments as part of my training. After a short course on news photography and another on economics reporting, I was at the Sports Desk on the morning of April 28 when a series of urgents started arriving from Sweden, where unusually high levels of radiation had been detected. Swedish officials said they believed the problem was emanating from the Soviet Union and demanded an explanation. It took several more hours before Moscow finally admitted that a nuclear accident had indeed occurred two days earlier at the Chernobyl nuclear power plant. For more than 48 hours, the world had been unaware that the worst nuclear accident in history had just taken place in Ukraine.

As Mikhail Gorbachev dealt with the first major international disaster of his rule, the Kremlin went into lockdown mode and stopped issuing journalists' visas. My departure got put on hold. It would be another month and a half – a frustrating time of wondering, like Chekhov's three sisters, whether I'd ever get to Moscow – before I finally received my visa as a correspondent authorized to report to the West from the Union of Soviet Socialist Republics.

MOSCOW
1986

Shortly after arriving in Moscow, I was at the Reuters bureau minding the desk when the phone rang. It was a fine June day, and my colleagues were out on stories. Rory Fraser, now my bureau chief, was upstairs at his place, presumably with the neighbors' nanny, his current love interest. In our small office with me was only Vartan, one of our three translators, a salt-of-the-earth Armenian of indeterminate age.

When Vartan passed me the call, the man on the other end introduced himself as a Finnish journalist.

"I have a tip," said the Finn. "Let me talk to Rory."

"He's taking a break," I replied. "Can I help you? I'm the new number two, Mona Venture."

"Oh, yes, I heard you were coming," said the Finn. "Thing is, we have it on good authority that some of the Chernobyl firemen who died of radiation poisoning have been buried at a Moscow cemetery. I can't touch it myself – my newspaper's too small, it wouldn't have any impact. That's why I'm passing it to the wires."

"What should I do?"

"Tell Rory and get him to send somebody out there. But for God's sake, don't take a camera. If anyone's spotted taking pictures, they're sure to be arrested."

I thanked him, hung up and told Vartan about the call. There was no point in dissimulating – the translators were there to keep an eye on us, and in any event our phones were bugged.

"It could be interesting," Vartan said. "You'd better call Rory."

This I was loath to do, as Rory had made exceedingly clear his wish not to be disturbed when with the willowy blonde nanny. But there didn't seem to be much choice. It took him a while to answer the phone.

"Can't you just handle it?" he said when I'd explained the situation. "Drive out there and check it out."

"I can't," I replied. "For one thing, I don't have a car yet. For another, I don't have the slightest idea where the cemetery is."

"Okay, okay, I'm coming down."

I was wondering nervously whether the call from the Finn had been monitored live when Rory came whooshing in on a skateboard, the nanny in tow. To say they looked like they'd dressed in haste would be an understatement.

"Right. I haven't got all day," said Rory, not even attempting to hide his exasperation with his clueless neophyte. "Which cemetery?"

"Something like Mitinsky," I replied nervously.

"That's Mitinskoye. I want you to go out there. Now."

"Now? Okay. Should I ask the office driver to take me?"

"No, definitely not. Call another reporter. Try Kara Gregory at the AP. She'll be happy to get the tip. I'm sure she'll take you." And out he flew.

Rory returned to mind the bureau half an hour later when Kara arrived to fetch me. Dark haired, tall, with the loping gait of a tennis pro, she had the reputation of being a dogged reporter. She'd agreed immediately to accompany me, hoping to get a scoop.

"Just don't take any photos," I warned as we veered northwest off Leningradsky Prospekt onto Volokolamskoye Shosse, a bumpy, crowded thoroughfare. Kara had her eyes on the rear-view mirror.

"I think we're being followed," she said, sending my blood

pressure soaring. In my short time in Moscow, I'd had time to become more than a little nervous about working as a Western reporter in the USSR. We were monitored constantly – not just the big fish, like correspondents for The New York Times or The Washington Post, but even the little fish, news agency hacks like Kara and me.

On my first full day in the Soviet capital, Rory had driven me over to the Foreign Ministry's press center to receive my official accreditation. Our chief ministry minder had spelled out very clearly the limits the Soviet state was imposing on my activities. It was unnerving. On the drive back to Sad Sam, I'd asked Rory how intensively he thought we were being spied on. Was his car bugged, for example?

"Are you joking?" he replied. "They've probably bugged your shoes by now."

As Kara made her way through dense traffic, I looked back but couldn't spot the tail.

"Look again," said Kara. "It's that dirty blue Lada."

And there it was, about eight cars back, weaving among the sputtering, mud-spattered Moskviches, sinister black Volgas and huge dilapidated trucks that clogged the road out of town.

"What should we do?" I asked in alarm.

"Don't worry, we'll lose him," she said. "Everything will be fine."

It was hard to imagine losing the tail given that our car had plates identifying the driver as an American journalist. But somehow Kara maneuvered so that by the time we got to the cemetery the Lada was no more in sight.

We parked and entered on foot through tall iron gates bearing red stars with the hammer-and-sickle insignia of the USSR. It was easy enough to find the 23 fresh graves on a grassy knoll within view of a guardhouse. White marble tombstones engraved in gold were being planted in the newly dug earth to identify each of the "liquidators of the consequences of the Chernobyl accident," the first emergency workers to succumb to acute radiation sickness.

We got out our notebooks, surreptitiously writing down the names and dates of birth and death of these unsung heroes, who had been secretly buried after giving their lives in a desperate fight to extinguish the fire at the damaged reactor despite the intense radiation emanating from its incandescent core. An elderly woman tending a nearby grave told us that the Ukrainian firemen had been sent to hospitals in Moscow to be treated, and were buried here because this is the city where they died.

I wandered away, not wishing to draw attention to our presence near the tombs of the firemen. Could the radiation that had killed them seep from their graves to poison us, I was wondering, when the peace was shattered by a loud cry.

"Halt!"

I spun around and saw a uniformed officer leading Kara away as she stashed a small camera in her purse. Another officer was heading straight for me. They marched us to the guardhouse, inspected our identity cards, confiscated our notes and Kara's film, and informed us that the cemetery was beyond the city limits, i.e. out of bounds to foreign journalists.

"You are intelligent correspondents," one of the officers sneered. "Surely you know that you need official permission to travel beyond Moscow. Wait here."

We didn't have much choice, as they locked us in a small anteroom while they phoned to get instructions.

"Oh my god," I moaned as soon as they left. "I told you not to take a camera. What do we do now?"

"We just have to wait," Kara said testily. "Don't worry."

"What did they mean by 'beyond Moscow?'" I asked.

"Well, actually, we did go beyond the outer ring road, which usually marks the city limits," she said. "But according to my map, Mitino is part of Moscow. Sorry about that."

Right – all Soviet maps were deliberately falsified. But that didn't improve the situation. I was already picturing my parents' reaction when they heard I'd been expelled or, worse, jailed by the KGB after just two weeks in Moscow.

After what seemed an interminable wait, the officers returned with a statement declaring that we had violated Soviet territorial integrity, and ordered us to sign. I turned to Kara, who already had a couple years in Moscow under her belt.

"This looks like a confession," I said quietly, trying not to panic. "Violation of Soviet territorial integrity – doesn't that mean spying?"

Kara nodded.

"I don't think we should sign it," I said. "If we do, we could be expelled."

"If we don't we'll be here all night," she replied.

"Well, I can't sign until I've spoken to Rory."

The senior officer reluctantly agreed to let me use his phone.

"I told you to be careful," Rory muttered. He was furious – less, it seemed, at our predicament than at the time it was taking me to return to relieve him.

"Just sign and get back here," he told me. "I'm late for a party."

"But we could be expelled! And I could be fired," I persisted.

Still fresh in my mind was the warning I'd received at Reuters headquarters on Fleet Street before taking up my post. If I got into trouble in Moscow by breaking rules, I'd been told, I'd be not just out of a posting but out of a job.

"Mona, for Christ's sake, sign the statement," said Rory. "Nobody's going to fire you unless you ruin my evening."

He hung up. Kara, who had already signed, was getting impatient.

"Listen," she said, "why not add a note explaining that you hadn't known the cemetery was in an area off limits to foreigners? That way, it's not your fault."

It was late, we were hungry and this sounded like a good idea. I signed – and never heard another word about the incident. But I never forgot about it, knowing that at the slightest misstep my "confession" could be hauled out and used against me.

From the very beginning in Moscow the dominant presence in my life was Sad Sam, the dusky yellow "ghetto" where I lived and worked. Our building was constructed around an asphalt courtyard where residents and their many KGB-affiliated housekeepers, drivers and translators came and went. Rory lived on the seventh floor. My apartment, identical to his, was on the fourth floor, just one story up from the Reuters bureau. The New York Times was across the hall from Reuters. Downstairs was The Daily Telegraph, upstairs the BBC and Agence France-Presse, in the next staircase the Los Angeles Times, European news organizations, British diplomats and Western businessmen of various stripes.

The quarters were spacious and comfortable, but it was a gilded cage. As Westerners we had to live where assigned by the Soviet authorities, and the fact that the building was guarded by militiamen – known by us as "milimen" – discouraged most Russians from dropping by. Oddly, though, these restrictions created an atmosphere of camaraderie that met or even surpassed my idealized vision of communal living dating back to the sixties. At Sad Sam, you had your own apartment, but one neighbor or another was always available for dinner or drinks.

At the center of my new universe was Reuters, where I worked in close quarters with Rory and two correspondents – Amanda Dorrington, originally from Yorkshire, and Ricky Prentice, a young Londoner, understated and extremely bright – and a brash but amusing trainee everyone knew as Rambo. We and our translators shared an office equipped with a couple of computers and a telex in the back room for when the computers stopped working, which seemed to happen regularly when a big story was breaking.

Ricky was not yet 30 and already balding, with quiet blue eyes behind wire-rim specs. His Russian was excellent, as he proved one June evening while playing Hamlet in a performance by a ragtag troupe of journalist-actors known as The Bard in the Yard. The play was proceeding in a variety of English, Scottish and American accents when Ricky suddenly took center stage and declaimed, *"Byt ili ni byt, vot v chyom vopros,"* and going on to pronounce the entire "To be or not to be" soliloquy in Russian. Ricky had received a first at Oxford, the rough equivalent of valedictorian. He had an occasional Russian girlfriend and wrote poetry in his spare time. He was helpful as a colleague and a wonderful drinking companion. We quickly became friends.

As for Amanda, a quiet young woman with short dark hair, we had met briefly in London while I was on the World Desk. She surprised me shortly before I got my visa by phoning up from Moscow to ask me to intercede for her with Rory. Amanda had made the fatal mistake of falling in love with a Russian, and Reuters was giving her an exceptionally hard time about it. They wanted to pull her out of Moscow for consorting with what, at that time, was still considered the enemy. Even with Mikhail Gorbachev in the Kremlin, it was still the Cold War, and our masters in London feared that our journalistic integrity could be tarnished if we got too intimate with the Russians.

"You've got to help me, Mona," said Amanda when she called, sounding dangerously close to tears.

"The thing is, Sima and I want to get married. I told Rory about it and now he's threatening to send me back to England. You know him from Paris. Please talk to him. I can't leave Sima, I just can't!"

Amanda's passion moved me, and I did speak to Rory. By the time I reached Moscow, the cloud over her head had largely lifted. Reuters agreed to let her stay. But she was hardly alone in that situation. As I got to know people beyond the borders of Sad Sam, I encountered several Western women involved with Soviet men. And in fact, I, too, had a Soviet man in my life.

On arrival in Moscow as a bona fide correspondent, one of the first things I wanted to do was to see Kolya. He had moved to a new place during the 22 months since we'd met, and the best news was that he now had a phone. I called him within a few days of arriving and we agreed to meet at a café down the street from Sad Sam.

I was surprised when I saw him. He looked different, tauter, with a new sternness about the mouth. We made small talk for a while, and then he asked me to come to a party at a friend's place out of town the next weekend.

"It's beautiful in the woods," he said. "We'll grill *shashlik* on the barbecue" – kebabs, Russian style. "I'm borrowing a car, so we can drive there."

This incident took place before my cemetery misadventure with Kara, but I knew the rules. Was Kolya's friend's place in an area off limits to foreigners?

He said no one would know as I'd be in a car with Soviet plates.

"Come on, you'll love it," he coaxed. "We'll get to be together."

I said I'd have to think about it and would phone him.

I never called. The whole thing smelled wrong to me, and I decided it would be best if I didn't see Kolya again. I remembered what had happened to my friend Henry Lambert, a former Moscow correspondent who had studied in Ukraine during a university year abroad and who knew the place too well for the comfort of his Soviet minders. While working for Reuters in 1971, Henry had been at a restaurant in Kiev when someone slipped a mickey into his drink. He awoke in bed naked and bruised, not knowing how he got there. Upon his return to Moscow, he reported the incident to the British Embassy. Although he assumed photos had been taken, he heard no more about it. But three years later the Soviet authorities accused Henry Lambert of having had a homosexual relationship in Kiev. They expelled him, abruptly ending the career of a remarkable and subtle Kremlinologist.

Why would I take the chance of something similar happening to me? I didn't like Kolya's insistence that I go out of town with him. I particularly didn't like it when, after a couple of days, I spotted him lurking down the street from my apartment building. Had he been an agent all along, I wondered, or had he been approached after his initial dalliance with me? I'll never know. But it seemed clear he was working for someone. Exit Kolya.

Reporting for a British news agency in Soviet Russia meant that I was "British" too, never mind my American passport. My *propiska*, or resident's ID card, said I was British. So did the license plates of the blue Volvo sedan I bought in Helsinki and drove back to Moscow via Leningrad. The cars of foreign diplomats and journalists were identified at the time by license plate numbers based on when each country had recognized the Soviet Union after the Bolshevik Revolution: Britain was 001, the United States was 004, and France, to the amusement of many, was 007.

On my first full day in Moscow, with the Chernobyl accident still very much on everyone's mind, I was summoned to a British Embassy briefing about how to buy food. Geiger counters were produced, and a couple of diplomats tried to explain what to do when we went to the market. Although the radioactive cloud had blown westward from Ukraine, theoretically sparing the Moscow area, there was no way to know the origin of the food sold in outdoor markets like the Tsentralny Rynok, conveniently located down a leafy path behind Sad Sam. The best plan was to check all fruit and vegetables with a Geiger counter, we were told. Trouble was, the embassy didn't have counters to hand out to us. We were advised to bring our fresh food over for testing before consumption. This might have seemed like a great idea, but in practice the embassy was across the Moskva River from Sad Sam, too far away to get to on a daily basis.

As far as I know, everyone at the briefing simply ignored the advice. For one thing, there was no way to avoid the effects of Chernobyl. We had to live with the consequences of the accident, just as our Soviet neighbors did. If you wanted to eat mushrooms, like the succulent chanterelles they sold at the market (golden orange in color, they were called *lisichki*, or "little foxes"), chances are they would be radioactive. We took this knowledge in stride. After all, Ricky Prentice had been in Kiev visiting a friend on the day the reactor exploded and discovered on returning to Moscow that his jeans were radioactive. He was okay – and so, we assumed, would we be, even if we ate the odd glowing salad leaf.

One of the benefits of being "British" was that I was invited to diplomatic functions like the Queen's birthday party, held every June in the gardens of the British Embassy. This was my introduction to high society, Moscow style, and I hoped I wouldn't flub it. I felt like I'd walked into a movie: Chinese trade officials exploring deals with East German diplomats, Brazilian journalists talking politics with their counterparts from Tass, waiters circulating with platters of fancy hors d'oeuvres, knots of elegant people crowding around the drinks tables. I did my best to keep up my end of the conversation, my faltering Russian improving the more champagne I consumed. Driving back to Sad Sam, Rory appeared suitably impressed by my collection of business cards and the bits of political gossip I'd picked up. Among the British, I had passed my first test.

Among the Americans, it was a different story. The U.S. Embassy also viewed me as British, which meant I was not invited to embassy briefings. Reuters had hoped to capitalize on the fact I was American to gain entry to such events.

But this didn't matter too much, because my American journalistic colleagues had no problem including me in – for quiet picnics at a wooded beach area along the Moscow River known as Serebryany Bor, for parties where far too much beer was consumed and, most importantly, for an information-sharing system worked out by Western press agencies in Moscow to ensure that news about dissidents did not go out on one wire alone, endangering both the dissident and the reporter. As Western correspondents we received many calls from Soviet citizens wanting to publicize various causes. Some of these calls were legitimate, others from cranks and still others apparently designed to entrap us.

In late August 1986, two and a half months into my posting, a seasoned American newsman was entrapped by the KGB when he accepted an envelope from a Soviet acquaintance that he thought held news clippings but that was said by the Soviet authorities to contain classified documents. It was a sobering moment for the entire Western press corps when Nick Daniloff, correspondent of U.S. News and World Report, was seized and led off to the KGB's Lefortovo prison. He was held for two weeks before pressure from the White House helped bring his conditional release. His mistake, we correspondents felt, was to have gone to the meeting with his contact alone. Our information-sharing system meant we didn't get exclusive stories, but it did offer a measure of protection at a time when the spy-versus-spy mentality still prevailed, and we – Western journalists in Moscow – were widely regarded as spies.

And not just spies but opponents worthy of denunciation. One of my first assignments from Rory was to write a preview of the Goodwill Games, a sports event sponsored by Ted Turner of Turner Broadasting at a time when the USSR and the United States were boycotting each other as hosts of the Olympics. The first edition of the Games was to be held in Moscow in July 1986, so in mid-June I went over to the grounds to check out preparations. Surprise, surprise – it was such a big mess at Moscow's Olympic Stadium that it seemed practically impossible the Games could open on schedule. I interviewed workmen and officials, returned to the bureau and wrote an account of what I'd seen and heard. The story went out on the Reuters wire that afternoon.

The next morning when I arrived at the bureau Vartan was all in a flutter.

"Mona, Mona, look," he said in his gravelly voice, waving a newspaper in front of my nose. "Sovietsky Sport. They wrote about you on the front page!"

"What? Let me see that."

Vartan handed over the paper, where he had carefully underlined several phrases in a front-page article headlined, "Toward the Goodwill Games, Ill Will."

Mona Venture, correspondent of the international news agency Reuters, does not know much about goodwill, Sovietsky Sport said. *In fact, as her article demonstrates, she has no goodwill at all toward the Goodwill Games. This alleged sports correspondent clearly knows nothing about an important event that will bring athletes from the whole world to the capital of the USSR. Here's a word of advice to Mona Venture of Reuters: from now on, keep your ill will to yourself.*

I didn't know whether to laugh or cry. In Moscow less than a month and already denounced in the official press? Rory, Ricky and Rambo were highly amused and told me to take it in stride. It was, they said, my christening as a member of the Western press corps.

Summer is magic in Moscow, an enchanted time when the light lingers until midnight at the horizon and returns glimmering in the dawn a mere two hours later. This produces a strange effect on the human body. The need for sleep diminishes in proportion to the presence of light, an odd wakefulness persisting sometimes right through the night. It is an almost poetic transcendence of time and space, as best described by the great Russian writers. That first Moscow summer hardly a night went by when I didn't see the sun go down and come up, so completely did I give myself over to the feeling of hovering outside the realm of the ordinary, of being not quite earthbound. As I embraced this sensation for the first time, it was like meeting a new lover, one who would carry me beyond my boundaries, into a state of bliss.

The Sad Sam Summer Soirée, held every year on the Saturday closest to midsummer night's eve, was my building's official bow to the power of Moscow nights. Our courtyard was turned into a barbecue pit and dance floor, with fairy lights strung overhead, an improvised bandstand in a corner, and tables overflowing with drink and food. That first June in Moscow, as preparations went into overdrive on the evening of the party, I had a hard time believing what was unfolding before my eyes. Right in the courtyard were the members of Moskovsky Dixieland, the band whose record I'd bought for my dad at GUM two years earlier. They had been escorted safely past the KGB militman and were now setting up, looking like they'd just arrived from Brooklyn. The American ambassador to Moscow was manning the barbecue, cooking up ribs, southern style, while at the same time maintaining a patter with the various dissidents and refuseniks who had managed to penetrate our stronghold. Kids, dogs, nannies, businessmen, moms, diplomats and hard-boiled journalists let down their guard, got down to the music and partied. We could have been anywhere, having fun – but it was impossible to forget this was Moscow, heart of the Communist universe, not only because of the high wall separating us from our Russian neighbors, but also because of the light.

Throughout the party I was up and down stairs, in and out of our bureau. As the new Reuters arrival, I had been given slot duty that evening along with Rambo, the trainee. We spelled each other, taking turns partying. I felt as effervescent as the bubbly *shampanskoye* being served in the courtyard by an impromptu team of bartenders, including at times myself.

As my apartment was close to the office I was in and out of that too, and at one point found myself opening beers for a knot of refuseniks including Ricky's 25-year-old Russian girlfriend, Tanya. Her father, a former Aeroflot navigator, had been interned in a psychiatric hospital for political reasons, and Tanya was doing everything in her power to try to get him released and win permission for the family to emigrate. She and her friends were speaking Russian, and I had to struggle to understand. But it was worth the effort.

I'd worked hard to improve my knowledge of the language before moving to Moscow, largely for fear that I'd mistranslate Pravda and create a diplomatic incident. But that was officialese. Now, at my own place, in the midst of this rowdy party, I was being initiated into the way real people spoke. Real Soviet people, not the cardboard-cutout Politburo figures we'd learned to fear as children in America, but generous, warm, ironic people with a deep inner sense of poetry who had been bruised or worse by their country's system and were now making light of it, even as they suffered. Some of the people drinking beer in my kitchen that night were to become good friends during my time in Moscow. They helped me understand not just their language but a Russian way of perceiving the world – with great humanity and the kind of acuity that we in the West are most often too comfortable to achieve.

At summer's end Rory was leaving as bureau chief and James Roberts was arriving from Paris to replace him. James wanted to install his family in the fourth-floor apartment where they'd lived before – my current home. So for a few weeks I shared my space with a Soviet renovation crew, mainly women painters dressed in dusty blue who, in the rough language of the Moscow streets, regaled me with stories. When Rory left, I moved upstairs to his seventh-floor flat. He left me his big brass bed, his modern-ugly living room furniture, his huge freezer and Sonya, his housekeeper, reputedly a KGB colonel.

I was not unhappy about the move – I'd always liked the feeling of lightness that comes with living on an upper floor – although it was a major hassle to relocate at a time when I was still trying to get to grips with my new job and the language. But there was an unexpected benefit to the switch. On the seventh floor, I quickly learned, my back door to the service stairs led across the landing to the flat of Anouk Rives, a correspondent for AFP. This created a passage between our two apartments that she and I used to exchange everything from a cup of coffee to political gossip or news from Paris. (Some years earlier, we learned, this same back-door passage had been used by two male reporters to exchange their wives.)

Freckled, with wise, mischievous eyes over high cheekbones, Anouk had arrived in Moscow around the same time as me. As a reporter, she was curious, committed and knew a good yarn when she saw one. Her sense of irony, honed in Paris and various farflung locations, was getting sharper by the day. As we were often covering the same stories, Anouk and I crossed paths regularly with other Western reporters. We naturally gravitated to a group of female correspondents who, like us, went in before the changing Soviet Union became a major story attracting star reporters. This group, more rightly this pack, had a core of half a dozen hard-working, smart-talking, fast-partying 30ish women. Together we covered the surprising events of the early Gorbachev era. We may have been rivals at work, but the friendships we formed were so strong that we still feel like family to each other 25 years on.

Thinking back to this time, I often wonder how it was that we became so close. Part of the answer is the siege mentality that prevailed among Westerners at the time. Our ability to go out and mingle with Russians was sharply limited, and so our social life was mainly confined to the Western community. But it was more than that.

By the autumn of 1986, based in Moscow as observers of Soviet life, we were on shifting sands. The good, the bad, the good, the bad proceeded in alternation, but the fact that there was any good at all was new. Nick Daniloff was jailed? Dissidents like Tanya's father remained imprisoned? Yes. But by the end of the year, Gorbachev's Kremlin had issued an order to the police to stop arresting innocent people – those were the actual words. The superpowers were still sparring over nuclear arms control and the Afghan war? Yes. But by the end of the year, Moscow had withdrawn 8,000 troops from Afghanistan and looked like it might pull out altogether. Soviet Jews were still being refused permission to emigrate? Yes. But before the year was out, the authorities had drafted a new emigration law that appeared to herald change.

Cultural censorship still persisted, with Russians unable to read works like Boris Pasternak's "Doctor Zhivago," as yet unpublished in the Soviet Union? Yes. But throughout the year, the first buds of liberalization began appearing in the arts. The poet Yevgeny Yevtushenko, backed by 40 writers, appealed to the authorities to rehabilitate Pasternak and turn his dacha into a museum. The literary journal Yunost took the bold step of publishing a work by another major poet, Andrei Voznesensky, that told the largely unknown story of a 1941 massacre by the Nazis of 12,000 people, mainly Jews, in the Crimean city of Simferopol, and that criticized the Soviet authorities for failing to erect a monument to the victims. "Unofficial artists" – those not belonging to the official Artists Union – were holding wildcat exhibitions of their paintings in underground galleries. Most striking of all, "Repentance," a film by the Georgian director Tengiz Abuladze about the terror of the Stalin era, was released with the blessing of the Soviet leadership after being suppressed for two years.

Yes. Change was in the air.

Change came two days before Christmas, on December 23, 1986, when Andrei Sakharov returned by overnight train from internal exile in Gorky.

Revered in the West, feared by the Kremlin, Sakharov was a giant of a man: a brilliant nuclear physicist in the Soviet atomic weapons program, he had been awarded the Stalin Prize, the Order of Lenin and was decorated as a Hero of Socialist Labor – three times – before falling out of favor through his turn to peace activism and human rights campaigning. In 1975, as one of the Soviet Union's most prominent dissidents, he received the Nobel Peace Prize for his activities as "a spokesman for the conscience of mankind." But Sakharov's Nobel prize didn't protect him. In January 1980, one month after the Soviet Union invaded Afghanistan, he was banished by Brezhnev to Gorky – a closed industrial city 250 miles east of Moscow – for denouncing the military intervention. He was held virtually incommunicado for nearly seven years in the city, which has since reclaimed its historic name, Nizhny Novgorod.

Sakharov and his wife, Yelena Bonner, lacked even a phone until December 15, 1986, when workers suddenly appeared and installed one in their Gorky apartment. The next day, Mikhail Gorbachev rang up in person to tell Sakharov that he was free to return to Moscow, resume his scientific activities and work for the public good.

The first we reporters heard of this dramatic development came on the Soviet evening television news a few days later. Vremya, the main newscast, broke into its regular programming of communal farm reports and factory statistics to announce that Sakharov was a free man. James Roberts quickly convened the Reuters bureau to plot our strategy. The trouble was, we didn't know when Sakharov would return. Whenever it happened, said James, the new trainee was to go to the Yaroslavl Station to meet Sakharov's train. I was to go to Sakharovs' apartment building to await his arrival. Ricky would stay at the office and man the slot.

On December 22, we learned that Sakharov and Bonner were traveling that night and would arrive the next morning at 7 a.m. I put fresh batteries in my tape recorder and set the alarm for 5:30. I didn't know how long it would take them to get from the station to their building on Chkalova Street, a couple miles from Sad Sam, and wanted to leave myself plenty of time.

As it turned out, this was a very good thing – for when I went downstairs in the early morning dark to warm up my Volvo, it was iced in. Someone had plowed a small mountain of snow up around the car and sprayed it with water. The miliman watched, smirking, as I tried to get into the vehicle. If I could open the door, I figured, I could turn on the heater. Maybe that would melt the ice. But this proved impossible, and time was short. What to do?

In those days it was a simple matter to flag down a car and pay the driver a small sum in exchange for a ride. In the frigid gloom, bundled up in my gray fur coat and shapka, slipping and sliding on the icy unplowed sidewalks, I made my way along the Garden Ring on foot. As soon as I was out of range of the miliman's vision, I hailed a car. We flew down the empty thoroughfare until we sighted a knot of reporters waiting patiently outside Sakharov's apartment building, some armed with thermoses of hot coffee. As I was paying him, the driver wanted to know what was happening. When I told him, he sped away.

We had to wait quite a while for Sakharov to appear. He had been thronged by reporters when his train pulled into the station. Accompanied to his apartment by a friend in a dented car, he emerged looking tired but happy to be home. We gathered around him as he made his way from the car to the apartment building, hoping he would take time to speak to the press, but he only wanted one thing – to be back in his own surroundings. Sakharov went inside and pressed the button for the elevator. As the great man rose to the eighth floor, I dashed up eight flights of stairs, my tape recorder running all the while. What I got was mainly the sound of a pack of reporters panting. Still, I was able to contribute a few words to the Reuters report that day – how moved Sakharov seemed to be home, how noble, how relieved.

For me, as for all the Western press, Gorbachev's decision to allow Sakharov to return marked a turning point. As the sun came up on that freezing December morning, we felt we were witnessing the start of a new era.

PROMISE

1987

The dozen people around the table were in that warm state of post-prandial comfort that ensues after a good meal and plenty of wine. There had been potatoes and herring, sour cabbage, roast beef and a dish called Russian Beauty, which turned out to be simply potato salad. The hosts' apartment had recently been searched by the KGB, a pretext for abundant jokes in the course of the evening.

Now the guests were singing funny songs in Russian, accompanied by a guitar. It was nearing midnight and this was Stary Novy God, the charmingly named Old New Year, celebrated every January 13 according to the old Julian calendar still used by the Russian Orthodox Church.

Not that anyone at the table was Christian – we were all Jewish. I'd been invited by Lisa and Tolya Rubinstein, new friends. Just in time someone switched on the radio. When the Kremlin chimes struck twelve, we all raised our glasses.

"A toast! A toast!" the guests cried in unison.

Lisa stood and solemnly held her glass aloft.

"Next year in Jerusalem," she said.

"Next year in Jerusalem!" the guests echoed as we touched glasses around the table.

I turned to Lisa.

"So this is how Russians welcome the new year?" I asked in mock confusion. "By wishing to leave Russia?"

Everyone laughed. But it wasn't really funny, for every single one of them was a refusenik. They had applied years earlier to emigrate, and all had been turned down. The adults had lost their jobs. The children had faced discrimination at school. No longer citizens in good standing, they were condemned to a kind of debilitating limbo with no resolution in sight. Like millions of other Soviet citizens across their vast land, they were celebrating the Old New Year not out of any Orthodox Christian fervor but rather as a small gesture of defiance toward the all-powerful Soviet state.

I had met the Rubinsteins a month earlier, taken to them one snowy December evening by Anouk and her new boyfriend, Stéphane Kramer, a French diplomat. With Anouk at the wheel of her blue Niva four-wheel drive, the headlights dimmed by swirling flakes, we made our way around the Garden Ring to a nondescript apartment bloc. Upstairs, over cheese pies and tea, we compared notes on the situation of the country's 380,000 Jewish refuseniks.

Although as a Jew I felt a sense of kinship with Soviet Jews, there were questions I hadn't been able to answer before moving to Moscow. Why, I had wondered, did Jews in particular sometimes qualify for permission to move abroad, while everyone else in the Soviet Union was effectively a hostage of the state? That was before I understood that the term "Jewish" was used in the USSR to indicate not a religion but a so-called nationality. All Soviet citizens had to carry an internal passport, or residence permit, that defined them by nationality based on notions of blood. A resident of Moscow could be "Russian" or "Ukrainian" or "Kazakh" or "Jewish" – never both. In other words, in the Soviet Union, a country with more than a million Jews even after the slaughter of World War II, there was officially no such thing as a "Russian Jew." This was seen as a contradiction in terms. Yet while most national groups had a territory of their own, Jews did not. Their territory was considered to be Israel. Whether or not they were allowed to go there was a matter of state policy that waxed and waned with the tides of anti-Semitism. In previous decades, the Kremlin had dealt with the "Jewish question" through cultural repression, purges, imprisonment or worse. In 1971 a period of relaxation began that saw more than 10,000 Jews a year allowed to leave the country. In the 1980s the Kremlin had cracked down again, reducing emigration to a trickle. But this had not stopped people from applying – and taking the consequences.

The Rubinstein family – Lisa, Tolya and their daughter, Natasha, now 18 – had applied to leave the Soviet Union in 1979. At the time, Lisa, a physician with a second doctorate in biochemistry, was working at the prestigious Vishnevsky Institute of Surgery, attached to the Soviet Academy of Medical Sciences. Tolya, an accomplished linguist, was writing and translating for the Soviet equivalent of National Geographic and also working freelance as a French-Russian translator. Natasha was in 4th grade in a neighborhood school.

Upon applying to leave, both parents lost their jobs. Lisa now earned what she could by writing dissertations for Ph.D. students and, during the holiday season, by dressing up as the Snow Maiden, the Soviet version of Santa's helper. Tolya had officially ceased to exist as a journalist/translator, but unofficially he continued working through the kindness of friends who let him sign their names to his translations. Natasha had been moved to a different school by her parents to spare her harassment by neighborhood children who knew the family wanted to emigrate. Lisa's father, a prominent doctor at the National Cancer Center, lost his job when he and his wife applied to go abroad, but continued to see patients privately. Lisa's sister and her family had also applied to emigrate, had lost their jobs and were on hold.

Like many Soviet Jews, the Rubinsteins were mainly seeking to leave not because they couldn't practice their religion, but because they wanted to live in a free society. They were dreaming of a better future. Eight long years after applying, they were still waiting, trying not to lose hope.

Were there any serious grounds for optimism? When I first met the Rubinsteins, in early December 1986, it hadn't seemed so — even though Anatoly Shcharansky, the country's most famous refusenik, had recently been allowed to leave for Israel after nine years in a Siberian labor camp. But things were moving quickly in Gorbachev's Russia. Now, in January 1987, after the electrifying release of Sakharov, Kremlin-watchers were awaiting the next move. A new emigration law had gone into effect at the start of the month, but nobody knew if it held the promise of real change for the people on hold.

A couple weeks after the Old New Year, Lisa invited me over for dinner, a meal usually served in the late afternoon. It was Moscow's bleak midwinter, when the sun rises at 10, hovers gingerly above the horizon and sinks back down at 4 to leave only blackness and endless snow. I had come early, around 3, in order to get there before dark and spend a little while alone in Lisa's company. I enjoyed her gravelly laugh, her sophisticated humor, the way her husky smoker's voice would lilt when an idea excited her. We were chatting in the tiny kitchen as Lisa prepared a chicken for roasting when suddenly she set aside her knife. Her eyes had welled up.

"What's wrong?" I asked, alarmed.

"Mona, you are American. How could you possibly understand?" said Lisa, her voice trembling.

"Tell me," I replied.

"You see, we are prisoners in this country," she said, struggling to maintain her composure. "My life is over. I cannot practice my profession. My husband, my daughter, all of us. We are prisoners here. We will never taste freedom!"

"No, no," I said. "I'm sure things will get better."

But that seemed far from certain. We were such new friends I couldn't take her in my arms, so I merely sat with her, wondering whether I could imagine how it would feel to be a Jew locked inside the giant penitentiary known as the USSR.

Of course I had encountered anti-Semitism in the States. I'd grown up in Wisconsin less than 10 miles southeast of the former Camp Hindenburg, set up by the pro-Nazi German-American Bund before World War II. I'd been the only Jew at a high school populated by many children of German ancestry. They told Jew jokes in front of me, not realizing I was Jewish. One boy confidently informed his friends that Jews had horns behind their ears. I told no one about this, not even my parents, not wishing to upset them. They had come of age at a time when anti-Semitism was legal in America. My father got his MD at Marquette University, a Catholic school – the University of Wisconsin School of Medicine having rejected him on the grounds that they had already filled their Jewish quota. Such discrimination persisted into my teenage years. When I was in high school my parents tried to join a country club that counted many of their friends among its members, but were briskly informed that the club didn't take Jews. So, yes, we'd faced discrimination. But nothing at all like the difficulties experienced by Soviet Jews.

Lisa and I were still sitting at her kitchen table. Could I help, I asked, by writing about their case? Lisa said she thought I could and went back to making dinner. An hour later, when Tolya and Natasha came in from the snow, we uncorked the red wine I'd brought, sat down together and shared a meal. Nothing more was said about the drama they were living through. We just enjoyed the roast chicken.

It was February, and Amanda's wish had come true. She and Sima were finally getting married – with the unofficial blessing of Reuters. The party would be at Amanda's place, in another ghetto for Westerners, Dobrininskaya, a modern building about a half circle around the Ring from Sad Sam. I was happy for Amanda, so happy that I volunteered to make the wedding cake and bought a small colorful model of St. Basil's Cathedral to set on top. I felt a sense of sisterhood with this quiet but determined woman who, in order to wed the man she loved, had endured the harassment of both her employer and the

Soviet secret services. I didn't know this for a fact but assumed it was the case, for that is how the Soviet state operated. Any close contact between a Westerner and a Soviet citizen could be used by the KGB to try to gain some advantage – usually, to gain an informer.

Many years later, Amanda confirmed to me that Sima had indeed faced harassment before the wedding, and that she had been targeted for recruitment afterwards. The venue was the headquarters of the traffic police, where she and Sima had been summoned to appear. He was made to sit in the corridor while she was questioned by a man in plain clothes seated beside a uniformed traffic cop.

"You love the Soviet Union, don't you?" asked the man in plain clothes, whom she instantly understood to be an officer of the KGB. "If you saw it was in danger, wouldn't you like to help?"

Amanda brushed off this clumsy attempt. A principled journalist, she was able to fend off the Soviet recruiters until they finally gave up.

Gabrielle Donalson, who worked for The Washington Post, had faced a similar situation, although I didn't know it at the time. A rangy honey-blond American with an inquisitive mind and a fluent command of the language, she had arrived in Moscow in 1984 and begun dating a Russian the following year. When Gabrielle first told me about Alyosha, she'd said merely that he worked at a gym. But in fact his father and brother were senior members of the Communist administration and he himself held a degree in engineering and was completing his doctorate in sports psychology. When they started seeing each other, Gabrielle told me much later, the KGB called in Alyosha's thesis supervisor to report that he was dating an American. Then they summoned his mother. When that produced no results, the KGB tried to convince Alyosha to break up with Gabrielle. When that also didn't work, they tried to recruit her as an informant. Gabrielle said nothing about this to her friends at the time, and in fact although I knew he existed I never met Alyosha while in Moscow, for he had been warned by the KGB to steer clear of the foreigner crowd and he followed that bit of advice. Only a few years later, when they were married, did I see the tall, swashbuckling bon vivant who had swept Gabrielle off her feet.

The harassment had been worse for Charlotte Hawthorn, a joke-cracking, frank-speaking Briton who worked with Kara Gregory at the AP. She had met Dmitri, a Russian musician, shortly after arriving in Moscow in 1983. By they time they got married two years later, Charlotte had been called in multiple times by the KGB, accused in court of helping an alleged would-be defector and denounced in a full-page article in the evening newspaper Izvestia. When top editors at the AP in New York found out she was dating a Russian, they urged her to leave Moscow for a new posting. Dmitri was warned by the KGB of bad consequences for his parents if he continued seeing Charlotte. But they held their ground – and when it became clear that they would marry, the AP switched tacks and began supporting Charlotte. By this time, with Mikhail Gorbachev in the Kremlin, falling in love in the USSR had become less of a geopolitical psychodrama for foreigners. Nonetheless, when the AP posted Charlotte to Vienna in the fall of 1986, Dmitri was refused an exit visa and she had to leave alone. Charlotte returned to Moscow in December for a task she'd been dreading – to separate their belongings and pack up her things. The AP convinced her to try to see Gennady Gerasimov, the Foreign Ministry spokesman, who was viewed as a relatively enlightened member of the Soviet bureaucracy. Two days later Charlotte's phone rang.

"This is Gerasimov," he said. "I have looked into the matter we discussed. Your husband may leave whenever he likes."

Farewell parties were quickly organized, and Dmitri soon joined Charlotte in Vienna.

With all this love and marriage in the air, I had to wonder whether I wasn't making a mistake in sticking to the vow I'd made before leaving for Moscow – don't get involved with a Russian. Yet it seemed to make sense. As a veteran reader of spy thrillers, in-Russia-in-love spelled potential entrapment. At 37, I hadn't stopped hoping I'd find a husband, but the complexities of marrying a Russian felt overwhelming. And then there was the killer factor: in Gorbachev's Russia, for the first time in my life, the men were less exciting than the story.

One of the prizes of working as a reporter in the USSR was travel. The country stretched across 11 time zones from the Baltic to the Pacific. Places with exotic names like Samarkand and Bukhara conjured up images of spices and silk. Of course, in Communist times, a trip to certain destinations could feel more like a booby prize. Just finding rudimentary food and drink was often a challenge, even to seasoned correspondents. But part of the deal when working in Moscow was, from time to time, to hit the road.

James Roberts tested me during my first winter by sending me into the Arctic night in Arkhangelsk, in Russia's frozen far north, where it was dark 22 hours a day. When I survived that experience, he sent me with Margaret Thatcher in March 1987 to Tbilisi, capital of Soviet Georgia. Discovering that city was like visiting the Italian Riviera for the first time, minus the tourist hordes. Surrounded by mountains, warmed by sultry breezes off the Black Sea, Tbilisi boasted magical light, spirited and generous people, fabulous food, charming architecture, banquets with singing and dancing by armed men in proud ancestral dress, even the occasional palm tree. Not to mention that it was already spring in Georgia. James sent me back there a month later with George Shultz, Reagan's secretary of state. I so enjoyed leaving dreary Moscow at that time of year, when it seemed summer would never come, that I barely hesitated when James offered to send me out on the road again, this time to Afghanistan.

Of course there was a war on, and I had no interest at all in being a war correspondent. But the Afghan government had assured Reuters that Western reporters would be kept far away from the hostilities. At the time, in early May 1987, Mujahedin "freedom fighters" had inflicted heavy losses on the Red Army, and the Kremlin was preparing to pull its troops out of Afghanistan. The aim of the trip apparently was to show us that Afghan forces of the pro-Soviet variety could step in and combat the Mujahedin once the Soviet forces withdrew.

We flew out of Moscow on an early morning Aeroflot flight to Tashkent, capital of Soviet Uzbekistan. Among the dozen or so journalists on the plane were two good friends – Anouk of AFP and Peter Martin of The Times of London. After a lengthy stopover we boarded an Ariana Afghan Airlines jet for the flight to Kabul. Anouk settled into a seat across the aisle from me, while Peter Martin, great teller of stories, was on my right.

Fueled by anticipation and multiple minis of Scotch, we were having a fine time until the plane suddenly tipped into its vertical corkscrew descent. Peter, a jovial Englishman, lost his ruddy complexion as I gripped his arm in terror. Even Anouk, whose sang-froid never deserted her, couldn't help asking, as she gazed out the window, "Do you think those are Stingers, darling? Or are they flares?"

The drop from 35,000 feet felt like it took forever but in fact we were on the ground within a few minutes. We were bused to the Kabul Inter-Continental – despite its name, a very basic hotel – and were told to be ready to leave the next morning for a day-long trip, destination unknown.

Fine, I thought. As long as it doesn't involve Ariana Afghan Airlines.

I quickly unpacked and got on the phone. From the window of my hotel room, I could see shells exploding in the nearby Hindu Kush mountains. How close was the war, I asked the British chargé when I got through to him on the phone.

"Very close," said the chargé. "A bomb exploded today on Chicken Street – you know, the bazaar in the center of Kabul. Might have been set off by the Mujahedin. They're very strong."

"Can I quote you on that?" I asked.

"No, absolutely not," he replied. "You can say 'well-informed diplomatic sources,' no more. By the way, I'm having a little party tonight at my place. Why don't you stop by?"

Next I called a senior Egyptian diplomat, who confirmed the bazaar explosion and invited me to his home for tea.

I wrote a dispatch on the bombing and went down to the lobby to file – only to find the international phones already in use by other reporters, who were already filing on the Chicken Street blast.

It was early evening by the time I reached the Egyptian's place, where I was treated to a sumptuous array of oriental pastries and a background briefing. Next stop, the British chargé, who lived in a modern villa on the outskirts of town.

Deep Afghan carpets over a black marble floor led from the front door into a lush garden of orange and lemon trees that could have been Eden but for the noise of distant explosions ricocheting off the Hindu Kush. Servants were grilling spicy kebabs on a large barbecue and the wine was flowing freely. I approached the chargé to introduce myself, but there was a loud bang and he silenced me with a wave of his hand.

"Is that incoming or outgoing?" he barked.

"Pardon me?" I didn't understand.

"The fire. The shells! Are they incoming or outgoing?"

"It's outgoing fire, sir," one of his subordinates said quickly. I took this to mean that the rebels weren't shelling Kabul, i.e. chances were we'd survive the evening.

The next day dawned sunny as we were bused back to the airfield and instructed to board a large plane painted in green and khaki camouflage. It was a Soviet-built Antonov troop transport, Anouk and I discovered as we made our way to what passed for seats – wooden benches running the full length of the walls of the plane. Where were we going? Nobody in the press corps knew, and the organizers wouldn't say. A bumpy hour or so after take-off, as we were preparing to land, they announced that we were arriving at Khost – a town near the Pakistani border where the American-armed rebels had been particularly active. But that, it turned out, was not our final destination.

Anxiously scanning the nearby hills, where puffs of smoke from shellfire were sprouting like mushrooms after a rain, we were herded onto open-back trucks with smiling Afghan drivers. They took us deep into a startlingly Asian landscape of green terraced hills, rice fields and water buffalo, up into the mountains over winding, rutted dirt roads. It took a couple hours of this before we reached a town where we were given lunch and a lecture about Americans who were arming the rebels. Then it was back into the trucks for another ride. When the road ended, they got us out and marched us through fields and trees to a clearing where, in the center, lay the charred remains of an Antonov troop transport plane identical to the one that had just flown us in.

"This is what happens when a civilian plane is shot down by Stingers," our guide said. "Everyone aboard died. Women, children, the pilot – everyone. You must write about this and tell the USA to stop killing innocent civilians!"

"Why are you calling this a civilian plane?" one of the reporters shouted out. "It's painted in military camouflage colors."

"Maybe, but it's a Red Cross plane as anyone can see."

We scrutinized the wreckage and eventually spotted a tiny red cross on a piece of the shattered tail.

"Bloody hell," Peter Martin muttered. "They can't really expect us to believe that this was a civilian plane! All the markings are military. There's no way anyone on the ground could spot a red cross that size."

"What worries me," said Anouk, raising an eyebrow, "is that we have to fly back in the same kind of plane." Although she would never have shown it, she was clearly as rattled as the rest of us.

"Did anybody notice a red cross on our plane?" I asked nervously as we were marched back to the trucks for the ride down the mountain to Khost. It was dark by the time we reached the airfield. Fine bright lines shooting upwards against the hills along the border marked the trajectory of shells being fired by the rebels and their opponents. They could take aim at us, no doubt. But we were so tired that we really didn't give a damn about flying in an Antonov. We took off without incident, arriving back at Kabul around midnight. Nobody filed.

The big event the next day was supposed to be a press conference by Najibullah, the Afghan president installed by Moscow. But we were told at breakfast to pack our bags. The organizers of our tour were sending us home two days early, apparently out of pique that we had filed on the bazaar bombing but not on the Antonov wreckage. We would have time merely to attend the presser and file, they said, instructing us to be ready to go to the airport by 3 p.m. for the flight back to Moscow.

We were bused to the press center, where Afghan security policemen posing as news photographers subjected us to a barrage of flashes, taking mug shots of us while we waited for Najibullah. He never showed. Instead he sent his foreign minister, who berated us for our uncomradely journalistic behavior and declined to answer questions.

Back on the bus we decided of a common accord not to file on the so-called press conference. There was just enough time before take-off, we figured, to visit the bazaar.

Anouk and I took a taxi to Chicken Street, where they were still clearing up glass shattered by the bomb. Merchants with significant mustaches and smiling eyes beckoned us to their stores, overflowing with carpets of every imaginable shape and color. I wanted an old carpet and found one in rich shades of red, from burgundy to fuschia. It now sits under my dining room table. Anouk found a long beige carpet with intricate designs for her front hall. The merchants rolled them up and taped them for our journey back.

When we got to the airport, we were ushered aboard a small jet boasting a salon fitted out with armchairs and tables. Why the luxury? The organizers had been in such a hurry to get us out of the country, it turned out, that they commandeered the Afghan president's plane. In great comfort, no longer fearing the Stingers, we were flown first to Samarkand, then on to Moscow via Aeroflot. Had we covered a war? Not really, but we had certainly weathered a war of propaganda, and we had trophies to show for it – our carpets.

It was three in the morning when the phone rang, and I did my best to ignore it. I'd had too much champagne at a cocktail party thrown by the British air defense attaché. But I was on call overnight, so I forced myself from the warmth of bed and stumbled into the hall.

"Mona?" It sounded like London.

"Yes?"

"Newsdesk here. Rob McAllister. Sorry to trouble you, but the AP is reporting that a young West German landed a light plane on Red Square. Could you please check it out?"

"That's impossible," I said. "No one can land on Red Square. Somebody's probably shooting a film down there. I'm sorry, but it's 3 a.m. I think you can safely ignore it."

I was drifting back to sleep when the phone jangled again. It was Rob, and this time he wasn't taking no for an answer.

"The AP says it's a Cessna," he said. "You'd better go down to Red Square or send someone. We have to confirm or deny, we can't just leave it hanging."

"Right."

Resigning myself to a sleepless night, I flipped through the Reuters phone list and guiltily called Amanda. She lived closer to Red Square and could get there more quickly.

"I'm sure it's bullshit," I said, laughing. "But I'm going to the office to make some calls. Just phone in as fast as you can so we can both go back to bed. Oh, and please take a camera – just in case."

When I got through to the duty officer at the West German Embassy, he denied knowing anything about the alleged incident. I messaged London and began pounding out a dispatch. While I was writing, the newsdesk messaged me back.

"AP reporting German under arrest. Grateful check with Russians before storifying."

I put aside my half-written dispatch and got back on the phone.

"*Nyet,*" a Foreign Ministry officer said grumpily. "No German has crossed the Soviet border in a Cessna. As is well known, anyone who tried such a stunt would be shot down by our border guards."

I added his comment and sent off the denial. London didn't waste time. I heard bells on the Reuter wire moments later as my story went out to the world.

The phone was also ringing.

"It's there, I saw it!" Amanda exclaimed.

"What are you talking about?"

"The Cessna. They were towing it away when I got to Red Square. I was just in time!"

"Oh no," I moaned. "I just put out a story denying it."

"Well, you'd better retract it," she said, "because there was definitely a plane on Red Square. I took a picture. They led away the pilot. I got his name – Mathias Rust. He's only 19."

"Oh God," I groaned. "I'll probably be fired for this."

Furiously backpedaling, I sent a new story. No sooner did I push the button than the bureau's phone rang with the rapid beeps that signaled an international call.

"Mona? Rob. What the fuck is going on up there?"

"I'm so sorry," I said. "But the Germans and the Russians both denied it. Anyhow, Amanda's coming to the office to file, so we're okay, no?"

But we weren't. We'd been scooped by the AP.

"By the way, whose name is on the AP story?" I asked Rob.

"Kara Gregory."

I should have guessed. It was the second time she'd landed me in major trouble. Still I had to admire her for getting the story.

When James Roberts arrived to take over the file, I crept home, intending to go straight to bed. But in my hall I encountered the neighbors' nanny, who was staying in my guestroom for a few days.

"I hope the phone calls didn't bother you," I said.

"No," she replied. "What's happening?"

"This sounds crazy, but a German teenager landed a Cessna on Red Square and the AP got the story and I blew it."

"The plane on Red Square? Oh yes, I know about that. A friend of mine saw it land yesterday when she was crossing the bridge toward St. Basil's. She told me about it."

Suppressing an urge to strangle the nanny, I asked why she hadn't mentioned it. If she'd told me before the cocktail party, Reuters would have scooped the AP. Come to think of it, what about that party? Every top European air force official in Moscow had been invited, along with many British diplomats – including close friends of mine. Surely they'd known, too.

Reuters didn't fire me. I think James Roberts even felt secretly sympathetic. After all, I wasn't the only Reuters reporter who had blown a story. At least I hadn't killed off a Kremlin leader, like one of my predecessors did when he noticed that a television anchorman was wearing a black tie and reported that Yuri Andropov, long absent from public view, might be dead – only to have to retract the story when the anchorman switched to a purple tie.

But never again did I laugh when the newsdesk called through with a request, no matter how improbable it sounded.

Improbable, unreal, unexpected – such events were becoming commonplace in Moscow. It seemed anything was possible.

So it felt one evening as I took another bite of tandoori chicken, willing myself to keep my cool in the presence of the Englishman beside me. We were having dinner at the Delhi, a new Indian restaurant in Moscow – a tableful of journalists brought together by one of our colleagues, the correspondent for the London newspaper The Independent. He had invited us to dine with him and his brother that evening. I was seated next to the brother. John le Carré.

Could it be? I'd read every spy novel ever published by Le Carré and here he was in Moscow, just a stone's throw from Dzerzhinsky Square, headquarters of the KGB, whose agents he had described so brilliantly in his thrillers. But if the reporters around the table felt the same awe as I did they didn't have time to show it, for the venerable author was quietly but persistently questioning us about Gorbachev's Russia. He was researching a new novel and was looking for details, the kind that we, as insiders, might know.

Jovial, attentive, slightly flushed, Le Carré was charmingly low key as we plied him with Cobra beer in hopes that in return he would tell us something about his work in progress. But he was, after all, a former intelligence agent, not to be so easily outwitted. Did he use anything we said that night in the work that became "The Russia House"? When I read the book a couple years later it seemed that he might have. I allowed myself to fantasize that this or that scene might have been drawn from something I'd casually said to my distinguished dining companion. But fiction is fiction, reality reality, and the truth is that, naïve or sentimental, I downed too much beer that night to remember exactly what I'd said to the perfect spy novelist on my right.

Improbable, unreal, unexpected. In April 1987, just three months after Lisa's moment of despair in the kitchen, the Rubinsteins received permission to go abroad. By early May they had left the Soviet Union, traveling first to Vienna and then to Rome to await entry visas for the United States. Before leaving they gave away all their possessions except for the clothes they could carry. Their most precious belongings – the family photos and some jewelry – they discreetly handed me one evening just before leaving, asking me to carry the items out to the West for them. For even if Gorbachev had opened the gates to emigration, nobody knew what would happen when refuseniks like the Rubinsteins actually crossed the border. It was assumed their belongings would be pawed through by customs officers who could confiscate items with impunity. And so it was that, the next time I left the USSR, it was with a pocket full of diamonds.

But even as Soviet security forces clung to old habits, Gorbachev was showing he was serious about changing things. In the course of 1987, more than 8,000 Jews received exit visas, a huge increase from the 943 allowed to emigrate the previous year. Cold War jousting between the superpowers continued, so deeply woven into the fabric of the second half of the 20th century that no one saw the threads beginning to fray. No one thought it peculiar in June 1987 when Ronald Reagan, in Berlin, challenged Mikhail Gorbachev to "Tear down this wall!" How were we to imagine that, in just over two years, the Berlin Wall would actually come down?

A year after the Chernobyl disaster, the Kremlin authorized foreign journalists to visit the accident site and report freely on what we found there. So it was that in June 1987 I flew to Kiev, capital of Ukraine, armed with my typewriter and an extra pair of shoes. For the reporters on the trip had been warned that the shoes we wore to the reactor would be so radioactive afterwards that they'd have to be thrown away.

On arrival, we met with a couple of firemen who had battled the reactor blaze, developing radiation sickness in the process. The fact that they had been decorated as Heroes of the Soviet Union was slight consolation. They had seen most of their colleagues die and knew their own chances of survival were slim. The encounter was so sobering that not a few of us went out that evening and hit the vodka. For there was no avoiding the Chernobyl effect on the heart: raw terror.

The next day we were loaded onto a bus for the drive to the damaged reactor, everyone joking and telling stories and making light of the whole business. Radiation was still so high in the Chernobyl exclusion zone that human habitation was prohibited. This we knew, but it was hard to imagine as we rolled north toward the exclusion zone through the verdant Ukrainian countryside, past lush fields bordered by trees in blossom and ramshackle cottages with peasants tending their gardens.

The atmosphere changed when we entered the zone, which began 18 miles from the nuclear plant. We disembarked while security guards in radiation protection suits checked our bus. It had grown eerily quiet outdoors. As we rode on through a forest, the soaring pines were bereft of needles, their branches spindly and yellow.

They drove us to a village not far from the plant where we were told about decontamination efforts to date and an experiment in growing oversize tomatoes. When we finally reached the Chernobyl power station, our guide handed out paper covers for our shoes, as though such slippers could stop radiation from penetrating the leather. He led us into one of the plant's three still functioning reactors, past its tubes and dials and cooling pools, and told us it was identical to the one that had exploded.

We toured the village where the Chernobyl workers had lived, a ghost town really, with laundry still on the line and dinner dishes abandoned in haste still lying on tables indoors. Thieves had broken into some of the houses to steal not televisions or stereos but jewels, apparently not worried that this merchandise, in a different way from anything else they stole, was hot. Our guide told us that the breaking and entering was not confined to thieves. It seemed that uprooted old folks, too, kept stealing back inside the exclusion zone and returning to their homes, stubbornly oblivious to the danger, more frightened by the alien towns to which they'd been transplanted than by warnings that their old familiar surroundings were radiant with lethality.

There was less joking on the bus ride back. People sat in silence and paid more heed to the environing absence, Zenlike noticing what wasn't there. The bird calls. The cat cries. The clucking of hens. The mooing of cows. The neigh of a filly or the honk of a goose. All the familiar sounds of a Ukrainian spring. All of them silenced by the invisible enemy that had turned this fertile countryside into a wasteland.

And what about men? I wasn't getting any younger and children were much on my mind, so much that I had again stopped using birth control. If I got pregnant, I figured, I'd just go ahead and have the baby, with or without a husband – never mind what my parents thought about that. This was my frame of mind when a former lover passed unexpectedly through Moscow on assignment. We hadn't seen each other for years, and I'm afraid to say my heart skipped a beat when I saw him. During his brief visit we renewed our erotic acquaintanceship. Before leaving, he asked me to join him for a week during the summer. It promised to be a happy vacation.

I flew out to meet him a month later, but something had changed. We couldn't renew the old magic. I stayed only a couple of nights before fleeing to Rome, where my old friend Tom from AFP was posted. He installed me in his guestroom, wined and dined me at trattorias and did his best – as a friend, just a friend – to ease the pain that had entered my heart.

Why had I been such a fool? The question tormented me long after my misguided attempt to rekindle an old flame. Why had I once again allowed myself to be seduced by eros? Why couldn't I be more practical, like other women, and make a man wait until I was sure of his intentions? And, by the way, were there no reliable men in the world? When would I find one who could take love seriously, who would want not just a few good times but a mate, a mother for his children?

Once again, I had to face facts. My love affairs weren't going the way they was supposed to, with a beginning, a middle and a happy ending. The same old faulty script kept repeating itself. Why did I cling to the illusion that all would be well in the end? That the rocky narrative of my life would magically right itself and make the story turn out fine? I thought back to my father, who kept his audience spellbound as he spun out the hilarious quid pro quos of whatever new shaggy dog story he had picked up. Those stories wandered all over the place, only to finish in a nonsensical anticlimax. Had I unconsciously integrated that pattern into my own life? Did I have no power to take control of the script?

DELIVERANCE
1988

It was January 1988 and James Roberts was sending me on another trip, this time to Bonn and Madrid with Eduard Shevardnadze, the Soviet foreign minister, who was visiting both cities. Fine by me, all the more so because I had a friend in Bonn — May Fredericks of UPI, one of the stars of our female rat pack in Moscow until she was posted to Germany.

When I phoned May to tell her I'd be coming, she suggested we meet at a bar she knew. She hinted she had some news but refused to say more. Before leaving Moscow I phoned a few more friends to find out about potential contacts.

"If you're going to Madrid," the correspondent of El País replied, "you really ought to look up Andrew Harris. He's new in town and he's the most eligible bachelor I know."

Good idea, I thought. I'd managed to get through the rest of 1987 with no major stumbles. I'd survived the wedding of Jacques and Nani, who were now man and wife — on paper, at least. There was nothing exciting on the horizon. I could use an eligible bachelor.

Grateful to James for sending me on the trip, I left lightheartedly for Bonn with my typewriter, my notebook, the Shevardnadze itinerary and the phone number of Andrew Harris, safely stashed in my pocket.

May was waiting for me when I found the bar, all blonde and glowing and prettily disheveled.

"You look great!" I said as we ordered a couple of beers. "Now spill."

"I met a guy," she said.

"And?"

"And he's been pursuing me. We're seeing each other this weekend."

"And?"

"I think he's going to propose to me. And I think I'm going to say yes!"

"Oh my god. That's huge."

"Yeah, I know! I can't really believe it."

"Who is it?"

"He's a hack. We met at a dinner party. I wasn't that interested in him, but he's been so persistent. I think he's really in love with me."

"And you?"

"Yeah, I think so. I really miss him. We haven't seen each other for a couple of weeks."

"Really? Why not?"

"He got posted to Madrid. That's where he lives now."

"So you'll be in Madrid this weekend? That's so great! We can meet up there."

"Sure," said May. "I'll introduce you."

"Wait a second," I said. "What's his name?"

But I already knew the reply.

"Andrew Harris."

As the world's most eligible bachelor bit the dust, I had to ask myself once again when I would find a man to marry. Had I taken more seriously some of the men who'd tried to woo me, could one of them perhaps have sought to wed me? If I'd given love a chance, I mused, maybe things would be different now.

Through these meditations an image appeared – the image of Tom, who had saved me when things went wrong the previous summer.

Tom was still based in Rome but he traveled frequently and phoned me from time to time. The last time we spoke, he'd mentioned that he'd be in the States in February. By coincidence, I'd be there too. I was joining my parents for a week at the beach in Florida and then going up to Washington. My mom had asked if I'd like to bring a friend along, as we needed a fourth for bridge. Tom played bridge...

"I'd love to," Tom said when I phoned. "But I have an interview in Washington at the start of the week. Could I join you for the last three days?"

The place in Florida was a rented condominium on a stretch of sand between the Indian River and the sea. It was the perfect antidote to Moscow – sunny, calm, with palms waving in the balmy breeze and a laid-back waterside restaurant nearby called Conchy Joe's that served giant mojitos in tin cups.

For the first few days I basked in the sun, baking the Moscow stress away and fantasizing about things to come. Awaiting Tom, my parents and I played three-handed bridge. As my freckles deepened and my skin turned brown, Tom's image appeared to me ever more clearly.

He had black hair over an intelligent brow, horn-rimmed glasses, a neatly trimmed beard and an internal tautness that undoubtedly served him well in his career as a foreign correspondent. I'd always found him good-looking. But what appealed to me most was his wit. He had a fine-tuned sense of wordplay that had delighted me when we worked together on the English Desk. He was married then, and when his son was born I'd given him a gift for the child. But Tom and his wife had split up, and the boy now lived with her in Paris.

On the drive to West Palm Beach to meet Tom's plane, I didn't know what to expect. We'd flirted for years but had rarely slept together. I knew he liked me, but could it go any further? Maybe.

Tom lit up when he saw me. Back at the condo he greeted my

parents cordially, and they took to him at once. After dinner we got out the cards and played bridge late into the night, my mom and dad against Tom and me. My dad was a masterful player with the killer instinct but Tom was also good. Was he letting my dad win on purpose, I wondered? Through the open balcony door, we could hear waves lapping at the shore, like a lullaby.

When bedtime came Tom waited until my parents were settled and then left the living room sofabed for my room, where we got reacquainted with each other. By the time morning came, it was clear this would be a great vacation.

The next day, when we joined my parents for dinner at Conchy Joe's, we were deeply in harmony. My father had no trouble demolishing us at bridge later that evening.

Then it was our last day in Florida, and I didn't want to leave. Tom and I strolled on the beach, basked by the pool, played a few last lazy hands of bridge with my parents. My mom and I made dinner together, my dad chose a superior wine. Afterwards, Tom and I took another walk along the sand. It was a balmy night, the moon low in the sky, a slim pink crescent casting pearly light on the sea. We stood for a moment under the stars.

"I'm glad I made the trip," Tom said, taking my hands.

"Me too," I said.

He pulled me towards him and kissed me, then looked at me intently, as though sizing up the moment.

"Why don't we get married?" he said.

I was speechless. Tom gently pulled me down with him to the sand. We were still holding hands. On bended knee, he spoke again.

"Mona?"

"Yes?"

"Will you marry me?"

"Are you serious?"

"Yes!"

"But we hardly know each other!"

"Mona – it's been nearly ten years. I've lusted after you all that time, as you very well know."

We kissed again.

"This is crazy," I said.

"Not really," said Tom. "We're very compatible, as these few days have shown. And there's another thing. How old are you now, 38?"

"I'm afraid so."

"The biological clock is ticking, Mona. We could have children together. We shouldn't wait."

"But we're not in love!"

"Not yet, but we can be."

Slowly we began making our way back to the condo. Was this some odd throwback to the way people used to marry, not for love but for reason? Often such marriages worked out well, I'd heard, with love budding between the sheets and flowering as the children were born. I liked Tom. We enjoyed each other's company. But could those feelings transmogrify into love? It was a question I could have asked myself many times before with men. But this was the first time someone I could realistically envisage marrying had actually asked for my hand.

"Mona, listen," Tom was saying as we neared the door. "I'm up for a new posting in the next few months. I want to be near my son, so I've asked for Paris. I think I'll get it. I've put my life on the line for the magazine and they owe me. You won't be in Moscow forever. We can commute for a while – and then, when the time comes, you can apply for Paris too."

"Maybe."

"These few days have been too brief," Tom went on. "I know you have meetings in Washington – I do, too. Since we'll both be there tomorrow that gives us an extra 24 hours. I've got a room at the Hay-Adams. Would you join me?"

We were booked out on separate flights the next morning. Tom landed first and was waiting for me when I arrived at the Hay-Adams.

I saw the editors of a major newspaper during the day. In the evening Tom and I dined together. We had another sexy, sleepless night. The next day, when it was time to part, Tom again raised the question of marriage. Would I or wouldn't I consider it?

"Yes," I said.

Back in Moscow, Lisa Rubinstein's sister, Yulia, had finally received permission to emigrate. She had been left behind when Lisa left because her husband's father had once had access to classified information. But then nearly everything in the Soviet Union was classified, even the jokes. Things were changing, though. Their exit visas in hand, Yulia, her husband and their son would soon make their way via Rome to Washington, where Lisa, Tolya and Natasha had settled.

The state's grip was loosening not just on Jewish refuseniks but on other dissidents too – among them friends of mine like Tanya, daughter of the imprisoned Aeroflot navigator. She had taken shelter in Sad Sam for months while struggling to get her family out of the USSR. The family wasn't Jewish – they simply wanted to leave. And who could blame them? Tanya's grandmother had been sent to a labor camp in 1946 for gleaning unharvested corn beneath the snow in order to feed her four starving children. A few decades later, Tanya's father had been subjected to psychotropic injections during forced confinement in a psychiatric hospital after applying to emigrate. They were ordinary Russians with no special grounds for applying to leave the country. What was extraordinary was the tenacity with which Tanya campaigned for their departure. With the help of Andrei Sakharov, she won the battle and the family left for Paris.

So, yes, things were changing in Gorbachev's Russia. I witnessed his charisma first-hand when he traveled to Yugoslavia in March 1988, captivating crowds with his talk of better relations, acclaimed by shouts of "Mikhail, Mikhail!" But even as he was lauded abroad, Gorbachev was mocked and derided at home. For the West,

Gorbachev was the first modern Kremlin chief, a man with whom leaders could do business. For many educated Russians, he was a hick from the south who spoke with a clumsy accent, whose velvet glove held an iron fist. Freedoms were few and far between, democracy as yet unborn.

Now it was April 1988 and Jews around the world were celebrating Passover, among them Soviet Jews who had never before attended a Seder. The new Moscow correspondent of The Washington Post and his wife, both practicing Jews, wanted to introduce some Russian friends to the yearly ritual. They organized a Seder at their place and invited me to join them.

It was curious to be sharing this familiar ceremony with Jews who had no idea how a Passover dinner proceeds. All was new to them – the unleavened matzo symbolizing bread that didn't have time to rise when Moses got the call from God to lead his people out of Egypt, the parsley dipped in salt water representing the hopefulness of springtime mixed with the tears of an enslaved populace. The Soviet guests were uneasy at first with the unfamiliar ritual – unfamiliar because it had been next to impossible for Jews to practice their religion in the Soviet Union. But as the evening wore on with the reading of the story of the exodus, as the four ceremonial glasses of wine were consumed, as a fine meal was enjoyed by all present, the warmth of the occasion worked its magic and everyone began to relax.

The Soviet guests, most of whom had been refused permission to emigrate, did their best to join in the singing of traditional Passover songs. And then it was time to finish the evening with a prayer. We stood, raised our glasses and pronounced the words: "Next year in Jerusalem!" I had been celebrating Passover all my life without grasping the prayer's symbolic power. A Jew of the diaspora, I had no desire to move to Jerusalem. But here, in Gorbachev's Russia, in the home of these generous friends, among kind, intelligent people who by force of Soviet history were unable to travel abroad, the prayer's promise of deliverance, of freedom from enslavement, could not have been more clear. As we made the toast some of the Soviet guests were weeping. To my surprise, I found that I was, too.

And what of Tom? Were we getting married, or weren't we? He came to Moscow a couple of times and appeared to be taking steps to leave Rome for Paris. But I had a bottom line on the matter.

"If you're serious about marrying me," I told him, "how about divorcing your wife?"

For Tom, although separated for many years, was still legally wed.

Nonetheless I informed Reuters that I wanted to leave Moscow before the end of my three-year tour and requested Paris as my next posting. James Roberts didn't understand. He felt I was just beginning to capitalize on the two years I'd spent mastering Russian and cracking the code of Soviet politics. But he reluctantly lent his support. In short order, I was offered a job in Paris starting in the autumn.

I was not unhappy at the idea of leaving Moscow, even though my job as a correspondent there had been by far the most thrilling experience of my life. As Tom had noted, I wasn't getting any younger. The time to have a baby was now, and I couldn't imagine that happening while I was working as a wire service reporter in the USSR. Whether or not things worked out with Tom.

And this was a real question. He had asked me to marry him on the spur of the moment, fair enough, but since then no ring had materialized. When we spoke on the phone, he sometimes mentioned his evenings out with various women – sometimes a bit too enthusiastically.

I decided to broach the subject with my mother.

"How did you and Dad like Tom?" I asked during one of our Sunday phone calls.

"He seems like a nice man," my mother said. "Why do you ask?"

"Well, we're kind of in a relationship."

"Oh? Since when?"

"Since Florida."

"Really? You certainly were discreet about it. Your father and I didn't notice anything."

"We were discreet, but it happened, Mom. And now we're thinking of getting married."

"Oh, sweetie!" she exclaimed, but I could hear the doubt in her voice. "That's wonderful, if you're happy. But is he in love with you?"

"I don't know," was all I could say. It sounded so wimpy. Ever since I could remember my mother had been after me to get married and have children. And now when I finally announced the news, she asked the one question I couldn't answer.

"You know what your father always says," my mom went on. "Marry in haste, repent at leisure."

"Don't worry, Mom. No one's marrying in haste because Tom's still married to his first wife."

"You can't be serious."

"I am. They've been separated for years but never got around to divorcing. They have a son together."

"Well, let me tell you something, young lady," said my mother, reverting to her scolding tones of my childhood. "Unless that man signs the divorce papers and produces a ring, he's not worth your time. Forget about him and start looking for someone who will treat you better."

I had a habit of ignoring my mother's advice. But this time I feared she might be right.

When I flew out of Moscow in July 1988 to tour the three Soviet Baltic republics, I was on my own with little idea what to expect. Usually foreign correspondents have a specific goal, but this time James Roberts had asked me to visit Lithuania, Latvia and Estonia simply to find out what was happening there. For hints were reaching Moscow that the formerly independent Baltic states, annexed by the Soviet Union in 1939, were taking timid steps toward autonomy.

My first stop was Vilnius, the Lithuanian capital, where I'd be staying in the special hotel for foreigners – the one with the bugged phones. I'd been assigned a "minder" from Elta, the Lithuanian branch of Tass, who would serve as a guide and report on me to the KGB. None of this dulled my excitement at being out on my own at the Western edge of the USSR in cities that had far more in common with Helsinki or Stockholm than Minsk or Pinsk. Despite nearly 50 years of Kremlin rule, the Estonians, Latvians and Lithuanians had stubbornly clung to their national languages and traditions, or so I'd heard.

Before leaving, I saw a couple of friends who had already visited the Baltics, including Anouk's diplomat boyfriend, Stéphane Kramer. He gave me a list of activists' phone numbers and the name of a new restaurant in the Old Town, where I headed for lunch after checking into the hotel. I'd go see the minder later.

The restaurant was charming, with fresh flowers on the table – unheard of in Moscow – but the menu was in Lithuanian and I couldn't read it. A man at the next table had a plate of something that looked delicious.

Gathering up my courage, I said hello in Russian and asked him what it was.

"*Bundukies*," the man replied. "Lithuanian meatballs."

"Thank you," I smiled. "I will order it."

I returned to reading the articles about the Baltics I'd printed out before leaving Moscow.

"Excuse me," the man said, "but you seem to have an accent. Are you from Estonia?"

"No," I laughed, "from much farther away than that."

"May I ask where?"

"You may," I replied. "I am currently living in Moscow, where I work as a correspondent for Reuters. But I'm actually from America."

"America? Really?! I've never met an American before. What are you doing here in Vilnius?"

"I'm on a reporting trip, just to find out what's happening. But I really don't know where to begin."

"If you want to know what's happening," said the man, "you need to go to the forest."

"Excuse me?"

"Yes, the forest. There is a Pan-Baltic student song festival on now. You must see it. You will be very impressed."

"But where in the forest? How will I find it?"

"It's easy," said the man. "Just walk down the hill to the river and follow the crowds."

After lunch I made my way down an ancient cobblestone street to the River Neris, which flows through the center of town. Sure enough, crowds of people were walking along a leafy path, quietly but determinedly, singly, in pairs or in knots. I slipped into the queue and followed along. After maybe half an hour, as the path made its way out of town and into the forest, sounds rose up through the trees. People were singing. The sounds heightened, deepened as we neared our destination, and then there it was, a clearing in the forest filled with thousands, tens of thousands of people, all singing. The sounds were deep and moving, their strains rising powerfully up from the clearing and scattering down upon the massive assembly, people of all ages, many wearing lapel badges of the pre-Soviet Lithuanian flag, some weeping with emotion.

During a pause, I turned to the woman beside me.

"I'm a foreigner," I said in Russian. "I don't speak Lithuanian. Could you kindly explain this to me? Who are these people? What are they singing about?"

"We are Balts who have come together to sing about freedom," the middle-aged woman said proudly. "This was supposed to be a student song fest, but in fact many came who are no longer students. I am a housewife from Estonia. Many thousands of people like me have come here to sing with our brothers and sisters from Lithuania and Latvia."

"What is this music?" I asked.

"We are singing patriotic songs," she said as a new group took the stage at one end of the clearing. "These are the songs we sang before we were occupied by the Soviets. Listen! That was the Estonian national anthem before the war. It was banned for so many years. But we kept it in our hearts, and here in the forest we may sing it again with pride."

I wandered through the crowd and spoke with many people – old men, pretty blonde students with braids wrapped around their heads, a photographer, young men in T-shirts brandishing homemade banners. All expressed a burning wish for independence. They told me excitedly about other singing events that had taken place recently, especially in Estonia, where rock musicians were leading the population in reviving the patriotic hymns of a previous era, songs where every note expressed their longing for deliverance.

After a while I made my way back to the city center and stopped in at Elta to meet my minder. He turned out to be a rare Lithuanian Jew, rare because nearly the entire Jewish population of Lithuania was wiped out by the Nazis during the war. At the time Vilnius had been known as Vilna. When I told my minder I was interested in learning about the history of the Vilna ghetto, where 40,000 Jews were first confined and then exterminated, this so-called journalist maintained, and actually seemed to believe, that nothing special had happened.

Writing off the minder as completely useless, I returned to the hotel and sat down to type up some notes about what I'd seen in the forest. There was no rush to file as the song fest would continue into the next day, a Sunday, and I planned to write a single piece from Lithuania before traveling on to Latvia on Monday. I also made a quick call to one of Stéphane Kramer's contacts, a little-known professor of music active in the independence movement, to get directions to his home. When we'd spoken before I left Moscow, the professor had invited me to come for Sunday lunch.

As the long northern evening faded to night, I thought back to what I'd experienced in the forest and felt grateful for what I'd seen. How amazing to be among these brave, extraordinary people. I thought back to other moments of high emotion. Sakharov's release.

The Rubinsteins' departure. The trip to Chernobyl. The Passover seder. The joy of Tanya's family when they were finally able to leave.

How rich my life had become, I mused. How fortunate to be here to witness repression receding, to watch people stand up and fight for their right to freedom. I thought back to my student days and our various quests for liberation. Now the word "liberation" had taken on a whole new cast. Not just personal but political in the deepest sense – powerful and revolutionary. The people in the forest knew that, and I was starting to understand, too.

Another revolutionary thought surged up. For so many years I'd been seeking something – love, a man, a family. I'd set my heart on these aspirations, paying no heed to the road I traveled while searching. And now here I was, at 38, in this farflung corner of the USSR, finally realizing something so liberating that I had to pour myself a shot of vodka to steady my nerves.

Had I misread the story of my life? All these years I'd been striving toward a goal, and feeling I'd failed – never considering that perhaps what matters most is not the destination, but the journey.

It was hot in Vilnius that July, so hot the following morning that I was typing away in only a T-shirt when there was a rap on my door. The hotel maid, no doubt.

"I'm busy – please come back later," I called out.

Moments later, another loud knock.

"Open up," a man shouted sternly.

"Just a minute," I said, throwing on some jeans.

I opened the door to find two uniformed officers.

"Citizen Venture, you are being expelled from the Soviet Socialist Republic of Lithuania," the older one said. "Please pack your things immediately."

"But why?" I asked in alarm. "What have I done?"

"You were granted permission to enter Lithuania on the grounds that you would be escorted everywhere by a journalist colleague from the Elta news agency. But you went alone into the forest yesterday, and now you have made an unauthorized appointment."

Oh no! I thought. What a fool I am! Why did I use the hotel phone to confirm my lunch? Of course it was bugged. Of course the KGB knew I was due to see Professor Vytautas Landsbergis in less than an hour. Now he would never know why I didn't show up – unless he, too, found himself in trouble because of my carelessness. As for me, I had no choice but to obey.

"Fine," I told the officers. "I will pack my things. But as you are expelling me, could you kindly expel me to Latvia? It's the next stop on my itinerary."

"*Nyet*," the senior man said sharply. "You are being expelled to Moscow in one hour. Hurry now. We must be on time."

In short order I found myself loaded into a police van and driven to the Vilnius airport, where I was put on an Aeroflot flight back to Moscow. During the journey, I ruminated on what I had done wrong – or right. I must have stumbled onto something important, I figured. Otherwise they would not have gone to the trouble to expel me.

Little did I know that the man I'd been due to meet for lunch would, in less than two years, become the first president of a free Lithuania.

Little did I know – little could I know – that what I'd witnessed in the forest was the start of a Singing Revolution that was to hasten not just independence for the three Baltic countries but the breakup of the entire Soviet Union, bringing to an end the world of two superpowers in which I'd come of age, the postwar world as we had known it.

Yes, the songs reverberating through the Lithuanian forest, rising high and clear above a tapestry of green, filling the summery air with hope, were to herald a new age.

Little did I know, as I stood amid thousands of Balts beneath the fluttery leaves of birches, lindens, oak, as we fell collectively under the spell of the music's call for freedom, as beside spruces soaring dark and blue I, too, let my heart dance in tune to the vision of a new future, little did I know that our dreams were within reach. Little could I imagine that happiness, even joy, might be just around the corner.

JOY

The Estonians declared sovereignty in November 1988, just four months after the song fest, followed half a year later by the Lithuanians and the Latvians. After these initial breaches in Soviet unity, it wasn't long before the entire house of cards came tumbling down. By November 1989 the Berlin Wall would collapse, and with it the Kremlin's control over Eastern Europe. In 1990, all three Baltic republics would unilaterally declare independence. By Christmas 1991, as Mikhail Gorbachev stepped down under popular pressure, all 15 of the Soviet Socialist Republics would become independent nations as the USSR ceased to exist.

This sudden determination of oppressed populations to risk taking their fate into their own hands captivated observers in the West. I was among them, for I had moved back to Paris, where things did not transpire as planned. I didn't marry Tom, his disinterest in obtaining a divorce proving fatal to our relationship. And I didn't rejoin the Paris bureau of Reuters. When they reneged on their offer to bring me back to Paris, I phoned an editor I knew at the International Herald Tribune to see if anything was available there. They hired me as a copy editor, a first step to the dream job I'd fantasized about for so long. But few dreams can stand up to banal reality. My excitement at working for a major American newspaper faded after a few weeks of tweaking grammar and writing headlines over the stories of Pulitzer Prize winning correspondents of The New York Times and The Washington Post.

Part of me – the ready-for-anything part – yearned to get back on the reporting circuit, to experience the adrenalin rush of pursuing a good story, to be doing something that mattered. But I had ceded my place at Reuters, and the IHT was not about to send me on assignment anytime soon. The other part of me – the happily-ever-after part – still wanted to find a good man, settle down and have a family.

I stayed on at the IHT, working my way up from copy editor to occasional editor on the news desk, effectively serving as one of the paper's two foreign editors. At the same time – again proving the triumph of hope over experience – I agreed once more to share a home with a man. We were an unlikely couple, and when the relationship failed I entered a new period in the wilderness. A period of wondering how things could have gone so badly wrong. Of wondering how I could have deluded myself yet again into thinking that powerful sex could translate into powerful love. Emotionally shattered at 41, I gave up my dreams of motherhood. I went to work, saw only my closest friends, ate, slept and grieved.

A few months after the breakup, a Dutch publisher phoned from Russia seeking to hire me as the founding editor of a new English-language daily newspaper in Moscow. I hesitated only briefly before accepting the job. It would be not just a fascinating new challenge, but a one-way ticket out of a situation where I regularly crossed paths with my ex.

And yet, as I boarded my flight back to Moscow, doubts assailed me. Was this adventure a new *fuite en avant* – fleeing forwards – or a movement backwards, a regression in search, as Proust says, of lost time? Would I manage to recapture the incredible camaraderie, the passion of covering earth-changing events that I'd known during my first posting in Russia?

The newspaper project was a professional success, but on a

personal level it failed. When I left, I'd helped create a respected publication that exists to this day. I'd also survived two coup attempts – one in the streets of Moscow against President Boris Yeltsin, and one within the newsroom against me. This took place when a few members of my very young staff rebelled against my authority as editor while I was out of town and the Dutch publisher failed to defend me. I stayed in my job for the full two years of my contract, but the psychodrama took its toll: I never again felt the exhilaration that should have accompanied my status as editor-in-chief of the first independent English-language daily in Russia. Yet I knew I'd done something that mattered, and had the consolation of seeing the young journalists I'd nurtured go on to successful careers, some of them brilliantly successful. This, I figured, was the closest I'd get to parenthood.

About a month after I left Moscow my father died of a heart attack, and four years later my mother succumbed to cancer. Both were young – in their early 70s.

When my mother fell ill, Ben and I took turns going to Wisconsin to care for her. I flew over from Paris, where I was back at the IHT, while Ben flew in from the Bay Area. More adept than I at love, he had been living for more than a decade with Cathy, a San Francisco lawyer. But on these visits he traveled alone. We organized our trajectories to overlap for a couple of days so that we could support each other during our mother's painful decline. This was the first time Ben and I had spent much time together since I left home for Madison at the age of 17. I rediscovered my brother as a deeply compassionate and thoughtful human being, a fabulous teller of tales, whose persona as a nonconforming and sometimes angry artist was perhaps his way of protecting a sensitive soul. After we buried our mother together and went our separate ways, I restored Ben to his rightful place as one of the most important men in my life.

And what of the other men?

Jake stayed married to Sally Katz for more than three decades until she died of cancer at 59. They had devoted their lives to working with Lyndon Larouche and never had children. After a period of mourning, Jake fell in love with a young woman, also part of the Larouche establishment, who soon announced she was pregnant. To Jake's astonished delight he is at last discovering fatherhood. We lunch together when he passes through Paris.

Jacques divorced Nani as planned before he, too, got married, to a French woman he'd courted for years before she finally agreed to wed. After The Paris Metro folded he continued in journalism, ultimately reaching the pinnacle of the French press with an editing job at Le Monde. Jacques and his wife never had children, although he now says he regrets having missed fatherhood. They are happy together, travel often, and live just down the street from me.

Magnus fell in love with a woman posted to Warsaw when Reuters decided the bureau needed a second reporter. They stayed together for many years, through another tumultuous posting in Eastern Europe and the birth of their two children. They live in southwest France now, in neighboring villages close enough to share parenting and support. Magnus rarely comes to Paris, but we talk on the phone occasionally and see each other when I travel to his region.

Tom ultimately obtained a divorce from his first wife. He is now remarried and living in New Jersey. We rarely communicate.

It has occurred to me, in thinking about my former partners, that despite their professed lack of enthusiasm for marriage and children, ultimately they all settled down. This has caused me to wonder whether just possibly the phrase "not the marrying kind" might apply more aptly to me than to the men in my life. Was my long quest for happily-ever-after merely an amusing distraction from accepting the reality that I was an independent soul who was never cut out to be settled? A diversion from embracing the subversive but ever more plausible reality that in my heart of hearts, during all those years, I was desperate ... not to be a housewife?

෯

When my mother passed away, I was 48 years old – old enough for her death to bring my own mortality sharply into focus. I had relatively little time left, I realized, if ever I was to achieve what I most desired in life.

With the money left to me by my parents I bought a rambling old cottage in Burgundy, in order, I told my mom before she died, to cultivate my garden. I raise organic vegetables there, and make jam from the cherries and plums and juice from the apples that grow abundantly on fruit trees planted decades ago, no two trees the same variety. There is a picnic table in the back beneath these trees where one can sit in the dappled sunlight of a summer afternoon, or after nightfall gaze up at a million points of light in the starry firmament. It is a kind of Eden. As I grow older I watch the seasons change with deepening appreciation of the closeness of all of us to nature, of our place in the natural world. I feel the spirit of my mother in the rustling of the leaves, in the sweet perfume of the roses and honeysuckle framing the pale green door. My dad's presence fills the kitchen each time I stoop to light a wood fire in the wide brick hearth – can I get it lit as he taught me, using just one match?

It's fun attempting to meet his challenge, all the more so because I have a helper now.

My daughter's name is Rokia. She is by my side when we light the fire, pick the fruit, make a crumble, plant some beans, water the roses, turn down the beds at night. When she was little, Rokia used to ride ponies in the country, but she's outgrown that now. She's blossoming into a young woman – spirited, creative, mischievous, tall and more beautiful every day. Born in Mali, West Africa, she came into my life thanks to a chance conversation shortly after my mother's death in which I learned it was possible in France for a single woman nearing 50 to adopt a child. I applied, and 18 months later the miracle happened.

"Wasn't it hard adopting?" people sometimes ask me, and I always have the same reply: not nearly as hard as waiting all those years for a man to decide to have a child with me.

"What about the cultural differences?" they say, meaning race, and I have to smile. That Rokia is black and I am white doesn't matter to her, at least for now. For children are color blind, I was to learn. They see beyond the skin, straight into the soul.

"But she doesn't have a father," they object, and I agree that Rokia and I sometimes dream about how our lives would differ if she had one. There have been men in my life since my daughter came along. But she lacks a special man to be her dad, and I regret it. Still, we have created a modus vivendi that works for us. She's a happy kid, surrounded by friends, with her Uncle Ben and Aunt Cathy popping in from time to time to give her a sense of family. And there's something more. Although Rokia and I don't discuss it, we know we saved each other's lives. Not having a man around? It's not the worst problem.

And what about the future? Rokia is growing up quickly. Soon enough she'll spread her wings and go. I'm ready. For this little girl has given me something I'd been seeking all my life but never found. With my daughter, for the first time, I've known unconditional love.

A memory. Rokia is four. We are standing in the vast blue rectangle of a public pool in a small town in Burgundy. The pale water ripples around my legs – it's up to her neck. Over and over she pushes off the bottom, trying to float toward me without touching down.

"Look, mama!" she demands. "Look, I'm swimming!"

I look at her, my wonder child, her compact black body glistening in the sun, the water beading on her braided hair, sparkling on her face as she takes a breath, pushes off, reaches for me, beaming with excitement.

"Look, mama!"

I look around me, at the pool for children, where we're playing, and its larger, deeper twin, both filled with kids and teens, their screams of glee punctuating the hot July afternoon. Behind the pool wall, the deep green trees with their rustling leaves form a perfect backdrop. I stretch out in the water and gaze up at the blue vault of the Burgundy sky, the ice cream clouds, as Rokia floats into me. We laugh as I find my footing and sweep her up in my arms, lifting her high up in the air as she squeals with delight, then sweep her back down into the water. She wriggles free and tries again.

Nothing could be more perfect, I think, and the shouts around us fade away into a hum. I'm there in the water, watching Rokia, but my mind is floating above us, seeing us there together, my girl's face, so joyful in the sun, my sense of peace in the moment. The feeling builds. Right here, right now. In this pool, with this small girl from Mali, our lives intertwined so closely by some miracle of fate, our pleasure in the sun and the water so intense. After searching all over tarnation for a way to feel at home in the world, it's so funny to think that I found what I was looking for where I least expected it. Right here, in this pool, in this small town in Burgundy, in this countryside, on this summer's day. With my child, with the joy she's brought me. Which is to say, within myself.

Could this be my happily ever after?

Yes, by some miracle of fate, I have come home.

ACKNOWLEDGMENTS

I would like to thank the many friends and colleagues who generously shared their thoughts and memories with me as I completed this work, among them Ann Mah, Celestine Bohlen, Mary Schmemann, Gilda Zwerman, Wilda Anderson, Erica Ellis, Julian Nundy, Linder Allen, David Lewis, Steve McDonnell, Susan Benda, Paul Chutkow, Niki Glen, Helen Womack, John Flattau, Anne Penketh, Sylviane Dungan, Julia Watson, Peter Agree, Reine Marie Melvin and Pauline Ridel. I am particularly indebted to my brother, Bruce Bortin, whose memory of our family life always comes through when mine falters. Special thanks are due to the Norman Mailer Writers Colony and the Southampton Writers Conference, which awarded me fellowships in 2010 and 2011 while I was at work on this book. In particular I'd like to thank Kaylie Jones, whose wise and witty classes on the art of memoir writing were an inspiration. As for the many men portrayed in these pages, I'd like to thank them all for their help in teaching me what it means to be an independent woman.

ABOUT THE AUTHOR

Meg Bortin is an American journalist and writer based in France. A former senior editor at the International Herald Tribune, she has written widely on French and Soviet affairs. Her articles on politics, culture and lifestyle have appeared in many publications. In 1992, she was the founding editor of The Moscow Times, the first independent English-language daily newspaper in Russia. Her personal essay *Dear Djeneba* was included in *Family Wanted*, an anthology on adoption published by Granta Books in 2005 and Random House in 2006. As a food blogger, she posts recipes regularly at *www.everydayfrenchchef.com*. She and her daughter divide their time between Paris and Burgundy, where they have a garden.